General Editor: JOSEPH BETTEY, M.A., Ph.D., F.S.A.
Assistant Editor: ELIZABETH RALPH, M.A., D.Litt., F.S.A.

VOL.51

WILLIAM WORCESTRE:

The Topography of MEDIEVAL BRISTOL

In memory of
ELIZABETH RALPH
1911-2000
Archivist of the City of Bristol 1937-71

This volume is dedicated
with respect and affection

The Bristol Record Society and the editor of this manuscript are particularly grateful to the Marc Fitch Fund and to The Society of Merchant Venturers of Bristol for grants towards the cost of this volume.

WILLIAM WORCESTRE:

The Topography of
MEDIEVAL BRISTOL

Edited by

FRANCES NEALE

Published by
BRISTOL RECORD SOCIETY
c/o Regional History Centre
University of the West of England
St Matthias Campus
Oldbury Court Road
Fishponds
Bristol BS16 2JP

2000

ISBN 0 901538 21 3

Bristol Record Society acknowledges with thanks the continued support of Bristol City Council, the University of Bristol, the Bristol & West Building Society and the Society of Merchant Venturers, and a grant from the Marc Fitch Fund towards the costs of this volume.

BRISTOL RECORD SOCIETY

The Society exists to encourage the preservation, study and publication of documents relating to the history of Bristol, and since its foundation in 1929 has published forty-eight major volumes of historic documents concerning the city. All the volumes, together with their authoritative introductions, are edited by scholars who are experts in the chosen field.

Recent volumes have included: *The Pre-Reformation Records of All Saints', Bristol*, edited by Clive Burgess (Vol. XLVI), the final part of *Bristol, Africa and the Eighteenth-Century Slave Trade to America (1770-1807)*, edited by David Richardson (Vol. XLVII), *The Topography of Medieval and Early Modern Bristol*, edited by Roger H.Leech (Vol. XLVIII), *The Goldney Family*, edited by P.K.Stembridge (Vol. XLIX) and *The Municipal Government of Bristol 1851-1901*, edited by David Large (Vol. 50).

Forthcoming volumes will include the correspondence of Edward Southwell (MP for Bristol 1739-54), the second part of the All Saints' Church Book, the account book of Thomas Speed, a seventeenth century Bristol merchant, and records relating to the Atlantic trade of Bristol during the eighteenth century.

In return for the modest subscription, members of the Society receive the volumes as they are published. The subscription for private members is £10 per annum, for U.K. Institutions £12.50, and for Overseas membership £15.00.

Subscriptions and enquiries should be made to the Hon. Secretary, The Regional History Centre, University of West of England, St Matthias Campus, Oldbury Court Road, Fishponds, Bristol BS16 2JP

Produced for the Society by
J.W.Arrowsmith Ltd
Winterstoke Road
Bristol BS3 2NT

CONTENTS

LIST of PLANS

Jacobus Millerd, Plan of Bristol 1673

Reproduced with permission of the Head of City Museums & Art Gallery, Bristol.

William Worcestre's signature on p.1 is a facsimile of one on a letter, ref. GRO D1637 M13, reproduced with permission of the County Archivist of Gloucestershire.

PREFACE
and Acknowledgements

William Worcestre's remarkable notes have attracted editors for over 200 years. James Nasmith first printed them in 1778. James Dallaway reprinted the Bristol material in 1834, still only in Latin, with a generous sprinkling of misreadings and disconcerting editorial quirks. When Dr John Harvey's massive and masterly *William Worcestre: Itineraries* was published, in Latin and English, in 1969, it was disappointing to find that the Bristol material was not included. The size of this volume indicates why. The time it has taken has been a test of faith for friends and colleagues past and present. The late Dr William Urry, Dr John Harvey and Elizabeth Ralph continue to inspire after their deaths. There are many who, with their encouragement over the years, helped more than they probably ever knew: among them Professors Philip Rahtz, Peter Fowler and Mick Aston, with Derek Keene on urban history and archaeology; Max Hebditch, Mike Ponsford and Eric Boore on specific Bristol buildings and sites; Roger Leech, both for past discussions, and for recent and future Bristol Record Society volumes which will form invaluable companions to Worcestre's descriptions. Latterly, the patience and encouragement of the General Editor, Dr Joe Bettey, has been invaluable in completing the volume.

The manuscript is published by kind permission of the Master and Fellows of Corpus Christi College, Cambridge, and I am grateful to Dr Raymond Page, former Librarian of the Parker Library, for his help at the start. The drawing on p.131 is reproduced with permission of Eleanour Harvey. I am most grateful to John Williams, City Archivist, and his colleagues at Bristol Record Office; to Jane Swinyard and colleagues at Wells Public Library, and David Bromwich, Somerset Studies Librarian; to Ursula Carlyle, archivist of the Mercers's Company, for investigating Robert Cobold, and to the Reverend Peter Thorburn of Wells for help with the Latin of some prayers and chronicles. Joan Hasler has gamely undertaken most intricate proof-reading. Most of all I owe a debt of deepest gratitude to the patience of my husband Richard. This volume is a tribute to all the people who made it possible. Any errors and shortcomings that remain are my own responsibility.

INTRODUCTION

Brittol, 1479.

WILLIAM WORCESTRE rode into Bristol from Castle Combe on 24th August 1480. From the house of his sister Joan Jay in Redcliffe Street, he would, in one direction, have come to Bristol Bridge, with St Nicholas's Gate and the central crossroads of the ancient town beyond, exactly as drawn a year earlier by the town clerk Robert Ricart, for his *Kalendar*. In the other direction, just beyond Redcliffe Gate, rose the magnificent church of St Mary Redcliffe, its spire dramatically broken off in a storm *c*.1445. Work was still in progress on the tower and west door. Worcestre had made a somewhat clumsy survey of Redcliffe church in 1478, and it may have been this earlier interest which suggested the idea of an extended survey of the whole town during his 1480 visit.

Worcestre's life and career have been fully described by John Harvey and need only be summarised here. Born in Bristol in 1415, and schooled at Newgate by Robert Londe, he left for Oxford in 1432. He then worked as secretary and agent to Sir John Fastolf in Norfolk and around the country, until that colourful knight died in 1459. Wrangles with the Paston family and others over Fastolf's will occupied another decade and more, and left Worcestre living in Cambridge and then Norwich in somewhat reduced circumstances. The travels and writings, 1477–80, for which he is now most highly regarded, are the product of his last years. By the autumn of 1485 he was dead.

The 1480 visit which is the main occasion of these notes was longer than usual – but even so, it lasted barely a month: from 24th August to about 26th September, with three days away in Wells at the end of August. Worcestre certainly did not retire to Bristol, as Dallaway and others have imagined. He came, it seems, to sort out problems relating to property, some belonging to him and some to his sister. He took the opportunity to obtain family history details from surviving relatives, and intended to enquire after family title deeds at the College of Kalendars. His concerns are perhaps a reflection of both his age, and his financial situation. It may not be just coincidence that Worcestre was with his widowed sister during the long wait for news of John Jay the younger and his voyage in search of Brazil. John Jay the younger was the namesake and probably half-brother of Joan's late husband. The incomplete date of 148... on the Jay brass in St Mary Redcliffe suggests that Joan might have been widowed quite recently. On 18th September came news that the storm-battered ship was safe in port in Ireland; a week later, Worcestre's Bristol notes end.

Meanwhile, Worcestre paced streets and measured buildings, jotting notes as he went. His handwriting reflects the circumstances: neat, careful extracts from a chronicle in a church, or almost illegible notes written awkwardly as he stood on the spot. His observations range from the length and width of streets and the size of churches, to the public latrines and washerwomen at the riverside. He was fascinated to the point of obsession with numbers, distances and angles – how to calculate the length of a slope (Ghyston Cliff), or the batter of a church spire (St Mary Redcliffe). Measurements are made sometimes in yards, rarely in feet and occasionally (when climbing up or down eight-inch stairs) in inches; vertical measurements are quite often in fathoms, suggesting he might have used a knotted rope borrowed from the quayside. Most of his measurements, however, are his own *gressus* or steppys: a deliberate heel-and-toe measure the length of his two feet, which Harvey demonstrated to be about 21-22 inches (56 cms.). In this slow, deliberate fashion Worcestre paced the length and breadth of Bristol. His reckonings are often multiples of 60, suggesting that he may have been counting on his finger joints as he went. His notes sometimes have gaps left for totals which are clearly added afterwards.

Roads and churches dominate his notes, giving a secure framework to his survey. He took an active interest in church-building in progress at St Augustine the Less, St Stephen's and St Mary Redcliffe. His lists of mouldings were probably dictated by the freemasons, Benedict Crosse at St Stephen's and John Norton at Redcliffe, and Benedict Crosse probably drew for him the highly professional section of moulding (worn but still recognisable) on St Stephen's porch.

Worcestre knew the great and the good of Bristol by repute, and where they lived; but he had been away for too long to have contact with them. He was, however, good at striking up casual acquaintance with people he met on his perambulations: the young blacksmith climbing in the Avon Gorge, or William Clark of Mary le Port street who could tell him about cellars.

Comments on appearances, such as the pitiful state the Castle, are rare. The window in the Bristol Bridge chapel showing merchants and their wives is the only stained glass he mentions. Worcestre's Bristol, however, is not just dry facts and figures. He describes goods and ships' equipment piled around the quays, and the arrival of ships in harbour on the tide. He was there: at the boundary stone outside Lawford's Gate, 'seen and touched by me', or scrambling up the cliff from St Vincent's chapel 'as walked and climbed by W.Botoner called Worcestre, walking and counting, on Sunday 26th September ... 1480 ... measures 124 steps.'

Alongside his obsession with counting he had a strong sense of history and the passage of time: 'the jousting place of olden days' and the Kalendars Fraternity, founded about 700 A.D., 'before the time of William the Conqueror ... as I have seen and read in confirmatory documents in an ancient hand, of the time of St Wulstan.' He has preserved for us Dynt the pumpmaker's folk-memory of a hawthorn tree standing at the central crossroads before the High Cross was set up in 1373, and details of the boat and worked timber found nearly fifty feet down in the mud near St Stephen's. Perhaps most remarkable is his description of the tumbled ruins of Clifton Camp, 'great stones piled up, and small ones scattered around ... in an orderly ring ... whereby a very strong castle is seen to have been there, which hundreds of years ago has been destroyed and thrown to the ground'. He includes a tantalising reference to a hill-figure; the closest parallel would be the Plymouth giants, also since vanished.

Sometimes Worcestre's notes are precise and vivid; at others they prove almost impossible to understand today. Michael Ponsford performed a *tour de force* to unravel Worcestre's Bristol Castle, alongside the archæological and documentary evidence. Michael Smith found his Redcliffe notes 'fascinating but infuriating'. The complete Bristol text and translation will, it is hoped, make more readily available to future historians and archæologists the work of the man whom John Harvey described as 'not merely our first antiquary, but in a true sense our first archæologist'.

EDITORIAL NOTE

The description and history of C.C.C.C. MS 210 given by Dr J.H.Harvey in *William Worcestre: Itineraries* cannot be bettered. Worcestre wrote on loose folded sheets, later bound together in no particular order. Harvey published the text in date order as he reconstructed it, but this led to some odd divisions of related material, such as Worcestre's diary and accounts, and cannot be applied safely to the Bristol notes. These are here printed in the order in which they are now bound. This volume includes not only the Bristol material omitted by Harvey, but all the other Bristol notes as well, so that the whole is available together. The notes have been divided into numbered items for ease of use and reference.

Following Harvey, Latin text and English translation are presented on facing pages, so that the original text is available. Worcestre's vigorous mixture of languages and cheerful disregard of case-endings is of interest in itself, and inevitably loses freshness in translation. The translation aims to keep the flavour of Worcestre's style. A chapel of St Mary, where it is clearly a Lady chapel, is translated as such. Items wholly in English are printed in **bold type**, although they too need careful translation. Grammatical errors are not normally noted; nor are his copious caret marks, brackets and boxes. Marginal headings are printed in capitals; other headings as Worcestre gives them. There are copious jotted figures in top margins, and sometimes elsewhere, as he works out his measurements; these have not been noted. Footnotes to the Latin text are noted as a, b, c; footnotes to the English as 1, 2, 3. Worcestre's symbols and abbreviations are discussed in the appendix.

A note on Bristol maps

The two maps most useful for understanding Worcestre's description of Bristol are Jacobus Millerd's plan of 1673, and G.C.Ashmead's plan of 1828. Millerd (Plans A, B, C and D in this volume) preserves in 1673 an astonishing amount of detail that Worcestre saw and recorded in 1480, down to the tiny but important water-conduit houses on The Key and The Back. His scale of yards tallies more often than not with Worcestre's measurements. Ashmead in 1828 accurately records property boundaries just before large areas of the ancient town centre were swept away for new housing, roads and factories.

The Topography of
MEDIEVAL BRISTOL

Corpus Christi College Cambridge
MS 210

pp.87–203
with additional Bristol references

CCCC MS 210

p.87[a]

(1)
PONS BRISTOLL
longitudo pontis Bristollie continet circa .72. virgas
latitudo eius continet .5. virgas.
Sed tota latitudo cum mansionibus domorum scituatorum super
pontem edificatarum continet ... [b]
Altitudo mansionum edificatorum supra pontem continet per
Estimacionem profunditas pontis ab altis arcuvj ad profundum
terre fundamenti, &c ... [b]

(2)
longitudo capelle beate marie in medio pontis scituate continet
.25. virgas
latitudo ejus continet .7. virgas

(3)
longitudo vici le Bakk proximo continuato ab occidentali dicte
pontis per longam keyam coram aquam de Frome[c] curret,
continet in longitudine .220. gressus vel tres .60. gressus et
40. gressus

(4)
longitudo marisci ex parte murorum ville propiendo a meridie
ab extrema banci aque Auene prope le Domum de Roperscraffte
vel latrinam officium extendo directe per calcetum ad aquam de
Frome, per rubeum calcetum, iuxta muros ville in orientali
parte ville scite continet sic in longitudine la dicti marisci
videlicet .7.cies .60. gressus. jdest .420. gressus

(5)
ā[d]
longitudo vie a porta sancti leonardi vsque le key transeundo
per le customhous vsque per le condyt directe per
Shyppardhous velut via trianguli continet, .90. gressus;

---

a   The top of the page is covered in unrelated later jottings and pen trials,
    including some Greek, probably by Aldrich
b   Blank in MS
c   First *aquam Auen* and then *Auen* have been successively deleted, and
    then *aquam de Frome* inserted, wrongly, as Worcestre is describing the
    Welsh Back quay alongside R.Avon. The reference *per longam keyam*
    perhaps caused the confusion, as The Key was the quay alongside
    R.Frome

CCCC MS 210

p.87

(1)
BRISTOL BRIDGE
The length of Bristol Bridge measures about 72 yards.
Its width measures 5 yards.
But the whole width, including the dwelling houses sited |and|
built upon the bridge measures ...
The height of the dwellings built upon the bridge measures by
estimation [to] the depths of the bridge from the top of the
arch to the lowest bedrock, etc. ...

(2)
The length of the chapel of the Blessed Mary, situated in the
middle of the bridge, measures 25 yards.
Its width measures 7 yards.

(3)
The length of the street [called] The Back extending
immediately on the west of the said bridge along the quay
beside [where] the river Frome[1] flows, measures in length 220
steps, or thrice 60 plus 40 steps.

(4)
The length of the marsh on the side of the town walls facing
south, from the furthest edge of the river Avon near the
Ropemakers' Hall or the public latrine, extending straight along
the path to the river Frome, along the red path, next to the
town walls sited on the east[2] side of the town – the said marsh
measures thus in length to wit seven times 60 steps, that is
420 steps.

(5)
The length of the road from St Leonard's Gate as far as The
Key, going past the Customs House as far as the conduit,
straight by Shipward's house, and likewise the triangular
roadway, measures 90 steps.

---

1   Error for Avon: see note c opposite
2   Error for west

---

d   Worcestre's *animadvertit* symbol; not noted in facing translation

(6)
BALDWYNE STRETE
longitudo vie Baldewynstrete.   Tyrcies .60. et 30 gressus
.210. gressus

(7)
longitudo vie^a venelle a porta sancti leonardi transceundo per
cimiterium in Smalstrete .214. gressus

(8)
SEYNT LAURENS LANE
longitudo vie vocate seynt laurens lane a Smalstrete per
sanctum laurencium .120. gressus

(9)
SMALLESTRET
longitudo vie vocate Smalstrete, de Smallestrete continet .240.
gressus vsque finem vie ad portam sancti Egidij ducentem ad
vnum vicum vocatum seynt laurens lane.

(10)
VOLTA ECCLESIE SANCTI JOHANNIS .29.
longitudo volte sancti Johannis baptiste continet preter le
chauncelle .29 virgas & dimidium^b
latitudo eius continet .7. virgas,

(11)
WYNCHESTRETE
longitudo a cruce alto eundo per vicum^c de Wynchstrete ad le
pilorye faciunt^d .150. gressus.   Et a le pylorye continuando
vsque Newgate^e nouies .60. id est .500. gressus   Et via de le
Newgate ad pontem de le Were continet ... ^{f} gressus

(12)
[V]IA AD [FRAT]RES PREDICA[TO]RES [.2]25.^{g}
Via de aqua de Weere eundo per fratres Predicatores & pontem
ad finem vie vocate Brodemede continet .225. gressus;

---

a   *vie* has been written on the line and *venelle* above it, without any
    deletion or caret mark
b   .29. also appears in margin opposite
c   *vsque* deleted
d   *.230.*, deleted
e   *60* deleted
f   Blank in MS
g   Heading partly obscured in centrefold by later binding

(6)
BALDWIN STREET
The length of the Baldwin Street road: thrice 60 plus 30 steps: 210 steps.

(7)
The length of the lane from St Leonard's Gate going past the churchyard into Small Street: 214 steps.

(8)
ST LAWRENCE LANE
The length of the road called St Lawrence Lane from Small Street past St Lawrence: 120 steps.

(9)
SMALL STREET
The length of the road called Small Street: Small Street measures 240 steps from as far as the end of the road at St Giles's Gate, leading to a street called St Lawrence Lane.

(10)
THE CRYPT OF ST JOHN'S CHURCH   29
The length of the crypt[1] of St John the Baptist measures, excepting the chancel, 29½ yards.
Its width measures 7 yards.

(11)
WYNCH STREET[2]
The length from the High Cross going along the street of Wynch Street to the pillory totals 150 steps. And continuing from the pillory as far as Newgate, nine times 60 that is 560 steps. And the road from the Newgate to the bridge of the Weir measures ... steps.

(12)
THE ROAD TO THE FRIARS PREACHERS 225
The road from the river at the Weir going past the Friars Preachers and the bridge to the end of the road called Broadmead measures 225 steps.

---

1   The crypt or undercroft of St John on the Wall, like that of St Nicholas (cf. **(15)**), is exposed at ground-level on the lower or outer side of the town wall, and this is what Worcestre measured as he walked past
2   The name *Wynch* derives from the pillory to which Worcestre refers, and was corrupted into what is now Wine Street

(13)
VIA AD,[a]
Item via a dicta fine vie de Brodemede eundo per
marshallestrete ad le barres vbi tenentes patris mei morantur
de fatuis mulieribus continet ... [b]

p.88

(14)
longitudo cimiterij sancti Jacobi Bristollie continet .150.
gressus.
latitudo eius continet, 100. gressus;

(15)
DE ECCLESIA SANCTI NICHOLAI
latitudo navis Ecclesie sancti Nicholai inter vicum vocatum
sancti Nicholai ex parte boriali & vicum subteriorem vltra
voltam vocatam introitus ad le bak, continet nisi .5. virgas;

(16)
Memorandum a porta turris vici Baldewynstret vsque
Cornerium magnum in principio de le key Bristollie per murum
ville sunt tres vices .60., id est .180.

(17)
Item a porta sancti Johannis eundo per Cristmasstrete vsque
principium pontis porte de Fromeyate sunt 124. gressus

(18)
ā
longitudo pontis de Frome[c] inter duas portas continet .24.
gressus;

(19)
VICUS DE LE WERE
Item via de principio vltra & prope Newgate ad finem vie vltra
le Weere & le wateryng place prope le graunt Orchard continet
occies .60[ta]. & 20. gressus continet .500. gressus

---

a   *sic*
b   Blank in MS
c   *pontis de Frome* underlined, probably by Talbot, with § in margin

(13)
THE ROAD TO
Also, the road from the said end of the Broadmead road, going by Marshall Street[1] to the Bars where tenants of my father dwell as wanton women, measures ... .

p.88

(14)
The length of the churchyard of St James, Bristol, measures 150 steps.
Its width measures 100 steps.

(15)
OF THE CHURCH OF ST NICHOLAS
The width of the nave of St Nicholas's church, between the street called St Nicholas's on the north side and the lower street the other side of the crypt, called the entry to The Back, measures less than 5 yards.

(16)
Memorandum: from the gate-tower of the street of Baldwin Street as far as the great corner at the beginning of The Key of Bristol, along by the town wall, there are three times 60, that is 180 [steps].

(17)
Also, from St John's Gate going along Christmas Street as far as the beginning of the bridge of the gate of Fromegate there are 124 steps.

(18)
The length of the Frome bridge between the two gates measures 24 steps.

(19)
THE STREET OF THE WEIR
Also, the road from [its] beginning just outside Newgate, to the end of the road beyond The Weir and the watering-place near the great orchard, measures eight times 60 plus 20 steps: it measures 500 steps.

1   More or less modern Merchant Street, in Broadmead

(19) [continued]

ā . +

Via de jnteriori parte de le Newgate per turrim[a] Bristollie &
per Ecclesiam sancti petri[b] et sancte Marie de la port continet
.nonies. .9.60.20. gressus .560[c]
.560.gressus

(20)

Via prope Ecclesiam sancti petri ducente de Wynchstrete ad
principium Cornerij[d] vie orientalis partis jncepcionis de le
bocherye continet ex transverso prope fontem de via prope
Ecclesiam sancti petri sic continet ... [e] gressus

(21)

SEYNT MARY [LE][f] PORT STRET

Via jncipiente ex parte orientali de le bochery eundo per
longitudionem vie de lez Shamlys[g] continuando ad finem porte
sancti Nicholai continet in longitudine quinquies .60. & .34.
gressus jdest .334. gressus.

longitudo de .4. domibus magnis de le bochery continet .25.
gressus
latitudo 4 domorum magnarum de bochery continet ...   [h]
gressus
Et[i] subtus dictarum magnarum domorum sunt grosse et magne
volte,

(22)

+

Vicus qui incipit a prima parte pontis & Finis de Radclyffstrete
vsque cornerium vie incepcionis de templestrete apud
Stallagecrosse[j] continet sexies .60 id est 360 gressus & finis de
dicta via apud le slepe de Avyn in angulo vie borealis
transceundo per magnam fontem,

---

a   *lond* (for *london?*) deleted
b   *ad* deleted
c   *.560.* is badly smudged, so it has been rewritten above the line, then at
     the beginning of the next line, and also in fainter ink in the margin
d   Worcestre started to write *orie* (for *orientalis*) then deleted it before
     writing *vie orientalis*
e   Blank in MS
f   Edge of page torn away
g   Worcestre originally wrote *Shameles*, then inserted the revised ending
h   Blank in MS

(19) [continued]
The road from the inner side of the Newgate by the tower of Bristol[1] and by the church of St Peter, and St Mary le Port, measures nine (9) [times] 60 [plus] 20 steps: 560 steps.

(20)
The road near the church of St Peter leading from Wynch Street to the beginning of the corner of the road, at the east end of the start of The Butchery, measures across the road next to the fountain[2] by the church of St Peter, thus measures ... steps.

(21)
SAINT MARY [LE] PORT STREET
The road starting at the east end of The Butchery, going along the length of the road of The Shambles, continuing to the end of St Nicholas's Gate, measures in length five times 60 plus 34 steps, that is 334 steps.

The length of the 4 great halls of The Butchery measures 25 steps.
The width of the 4 great halls of the Butchery measures ... steps.
And beneath the said great halls are massive great vaults.[3]

(22)
The street which starts from the first side of the bridge and the end of Redcliffe Street, as far as the corner of the road at the start of Temple Street at Stallage Cross, measures six times 60, that is 360 steps; and the said road ends at the Avon Slip, at the northern corner of the road going past the great well.

---

1   The keep of Bristol Castle, described **(396)** and **(422)**, would seem (see note a opposite) to have reminded Worcestre of the Tower of London
2   St Peter's Pump
3   Worcestre's use of *volta* (a church crypt, cf. **(10)**, **(15)**), implies that these were more than ordinary cellars, and had vaulted roofs

---

i   Worcestre wrote *Et s* at the start of the line, crossed it through and began the entry again immediately below
j   Originally written as *Cheryncrosse* (Charing Cross, another confusion with London? cf. **(19)**), deleted and *Stallagecrosse* written above

(23)
Vicus incepcionis apud le Avyn in parte boriali[a] de Stallage crosse[b], eundo per longam viam ad templeyate continet .110. gressus vsque crucem vocatum Stallage crosse Et continuando dictam viam de cruce prope[c] ibidem vocata Stalygecros Vsque Ecclesiam Crucis sancti Templi jntroitus Ecclesie predicte continet .300. gressus.   et sic continuando ad finem porte vocate templeyate continet[d] .320. gressus.   Summa in toto …[e]

(24)
Portus templi longitudo continet .9. virgas.   latitudo porte templi continet 3 virgas

(25)[f]
Templestrete,
Vicus vltra portam Templi versus Ecclesiam sancte marie de Radclyff continet 420. gressus

(26)[f]
latitudo vie de le Templestrete prope portas Ecclesie fratrum sancti Augustini continet 20 gressus

latitudo principij vie templestrete ex parte boriali apud Staligecros continet … [g] gressus
latitudo vie in fine apud Templeyate continet .20. gressus.

p.89

(27)
SHAMELYS,
　　　Domus altissime et late Regis cum voltis in vico de
　　　Worshypstrete, alias Shamellys sive bocherye,

In vico vocato le Shamelys sunt .3. profundissimi Cellarij[h] Regis sub tribus domibus magnis quantitatis & alte edificature que fuerunt ordinate pro lanis et mercandisis custodiendis, ad onerandas naues Bristollie ad exteras partes .Vltra marinas. Et similiter sunt in dicto vico .4. alie Cellarij;

---

a　Worcestre first wrote *meridionali*, deleted it and wrote *boriali* above
b　Worcestre first wrote *Caryncrosse* (cf. **(22)**), deleted it and wrote *Stallage crosse* above
c　*Stallage crosse* is written again between the lines, above *prope*
d　*continet* repeated
e　Blank in MS
f　Items **(25)**–**(26)** have been inserted in the margin alongside **(23)**–**(24)**

(23)
The street starting at the Avon on the north side of Stallage Cross, going along the road to Temple Gate, measures 110 steps as far as the cross called Stallage Cross. And continuing the said road from next to the cross there, called Stallage Cross, as far as the church of Holy Cross Temple, [to] the entry of the aforesaid church, measures 300 steps. And continuing thus to the end [at] the gate called Temple Gate measures 320 steps. The sum total ...

(24)
The length of Temple Gate measures 9 yards; the width of Temple Gate measures 3 yards.

(25)
Temple Street:
The street beyond Temple Gate towards the church of St Mary Redcliffe measures 420 steps.

(26)
The width of the road of Temple Street near the gates of the church of the Augustinian Friars measures 20 steps.

The width of the beginning of Temple Street road, at the north end at Stallage Cross, measures ... steps.
The width of the road at the Temple Gate end measures 20 steps.

p.89

(27)
SHAMBLES
The extremely high and spacious halls of the King,
with vaults, in the street of Worship Street,
otherwise the Shambles or Butchery.

In the street called The Shambles there are 3 extremely deep cellars of the King, beneath three halls of great size and built high, which were established for the safekeeping of wool and merchandise, for loading Bristol ships [bound] for foreign parts beyond the seas. And likewise there are in the said street 4 other cellars.

---

g   Blank in MS
h   *Cellarij* repeated

(28)
Volta profundissima sive Cellarium fortissimum subtus portam
Newgate[a]

(29)
VOLTA SUPER PONTEM BRISTOLLIE
Super pontem Bristollie est pulcra volta larga artificiose
operata subtus Capellam beate marie pro Consulibus et juratis
ville Bristollie sedendus et ad conciliandum super comuni
vtilitate[b] ville

Super dictum pontem Bristollie sunt .4. Cellaria in fine &
principio pontis.

(30)
TOLSYLLE
Spacium super le Tolsylle[c] vbi maior et conciliarij ville obviant
de die in diem quando videtur exspediens. sub coopertura de
cylynge cum plumbo coram hostium occidentalem Ecclesie
Christi continet .5. virgas et ex alia parte coram hygh Strete
continet ... [d] virgas

(31)
DOMUS CONCILIARIJ PRO RE PUBLICA VILLE PROPE
ALTAM CRUCEM.
Officium Domus conciliarij tam maioris vicicomitis ballivorum
ville ac conciliariorum principalium eorundem tam de
principalibus mercatoribus cum exspediens fuerit est scitum
prope le Tolsylle Court est proximo sequens spacium apertum
de stacione super le Tolsylle ex opposito Cancelle Ecclesie
omnium sanctorum cum cameris desuper honestissimo
preparatis pro conciliarij gubernatorum dicte ville annexis in
parte meridionali Ecclesie sancte Adoeni.

p.90

(32)
Pyll strete, in parochia sancti Stephani,

PARS VIE DE PYLLSTRET
Via a Porta sancti leonardi incipiente sub porta sancti leonardi[e]
videlicet a fine vie de Baldwenstrete directe eundo per

---

a   Worcestre wrote *portam New*, ran out of space at the end of the line,
    and rewrote *Newgate* in full more clearly above
b   *vtilitate* written a second time, more clearly
c   *continet* deleted

(28)
[There is] an extremely deep vault or strong cellar under the gate [of] Newgate.

(29)
THE CRYPT UPON BRISTOL BRIDGE
Upon Bristol Bridge there is a beautiful large crypt, skilfully worked, below the chapel of the Blessed Mary, for accommodating the councillors and officers of the town of Bristol, and for meetings on the public business of the town.

Upon the said Bristol Bridge there are 4 cellars, at the beginning and end of the bridge.

(30)
TOLSEY
The place over against the Tolsey, where the mayor and councillors of the town meet from day to day, when it seems needful, beneath the cover of a flat lead roof, fronting the west door of Christ Church, measures 5 yards; and on the other side fronting High Street it measures ... yards.

(31)
THE HALL OF THE COUNCILLORS FOR THE GOVERNMENT OF THE TOWN, NEAR THE HIGH CROSS.
The Meeting-hall of the councillors, as well of the mayor, sheriff and bailiffs of the town and their chief councillors, and of the chief merchants when it shall be needful, is situated next to the Tolsey Court. It is right next to the open meeting-place over against the Tolsey, opposite the chancel of All Saints' church, with rooms above, most worthily furnished for the ruling councillors of the said town, attached onto the south side of St Ewen's church.

p.90

(32)
                    Pill Street, in the parish of St Stephen.

PART OF THE ROAD OF PILL STREET
The road from St Leonard's Gate, starting under St Leonard's Gate (to wit, from the end of the road of Baldwin Street),

---

d   Blank in MS
e   *incipiente sub porta sancti leonardi* has been inserted above the line
    in different ink

(32) [continued]
venellam conducentam ad le key Bristollie vbi le custom hows[a]
in principio trianguli super le key[b] qui[c] quidem triangulus est
in parte meridionali de le key in medio cuius trianguli exellens
domus conducti de Frestone scita est & construitur, Et dicta
via modo est finis de la pyllestrete, continet .100. gressus

latitudo dicte venelle continet .5. virgas ad jncepcionem anguli[d]
dicti Trianguli de le Custom hows & ibidem finiente

(33)[e]
scribatur ista pagiam cum vico de hyghstrete

VENELLA PARVA DE HYGHSTRETE PER CIMITERIUM OMNIUM SANCTORUM[f]
ā
Venella parvissima et stricta eundo de hyghstrete prope altam
Crucem inter Ecclesiam omnium sanctorum & officium artis
Cocorum ville extendo per cimiterium eiusdem Ecclesie et
meridionalem partem dicte Ecclesie. iuxta murum noue ale
edificatum diebus juuentutis mee per hostium meridionalem
Ecclesie predicte. et iuxta quem murum Dominus Thomas
Botoner presbiter fuerit sepultus in parte orientali hostij
meridionalis sed credo ossa dicti domini Thome sunt remota
tempore edificationis nove ale. et Tumba de Frestone eius
similiter est remota, Et dicta stricta venella in longitudine
extendit ad parvam et Curtam viam in occidentali parte dicte
Ecclesie ad finem hospicij alti[g] prioris Collegij vocati lez
kalenders vbi dictus dominus Thomas Botoner fuit vt
supponitur consocius. et in domo[h] prioratus hospicij obijt ex
certa scientia Elizabet fratris[i] sue matris mee michi relate. circa
etatem juuentatis mee quinque vel sex annorum vt suppono;
quia quamvis fui presens secum die mortis sue cum matre mea.
vale faciendo die vltimo vite sue non habui discrecionem ad
noticiam persone sue. Et vt credo Carte & evidencie tam
hereditatis sue in tenemento suo prope yeldehall in Bradstrete

---

a *custom hows* written again more clearly above the line
b *key* written twice
c *quod* deleted and *qui* written in its place
d Worcestre originally wrote *...ad angulum dicti...* and then inserted
   incepcionem anguli in front of *angulum* without deleting it
e In the margin is *q'* (for *questio* or *query?*)
f Because of its family interest, this item has been annotated and
   underlined by at least three other hands, although one of these might
   perhaps be Worcestre himself on a later occasion. Only amendments
   and underlinings by Worcestre are shown here. For details of
   annotations by others see Appendix

(32) [continued]
going straight along the lane leading to The Key of Bristol
where the Customs House [is] at the beginning of the triangle
upon The Key (which same triangle is on the south side of The
Key) – in the middle of which triangle a fine conduit house of
freestone is sited and built. And the end of the said road is
now the end of Pill Street; it measures 100 steps.

The width of the said lane measures 5 yards at the start of the
corner of the said triangle at the Customs House, and it
finishes there.

(33)
This page to be written up with the street of High Street.

A SMALL LANE FROM HIGH STREET PAST THE
CHURCHYARD OF ALL SAINTS.

A very small and narrow lane, going from High Street near the
High Cross, between All Saints' church and the hall of the
Cooks' guild of the town, extending past the churchyard of
that church and the south side of the said church, next to the
wall of the new aisle, built in the days of my youth by the
south door of the aforesaid church. And next to which wall
Sir Thomas Botoner, priest, may have been buried, on the east
side of the south door; but I believe the bones of the said Sir
Thomas were removed at the time of building the new aisle,
and his tomb of freestone was likewise removed. And the said
narrow lane extends in length to a small and short road on the
west side of the said church, at the end of the tall lodgings of
the prior of the College called the Kalendars, where the said
Sir Thomas Botoner was, as I have understood, a fellow. And
he died in the house of the priory lodgings, to the certain
knowledge of his sister[1] Elizabeth, my mother, [as] told to me,
about the fifth or sixth year of my childhood,[2] as I suppose;
because although I was present with him on the day of his
death, with my mother, for leave-taking on the last day of his
life, I did not have understanding [enough] to notice his
appearance. And, as I believe, deeds and documents both of
his inheritance in his house near the Guildhall in Broad Street,

---

1   See note i below
2   Worcestre was born in 1415, so this would be about 1420

---

g   *fratrum* deleted
h   *hospicij* deleted
i   *sic*, error for *sororis*

(33) [continued]
ex parte meridionali dicte Gyldhall necnon de hereditate eius
per Thomam Botoner patrem eius et matris mee in villa de
Bokyngham in Westrete jacentem versus aquam in parte ...[a]
scitam ac in villis adiacentibus iacent[b] de racione deberent
remanere quando queratur de priore kalendarij si remanent
inter eorum evidencias de evidencijs Domini Thome Botoner
consocij eorum;

ā
longitudo dicte venelle stricte continet .60. gressus
ā
latitudo dicte venelle continet tres pedes siue vnam virgam;

(34)
ALLEHALOWIS LANE BREVIS VIA
ā
Via breuis de Cornstrete returnando[c] per occidentalem partem
hospicij prioris de kalenders continet in longitudine .170.
gressus
ā
latitudo vie continet .5. virgas prope Cornstrete
ā
Cellarium vnum vel duo pro vinis vendendis est in dicta via
parua

p.91

(35)
                    versus montem sancti michaelis[d]
circumgirata que quidem venella alciora et ulteriora trium
dictarum venellarum quarum vna jncipit venella in medio vici
vocato   horstrete   ad   angulum   muri   gardini   fratrum
Carmelitarum ad ymaginem beate marie in muro predicto scita,
& continuat vsque crucem de lapide & fontem[e] remociorem ad
caput montis vie de Stepestrete,

---

a   Blank in MS
b   *sic*
c   *ad* deleted
d   **(35)**, with its abrupt start, is in fact a continuation of **(36)**, and the
    apparent heading is a catchphrase to link the two
e   *Vlter* (presumably for *Vlteriorem*) deleted

(33) [continued]
on the south side of the said Guildhall, and also of his
inheritance from Thomas Botoner, father of him and of my
mother, in the town of Buckingham, in West Street, situated
and lying next to the river on the ... side, and in neighbouring
villages, by reason ought to survive – sometime enquire of the
Prior of the Kalendars if there remain among their documents
any documents of their fellow Sir Thomas Botoner.

The length of the said narrow lane measures 60 steps.

The width of the said lane measures three feet or one yard.

(34)
ALLHALLOWS LANE, A SHORT ROAD

The short road turning off from Corn Street, past the west
side of the lodgings of the Prior of the Kalendars, measures
170 steps in length.

The width of the road measures 5 yards next to Corn Street.

There are one or two cellars for the sale of wines in the said
small road.

p.91

(35)
...towards St Michael's Hill[1]
[winding around];[2] the which lane is highest and furthest of
the three said lanes, of which one lane begins in the middle of
the street called Horestreet[3] at the corner of the garden wall of
the Carmelite Friars, at the statue of the Blessed Mary set in
the aforesaid wall, and continues as far as the stone cross and
the further well at the top of the hill-road of Steep Street.

---

1   Continuation of **(36)**: see note d opposite
2   Transferred to **(36)** in translation
3   Host Street on Millerd plan, 1673

(35) [continued]
<u>FROGLANE</u>
et venella secunda jncipit ad dictam Fontem siue crucem &
vocatur Froglane & continuat in parte retro^a ortorum^b Ecclesie
de Gauntes et^c sanctuarium

(36)
<u>IN HORSTRETE</u>
1   Venella in horstrete iuxta occidentalem partem Ecclesie
sancti Bertholomei vocata Stypestrete jncipiendo & Ascendendo
ad Ecclesiam sancti Michaelis vsque ad crucem & fontem de
Frestone continet ...^d

2   Venella secunda in horstrete incipiendo ad finem muri
fratrum Carmelitarum vbi ymago sancte marie ponitur in
tabernaculo muri fratrum.   et transceundo versus montem
sancti michaelis vsque ad finem dicte venelle vocate ...^d
continet ...^d gressus

MURUS FRATRUM CARMELITARUM
Via de jncepcione dicte venelle in horstrete ex dextra manu
eundo per murum fratrum ad jntroitum Ecclesie Fratrum^e
coram le bak fratrum in opposito de le key Bristollie continet
.80. gressus

3   Venella alia ex sequenti via de horstrete ad sanctum
augustinum eundo sed jncipit ad portam jntroitus Ecclesie
fratrum Carmelitarum per viam de le bak & sic eundo ad
borialem plagam per <u>Froglane</u> scindendo^f viam & sic
continuando dictam venellam borialiter ad finem dicte venelle
continet .240. gressus versus montem sancti michaelis^g

(37)
<u>VENELLE SUPER LE KEY CORAM AQUAM DE FROME
CURRENTEM</u>
prima venella super le key eundo ad Mershstrete jncipiendo ad
domum principalem lapideam jncepcionis de le key versus le
mersh ex opposito ...^h continet .80. gressus.ⁱ

---

a   *de* deleted
b   presumably intended for *hortorum*
c   *Abbathium* deleted, referring to St Augustine's abbey
d   Blank in MS
e   *continet* deleted
f   *sic*, perhaps an error for *ascendendo*
g   Continues as **(35)**
h   Blank in MS, presumably intending St Augustine the Less
i   *gressus .80.* repeated on the line below, where there is more space

(35) [continued]
FROG LANE
And the second lane begins at the said well or cross, and is called Frog Lane; and it continues on the back side of the gardens of the Gaunts' church, and of the precinct. [1]

(36)
IN HORESTREET
1   A lane in Horestreet, next to the west side of St Bartholomew's church, called Steep Street, beginning and climbing to St Michael's church, measures as far as the cross and well of freestone ...

2   The second lane in Horestreet, beginning at the end of the wall of the Carmelite Friars, where the statue of St Mary is set in a shrine [in] the Friary wall; and going along towards St Michael's Hill as far as the end of the said lane called ... , measures ... steps.

THE WALL OF THE CARMELITE FRIARS
The road from the beginning of the said lane in Horestreet, on the right hand, going along the Friars' wall to the entrance of the Friars' church, fronting The Friars' Back, opposite The Key of Bristol measures 80 steps.

3   Another lane, next along the road of Horestreet going towards St Augustine's; but it begins at the entry gate of the Carmelite Friars' church along the road from The Back, and so going to the northern area, cutting across the Frog Lane road, [2] and so continuing [along] the said lane northwards to the end of the said lane, [winding around][3] towards St Michael's Hill. It measures 240 steps;[4]

(37)
LANES UPON THE KEY FRONTING THE COURSE OF THE RIVER FROME
The first lane upon The Key going to Marsh Street, beginning at the foremost stone house at the start of The Key towards The Marsh, opposite ... , measures 80 steps.

---

1   The deleted reference to the abbey (note c opposite), makes it clear that this refers to St Augustine's abbey precinct or burial ground, now College Green
2   Alternatively (cf. note f opposite) ... by Froglane, climbing the road,...
3   Supplied from **(35)**
4   Continues as **(35)**

(37) [continued]
Secunda venella sequens versus Ecclesiam sancti Stephani infra
de le Key versus mersh strete intrando[a] latitudinem vie .30.
gressuum continet eius longitudo .90. gressus

Tercia venella de Keya eundo ad Ecclesiam sancti Stephani per
portam meridionalem nouam Ecclesie vsque ad finem Ecclesie
orientalem continet .180. gressus

Quarta venella de le key eundo per alteram partem Ecclesie
sancti Stephani per le north dore vsque le Mershstrete continet
.84. gressus

Quinta venella eundo ab domo jncipit coram portam
meridionalem ex novo factam Ecclesie eundo nouum Campanile
& costeram parietis borialis Ecclesie continet .90.[b]
Continet 90 gressus[c]

Sexta[d] venella a loco trianguli de le key de domo magistri
Shyppard subtus celarium sic eundo ad Ecclesiam sancti
Stephani ex parte boriali vsque ad ...[e] continet .90. gressus

(38)
KEYA[f]
Triangulus vicus de le key in quo loco magni spacii dicti
trianguli vbi pulchrum conductum aque scita est de Frestone
erectum pro commodo ville computando siue numerando ab
angulo de vico vocato le key coram aquam de Frome et eundo
directa via ad oppositum loci. viz versus cimiterium sancti
leonardi vbi jncepcio solarij domorum edificatur super trabes
jta quod homo potest sicco pede transeire[g] per keyam ad
Ecclesiam sancti laurencij. continet .54. gressus.

---

a　*de le Key versus mershe strete intrando* has been added below, with a
　　mark to suggest its insertion at this point
b　This paragraph appears to have been squeezed in afterwards, so that *ab
　　domo* refers to *domo magistri Shyppard* below.
c　Written in margin opposite, for lack of space in the text (note b)
d　*Quinta* deleted. Having miscounted the network of lanes, Worcestre
　　then inserted the paragraph above (see note b)
e　Blank in MS
f　In the margin below the heading is *q'* (for *questio* or *query*?)
g　*ad* deleted

(37) [continued]
The second lane along towards St Stephen's church, entering in from The Key towards Marsh Street: the width of the road measures 30 steps, its length 90 steps.

The third lane from The Key, going to St Stephen's church, past the new south door of the church as far as the east end of the church, measures 180 steps.

The fourth lane from The Key, going past the other side of St Stephen's church, past the north door as far as Marsh Street, measures 84 steps.

The fifth lane, going from the house,[1] begins in front of the newly built south door of the church, going [by] the new bell-tower and beside the north wall of the church; it measures 90.[2]
It measures 90 steps

The sixth lane from the triangular place off The Key, from Master Shipward's house, [with] warehouse below,[3] so going to St Stephen's church on the north side as far as ... measures 90 steps

(38)
THE KEY
The triangular street off The Key, in which place [is] the said great triangular space, where a fair water-conduit, built of freestone, is situated for the convenience of the town, counting or reckoning from the corner of the street called The Key, fronting the river Frome, and going straight across to the opposite spot, to wit towards St Leonard's churchyard, where [is] the start of the upper room of the houses built out upon jetties, so that a man can pass dry-shod along The Key to St Lawrence's church: measures 54 steps.

---

1   The house of Master Shipward, below (see note d opposite)
2   see notes b,c opposite
3   *sic*, or could perhaps be an error for *subtus solarium*, [going] below the solar: cf. **(38)** and **(62)** note e

p.92

(39)

De Muro ville ad finem de le bakk
DE MURO VILLE CIRCA LE MERSH & LE KEY

Murus Ville longitudo viz a prima porta vocata le mersh yate prope finem vie de le bakk ab aqua de Avyn[a] sic transceundo per le mersh prope dictum murum. vsque portam secundam ville ad finem vie de mershstretet[b] continet in longitudine .440. gressus[c]. ∴ Locus facture navium[d] ∴ Et continuatio dicti muri vocati le towne walle eundo de dicta porta secunda vocata le Mershyate transceundo per locum vbi naves de nouo sunt erecte et composite. ac arbores & mastys de vyrre[e] cum anchoris jacent et cellarij plures et spacium magnum jnfra dictum murum vsque primum angulum de le key Bristollie in occidentali parte de le kay vbi naves magne iacent in le woose in parte occidentali de le kay aque de Frome[f] currentis que est primus locus de le key eundo versus Ecclesiam sancti Stephani & Ecclesiam sancti laurentij continet longitudo dicti muri .320.[g] gressus.[h] Et in toto[i] dictus murus a prima porta de le bak vsque eundem primum locum incepcionis pavimenti de le key continet .760. gressus

Altitudo dicti muri continet per estimacionem .40. pedes latitudo dicti muri continet .8. pedes;

p.93

(40)

Apud hygh crosse .4. vie quadriuiales[j] videlicet hyghstrete Bradstrete Wynchstrete & seynt Collas strete

(41)

[k]at seynt Collas yate[l] in the north syde of the yate meten a crosse wyse .iiij. weyes. whych ben the shamelys. and seynt Nicholas strete. the waye entryng to the brygge yate. and the seyd hyghstrete

---

a   *aqua de Avyn* underlined, with § in margin opposite, by Talbot
b   *sic*
c   *gressus* written again above
d   Marginal note intended as an insert at the point marked ∴ in the text
e   *vyrre* underlined in the same ink as note a (above), with *fyrre abies* (silver fir) written in the margin, probably by Talbot
f   *aque de Frome* underlined in the same ink, with § in margin opposite, by Talbot
g   *.320.* underlined, with *320* written again above it
h   *320* repeated and deleted
i   *altitudo* deleted

p.92

(39)

Of the town wall to the end of The Back
OF THE TOWN WALL AROUND THE MARSH & THE KEY
The town wall: length, to wit from the first gate called the
Marsh Gate near the end of the way from The Back, so passing
from the river Avon by the marsh next to the said wall, as far
as the second town gate, at the end of the road of Marsh
Street, measures 440 steps in length. The ship-building place:
And the continuation of the said wall called the town wall,
going from the said second gate called the Marsh Gate, passing
by the place where new ships are set up and fitted out, and
where poles and masts of fir as well as anchors lie; and [where
are] many warehouses and a great space within the said wall,
as far as the first corner of The Key of Bristol, at the western
end of The Key, where great ships lie on the mud at the
western end of The Key (the course of the river Frome) which
is the main part of The Key, going towards St Stephen's
church and St Lawrence's church: the length of the said wall
measures 320 steps. And the said wall, overall, from the first
gate of The Back as far as that first spot at the beginning of
the pavement of The Key measures 760 steps.

The height of the said wall measures, by estimation, 40 feet.
The width of the said wall measures 8 feet.

p.93

(40)
At High Cross [is] a 4-way crossroads, to wit High Street,
Broad Street, Wynch Street and St Nicholas Street.[1]

(41)
At St Nicholas's Gate, on the north side of the gate, 4 roads
meet as a crossroads: which are The Shambles, and St Nicholas
Street, the road leading to the bridge gate, and the said High
Street.

---

1   *sic*, error for Corn Street

---

j   *tam* deleted
k   *Int* deleted
l   *ben* deleted

(42)

at the soutsyde of seynt Collas yate meten twey chyff weyes, the chieff brygge uppon iiij. grete arches of .viij. x[a] vethym yn hyth and the fayre Chapelle vppon the .v. arch
and the second way havyng the space of a Tryangle goyng to bak by seynt Nicholas Chyrch

(43)

ā

Item at the begynnyng of the bakk there the fyrst Gryse[b] called a slypp ben twey weyes. the fyrst way ys the seyd slepe of … [c] yerdes long goyng to the water called Avyn water[d] to wesshe clothes and to entre ynto the vessells & shyppes that comen to the seyd bak & the second way entryth yn Baldwynestreet

(44)

ā

at the[e] Crosse yn Baldwynestrete been .iiij. crosse wayes metyng. one way goyng and ys a grete wyde way goyng to Bafftstrete.[f] The[g] second othyr way[h] goyng northward bye a hygh Gryse called a Steyr of xxxij. steppys ynto seynt Collas Streete. The othyr tweyn metyng wayes at the seyd cros of Baldwyne streete

(45)

ā

At the southsyde of seynt John ys[i] yaate meten also .iiij. crosse weyes. whych one chieff way ys Bradstrete, the second ys Toure strete[j] bye seynt John ys chyrch goyng streyt too Wynch streete. and ys but a streyt way goyng by the old towne walle and the old toune yate called blynde yate streyt by the auncient fyrst yaate called pyttey yate vppon the hylle[k] entryng ynto Wynchstrete. called Castel streete,

p.94

The .iij[d]. way[l] ys seynt laurens strete goyng from seynt John yate ynto Smallestrete

---

a .viij. with x written immediately above; since this cannot be 8x10 fathoms (480 feet), it is probably 8 fathoms amended to 10 without deletion
b Gryse repeated above and in front, rather more neatly
c Blank in MS
d Underlined in Worcestre's characteristic style, but with § by Talbot, in margin opposite
e the repeated

(42)
At the south side of St Nicholas Gate, two main roads meet: the main bridge upon 4 great arches 10[1] fathoms high, and the fair chapel upon a 5th arch.[2]
The second road being a triangular space going to The Back past St Nicholas church.

(43)
Also at the beginning of The Back, at the first alley called a slip, are two roads; the first road is the said slip, ... yards long, going to the river called Avon-water, for washing cloths[3] and boarding the vessels and ships that come to the said Back; and the second road leads to Baldwin Street.

(44)
At the cross in Baldwin Street 4 cross-roads meet. One road leading off is a great wide road going to Back Street.
The other, second way goes northwards by a steep alley called a stair, of 32 steps, into St Nicholas Street. The other two roads meet at the said cross of Baldwin Street.

(45)
At the south side of St John's Gate 4 cross-roads also meet: of which one main road is Broad Street; the second is Tower Street, going past St John's church, direct to Wynch Street, and is but a narrow road going beside the old town wall and the old town gate called Blind Gate, straight past the ancient first gate called Pithay Gate, up the hill called Castle Street, leading to Wynch Street.

p.94

The 3rd road is St Lawrence Street, going from St John's Gate to Small Street.

---

1 i.e. 60 feet; or 8 fathoms (48 feet): see note a opposite
2 Bristol Bridge had four arches (Millerd plan, 1673). For the fifth arch beneath the Chapel on the Bridge cf. **(261)**
3 cf. **(250)**

---

f *sic*, clearly written as *Bafftstrete*, not Basststrete
g *The* repeated
h Worcestre wrote *the* at the end of the previous line, deleted it, and inserted *The second* in front of *othyr way* on the next line
i *ys* repeated
j *by* deleted
k *goyn* deleted
l *goeth* deleted

(45) [continued]
The .iiijth. way throw the seyd yate of seynt John Goyng ynto Cristmastrete called knyfsmythstret

(46)
ā
In the north syde of seynt Johnys yate. ys a .iij. Triangle ways. one way goyng north to Cristmasse strete warde

The second way goth ryght Est^a the woult of seynt John chyrch goyng yn to Gropecount lane to monken brygge a pryson^b place somtyme

The .iij. way goyng a crosse way to the kay. by the lower way of seynt laurens and by the old temple of yewys. where be grete Vowtes vnder the^c hyghest walle of Bristow and the olde Chyrch of Seynt Gylys was bylded ovyr the Vowtes yn the way goyng by Seynt laurens laane yn to Smalstrete,

(47)
ā
At Seynt leonard yate yn the East syde meten wythynne the yate .iiij. quadryvyalle weyes. as Corn strete in the Est part. the second way toward the north ys seynt leonard way goyng from the chyrch streyt ynto Smallestrete The .iij^d. way goth Esterly from seynt^d leonard chyrch ynto seynt Collas strete,^{e}

(48)
The yate of Seynt leonard vnder the seyd Chyrch crosseth .ij. weyes. the south East way ys Baldwyne strete goyng to the^f bakk

The second way ys called pylle Strete. there of old dayes renne the water called Frome by^g Baldwynestrete. to the bakk fallyng yn to Avyn^h water and whych Pylle strete gooth strayt northly by the old Custom house to the kay where ys a grete space lyke to a large Tryangle^i and yn the myddell of the seyd Tryangle ys a fayre Tour of Frestone bylded,

---

a   *by* deleted
b   *pryson* repeated
c   *an* deleted and *the* written above
d   *N* deleted
e   *strete* repeated
f   *the* repeated

(45) [continued]
The 4th road [is] through the said Gate of St John, going to Christmas Street, [also] called Knifesmith Street.[1]

(46)
On the north side of St John's Gate is a triangle of 3 roads: one road goes north towards Christmas Street.

The second road goes sharp east past the crypt[2] of St John's church, going to Gropecount Lane, to Monkenbridge, once a prison.

The 3rd road goes the opposite way, to The Key, along the lower road of St Lawrence and past the old Jews' Synagogue, where there are great cellars under the highest wall of Bristol; and the old church of St Giles was built over the cellars, in the road going along St Lawrence Lane to Small Street.

(47)
At St Leonard's Gate, on the east side, a 4-way crossroads meets under the gate: that is, Corn Street on the east side; the second road, northwards, is St Leonard's road going from the church direct to Small Street. The 3rd road goes eastwards[3] from St Leonard's church to St Nicholas Street.[4]

(48)
St Leonard's Gate, under the said church, faces two ways. The south-east road is Baldwin Street, going to The Back.

The second road is called Pylle Street. There, in the old days, the river called the Frome flowed beside Baldwin Street to The Back, falling into the river Avon. This Pylle Street goes due north past the old Customs House to the Key, where there is a great space like a large triangle; and in the middle of the said triangle a fair tower of freestone is built.

---

1   cf. **(93)** which confirms that this street had two names
2   cf. **(10)**
3   *sic*, presumably an error for southwards
4   The fourth arm of the crossroads is St Leonard's Gate: see **(48)**

---

g   *of old dayes renne* the water *called Frome by* is underlined, probably by Talbot, with § in the margin opposite
h   *fallyng yn to Avyn* is underlined, probably by Talbot, with § in the margin opposite
i   *Tryangle* repeated more clearly

p.95

(49)

Item yn the myddys of Pyllestrete toward the new chyrch[a] Toure of Seynt Stevyns metyn .iiij. wayes dyuersly. at the entree of Seynt Stevyns Chyrch yerd at the style or lytille yate the fyrst way westward ys a large way & a long called mershstrete during[b] to mershyate.[c] there many merchauntes and also maryners duellyn.

ā

At the seyd Chyrch style ys a laane goyng yn the south syde of Seynt Stevyn chyrch goyng by the chyrch yerde to the kay by olde[d] leycetyr dore yn the north syde of the Toure of the chyrch by the new doore to the seyd kay

ā

Item at the eende of the seyd Pyllestrete by the seyd lane that retorned by the begynnyng of the seyd fyrst lane. ys a nother laane that goth evyn ryght by the Este ende of Seynt Stevyn chyrch vnder the hygh auter and so contynewyth the seyd laane to the seyd kay northly

Item owt of that laane that gooth by the Este eende of Seynt Stevyn chyrch returnyth another laane from the north syde of Seynt Peter[e] chyrch. by the west dore of the seyd church. turnyng to a forseyd fyrst laane so entryng to the kay.

(50)[f]

At Newyate vbi quondam scola gramatica per magistrum Robertum Land principalem didascolum cum ... [g] leyland magistri gramaticorum in Oxonia dicebatur fuisse flos gramaticorum[h] & poetarum temporibus annis plurimis revolutis. & tempore quo primo veni ad Oxoniam universitatem scolatizandi obijt in termino pasche anno christi .1432. circa mensem Junij quando generalis Eclipsis die sancti Botulphi accidebat

---

a   Worcestre started to write *of* but substituted *Toure of*
b   *sic*, an eccentric combination of Latin *ducens* and English *leading*?
c   *Mershyate* is unclearly written, and therefore repeated
d   *leyyC*, suggesting a false start and spelling difficulties with *Leycetyr*
e   *sic*, error for St Stephen
f   Because of its personal interest this item has been extensively annotated by others: see Appendix
g   Blank in MS

p.95

(49)
Also, in the middle of Pylle Street, in the direction of the new church tower of St Stephen's, 4 assorted roads meet at the entrance of St Stephen's churchyard at the stile or little gate. The first road, westwards, is a broad and long road called Marsh Street, leading to Marsh Gate; many merchants, and mariners also, dwell there.

At the said church stile, is a lane along the south side of St Stephen's church, going past the churchyard to The Key, past old Leicester's door[1] on the north side of the church tower, past the new door, to the said Key.

Also, at the end of the said Pylle Street, past the said lane which turned back at the beginning of the said first lane, is another lane which goes sharp right past the east end of St Stephen's church below the high altar; and the said lane thus continues northwards to the said Key.

Also, from that lane which goes past the east end of St Stephen's church, another lane turns back along the north side of St Peter's church,[2] past the west door of the said church, joining the aforesaid first lane [and] so leading to The Key.

(50)
At Newgate, where [was] formerly the grammar school of Master Robert Londe, head teacher with ... Leland, master of grammatical studies in Oxford,[3] said to have been the flower of grammarians and poets in times long gone by. And he[4] died at the time that I first went to Oxford University to study, in Easter term in the year of Christ 1432, about the month of June, when a general eclipse occurred on St Botulph's Day.[5]

---

1   John Leycestre, burgess and merchant, was a benefactor of St Stephen's church who died in 1437 (Wadley, *Bristol Wills* pp. 128-9)
2   Error for St Stephen's church
3   John Leland the elder, grammarian
4   Leland, although according to *D.N.B.* he died 30th April 1428. Robert Londe died in 1469: see **(237)**
5   17th June; 1432 may be an error for 1433: cf. **(119)**

---

h   *flos gramaticorum* refers to the popular saying about Leyland, which Talbot notes in full at the foot of the page: see Appendix

(51)

at the seyd Newyate yn the west part of yt wythynne Bristow. there meten .ij. large weys and the norther way ys called Towrstrete aliter wynchstrete. and so goth by the old yate of the toune about .120. steppys yn lenght, to the hygh Crosse ward where the old towne walle stode[a]

p.96[b]

(52)

Informacio cuiusdam Feryman marinarij custodientis. anglice[c] le Fery idest eundo & redeundo cum parua cimba. ex transuerso aquas de avyn et Frome venientibus de Bristollia apud Rownam,

IN PRIMIS

ā   From Bristow to Rownam j myle in longitudine vbi there as Gyston Clyff begynnyth. that ys .60. vethym hygh

ā   Froo Rounham to hungrode .2. miliaria

ā   De hungrode vsque kyngrode .2. miliaria[d]

ā   De kyngrode vsque[e] duas jnsulas de Holmys. anglice vue syght kennyng .21. myle

ā   De jnsulis Holmys vsque jnsulam londay[f] duo kennynges jdest twey syghtes continet quelibet kennyng .20. miliaria .40. miliaria

De jnsula holmys vsque ad England eende[g] versus Cylly[h] .7. kennyngys continet .147. miliaria.[i]

Ad jnsulas Syllye .21. miliaria
Summa de Bristollia vsque England eende .83. miliaria. summa totalis 124. miliaria
De England Ende[j] vltra montem sancti michaelis per ... [k] miliaria
Continet miliaria summa totalis .124.[l]

---

a   followed by the letters *ge*
b   This page, items **(52)**–**(54)**, is written upside down. **(52)** was included in Harvey, *Itineraries*, pp. 302-3, with some variations in transcription and translation
c   An illegible word, ?*f-er*, written above
d   *Qu'* (for *questio* or *query*?) in margin
e   *Holmys* deleted

(51)

At the said Newgate, on the west side of it, within Bristol, 2 broad roads meet; and the northern road is called Tower Street, otherwise Wynch Street, and goes past the old gate of the town (where the old town wall stood) about 120 steps in length towards the High Cross.

p.96
(52)

Information from a certain ferryman, a sailor in charge of (in English) 'the ferry' (that is, for going to and fro in a small skiff) across the rivers Avon and Frome, coming from Bristol, at Rownham.[1]

FIRSTLY,

> From Bristol to Rownham: 1 mile in length, to where Ghyston Cliff, which is 60 fathoms high, begins.
> From Rownham to Hungroad, 2 miles.
> From Hungroad as far as Kingroad, 2 miles.
> From Kingroad as far as the two islands of the Holms (in English a 'view sight kenning'), 21 miles.
> From the Holms islands as far as Lundy Island, two kennings, that is two sights, each kenning measures 20 miles: 40 miles.
> From the Holms islands as far as Lands End, towards the Scillies, 7 kennings: measures 147 miles.

> To the Scilly Isles: 21 miles.
> Total from Bristol as far as Lands End: 83 miles.
> Grand total 124 miles.
> Lands End [is] further than St Michael's Mount by ... miles.

The grand total measures in miles: 124

---

1 Probably the occasion noted in **(437)**, diary: 26th September 1480

---

f *.40. miliaria* deleted
g *England eende* underlined by Talbot, with § in margin, and the comment interlined, *is nott this Penwyth strett* (is not this Penwith Strait?)
h *Cyllys* written above
i *sic*: a kenning is clearly a somewhat variable measure
j *England Ende* underlined with a rough double line by Talbot
k Blank in MS
l Written in margin for lack of space

(53)

Memorandum quod a principio Franchesye de sanctuario sancti Augustini Abbathie incipiendo ad metum cimiterij antique Ecclesie isto anno christi 1480. noviter constructe eundo per medium sanctuarij ad finem eiusdem videlicet ad descensum terre & finem sanctuarij vocatum le west partye per primum murum & viam domus lapidee in eadem parte vie eundo versus lymotes[a] vbi Ecclesia de Gauntes habet jntroitum in ecclesiam predictam continet .360. gressus

ā

latitudo dicte vie eundo ad lymotes sub Brandonhille continet .42. gressus[b]

(54)

Et a dicto angulo domus muri in occidentali parte Ecclesie de le gauntys continet .720. gressus.[c] videlicet sub monte sancti Brendani Ecclesie de Gauntes ex parte boriali sanctuarij sancti Augustini jn eundo ad mansionem versus villam Rownam & Ghyston Clyff vocatem lymotes. vbi lapis altus de Frestone longitudinis unius virge siue trium pedum pro meta limita siue butta que est vltimus finis libertatum et Franchesie de villa Bristollie super aquas de Avyn & Severn[d] currentes ad Rownam directe sub pede montis sancti Brendani[e] continet a principio jntroitus sanctuarij vsque dictam domum de lymotes; hoc est intelligendo dictum jntroitum ad dictum sanctuarium sancti augustini computando ad vetus & primam Ecclesiam dicte Abbathie que modo est Ecclesia parochialis nouiter edificata, continet in toto .980. gressus

p.97

(55)

Apud[f] Rupem altissimam de Ghyston Clyff quam jncipit prope villam passagij de Rownam. vsque heremitagium. & Castellum in altera parte aquarum de Avyn & Frome. que Rupis altissima jncipit per vnum miliaris spacium de villa Bristollie et continet dicta Rupis in altitudine per longitudinem vnius miliaris & vlterius versus Rownam Rode pro navibus[g] reponendis.

---

a   *eundo versus lymotes* has been inserted above the line
b   Written in the margin for lack of space
c   *720. gressus* repeated in the margin
d   *sic*, error for Frome. *Avyn & Severn* underlined in darker ink, probably
      by Talbot
e   *montis sancti Brendani* underlined in darker ink, probably by Talbot
f   O in margin alongside start of this paragraph, by Talbot
g   *Navibus* repeated, Worcestre having partly deleted the first *navibus*

(53)

Memorandum, that from the beginning of the liberty of St Augustine's abbey precinct, starting at the boundary of the churchyard of the old church (rebuilt this year of Christ 1480) going across the middle of the precinct to its end, (to wit, to [where] the ground drops away and [to] the edge of the precinct called the west side), by the first wall and the road, [and] the stone house on that side of the road going towards the Bounds, where the Gaunts' church has an entry into the aforesaid church, measures 360 steps.

The width of the said road, going to the Bounds beneath Brandon Hill, measures 42 steps.

(54)

And from the said corner of the house-wall on the west side of the Gaunts' church measures 720 steps, to wit in going beneath St Brendan's Hill at the Gaunts' church, on the north side of St Augustine's precinct, to the dwelling house called The Bounds, towards the hamlet of Rownham and Ghyston Cliff: where [there is] a standing stone of freestone, one yard or three feet in length, as a boundary point or mark, which is the furthest point of the liberties and franchise of the town of Bristol, over against the rivers Avon and Severn[1] flowing to Rownham, right under the foot of St Brendan's Hill. It measures from the start, at the entrance to the precinct as far as the said Bounds House (that is, taking the said entrance to the said precinct of St Augustine's, [for] reckoning, as the old, original church of the said abbey, which is now the newly built parish church): it measures in all 980 steps.[2]

p.97

(55)

At the highest rock of Ghyston Cliff, which begins near the hamlet of Rownham Passage, as far as the hermitage and hill-fort on the other side of the rivers Avon and Frome; which highest rock begins one mile distant from the town of Bristol. And the said rock measures in height for the distance of one mile and more towards Rownham Road, where ships are held.[3]

---

1 *sic*, error for Frome
2 *sic*, Worcestre has mislaid 100 steps in this lengthy calculation, as 360 steps **(53)** + 720 steps **(54)** should total 1080 steps in all
3 i.e. until the tide permitted incoming ships to pass up the Avon Gorge to Bristol

(55) [continued]
et dicta Rupis[a] continet in altitudine[b] ab aqua de avyn &
Frome[c] .60. brachia videlicet de Firma terra ad quoddam
heremitagium cuius Ecclesia fundatur et dedicatur in honore
sancti vincentij[d] sunt in altitudine .20. brachia. Et a dicto
heremitagio ad profundum aquarum predictarum sunt .40.
brachia. et intellige quod brachium continet .6. pedes
longitudinis,

(56)
Castellum[e]

Castellum[f] super altitudinem terre non distans per quartam
partem miliaris de Ghyston cliff. vt dicitur a vulgaribus
plebeis,[g] ibidem fore Fundatum ante tempus Willelmi
Conquestoris per Saracenos vel Judeos per quondam Ghyst
gigantem in terra portraiatum Et quod tale Castellum
verisimile erat antiquis temporibus fundatum. remanet in
hodiernum diem in magno circuitu congeries magnorum
lapidum et parvorum sparsim seminatorum valde mirabili visu
dictas lapides ita globose iacentes.[h] in ordine et circuitu
maximo. quod ibi videbatur fuisse castrum fortissimum quam
centenarijs annis preteritis fuisse dirutum et ad terram funditus
prostratum et ideo quod est decus & honor patrie Bristollie et
Comitatui Gloucestrie habere vel audire fundaciones nobilium
Fortaliciorum & Castrorum hic inter alia scribo per modum
memorandi de isto Castro siue Fortalicio,

p.98   *[Blank]*

p.99

(57)
Via trianguli a Porta sancti Nicholai ad le
Bakke vsque le bakke[i] per principium pontis Bristollie

Trianguli longitudo de angulo domus conducte aque de
Frestone in prima introita ad le bak eundo ad portam sancti
Nicholai citra hyghstrete. et eundo per & prope vol dictam le
Croude. continet .40. gressus

---

a   *dicta Rupis* underlined by Talbot
b   Worcestre repeats this phrase, having been diverted from it by his
    description of the length of Ghyston Cliff
c   *ab aqua de avyn & Frome* underlined by Talbot
d   *sancti vincentij* underlined, with ⊗ *S. Vincent* in margin, by Talbot
e   *Castellum* is written in a large space left between **(55)** and **(56)**
f   O in margin alongside the start of this paragraph by Talbot

(55) [continued]
And the said rock measures 60 fathoms in height above the
river Avon and Frome: to wit, from the solid ground[1] to a
certain hermitage, the chapel of which is founded and dedicated
in honour of St Vincent, there are 20 fathoms in height; and
from the said hermitage to the depths of the aforesaid rivers
there are 40 fathoms, taking that a fathom measures 6 feet in
length.

(56)
The hill-fort

The hill-fort upon the high ground not a quarter of a mile
distant from Ghyston Cliff, as it is called by the common
people, was founded there before the time of William the
Conqueror by the Saracens or Jews, by a certain Ghyst, a
giant portrayed on the ground. And because so great a hill-
fort was probably built in ancient times, it remains to this day
as a large circle of great stones piled up, and small ones
scattered around, most remarkable to see; the said stones lying
thus, in an orderly ring and great circle, whereby a very
strong castle is seen to have been there, which hundreds of
years ago has been destroyed and thrown to the ground. And
because it is a credit and honour to the district of Bristol and
the county of Gloucestershire to have, or to hear of, the
origins of impressive fortresses and castles, I write this among
other things by way of a reminder of this castle or fortress.

p.98   *[Blank]*

p.99

(57)
The triangular roadway from St Nicholas's Gate to
The Back, by the beginning of Bristol Bridge.

The length of the triangle from the corner of the freestone
water-conduit house at the start of the entry to The Back,
going to St Nicholas's Gate this side of High Street, and going
close by the crypt called The Croude, measures 40 steps.

---

1   i.e. the cliff top

---

g   ⊗ in margin alongside by Talbot
h   *a castell* alongside, in Talbot's hand
i   *sic*

(57) [continued]
latitudo vie[a] ad dictum jntroitum de le bakk ad angulum cornerij proximi continue dictam domum de Frestone prope angulum strictum unius Grocer ibidem in parte dextra continet .5. gressus

Pars latus trianguli predicti eundo[b] de le Boteras in parte de le bocherey viz[c] infra principium pontis vsque ad supradictum angulum prope principium de le bak prope dictam domum conductus aquarum continet .40. gressus

Caput trianguli predicti de jncepcione prime partis pontis Bristollie ad & ex parte sinistra vsque directe eundo ad angulum oppositum vie latitudinis pontis predicti continet .20. gressus siue ... [d] virgas

(58)
.Via[e] latitudo
latitudo vie Toukerstre[f] ad finem pontis Bristollie eundo versus Stallage cros continet .14. gressus ... [g] virgas

(59)
VIA SANCTI THOME
latitudo vie de Seynt Thomasstrete stricte ad jncepcionem[h] & jntroitus vie stricte in longitudine circa .66.[i] gressus continuando per murum longum. eundo continue ad[j] Seynt Thomas strete. continet illa latitudo[k] .5. gressus   Et sic continuando per vicum Seynt Thomas strete & per domum quadratam de Frestone pro aqua gentibus illius parochie et circummanencium vsque ad murum ville Bristollie retornando versus Radclyffyate continet in longitudine[l] .305. gressus

---

a *de l* deleted
b *a le Pil* (possibly *Pillar*, changed to *Boteras*?), partially deleted
c *citra* deleted
d Blank in MS; *virg* smudged and deleted
e *qu* deleted
f *sic*
g *sive* deleted, followed by blank in MS
h In the margin opposite this point is written *memorandum de 145. gressus*; it is not clear to what this refers, or whether it is simply part of Worcestre's long calculation of 395 steps in all

(57) [continued]
The width of the road at the said entry of The Back, at the angle of the next corner along the said freestone house, [and] by the sharp corner of a grocer's there on the right-hand side, measures 5 steps.

The broad side of the aforesaid triangle, going from the buttress on The Butchery side, to wit below the beginning of the bridge, as far as the above-mentioned corner next to the beginning of The Back, by the said water-conduit house, measures 40 steps.

The top of the aforesaid triangle, from the start of the first side of Bristol Bridge, at and on the left-hand side, going straight as far as to the opposite corner of the road, across the width of the aforesaid bridge, measures 20 steps or ... yards.

(58)
The width of the road.
The width of the road of Tucker Street at the end of Bristol Bridge, going towards Stallage Cross, measures 14 steps, [or] ... yards.

(59)
ST THOMAS'S ROAD
The width of the road of Narrow St Thomas Street, at the start and entry of the narrow road, [and] continuing in length for about 66 steps beside a long wall, going on to St Thomas Street: that [part] measures in width 5 steps. And so continuing along the street of St Thomas Street, and past the square house of freestone for water for the people of that parish and living in the area, as far as the town wall of Bristol, turning towards Redcliffe Gate, measures 305 steps in length.

---

i   *.66.* written twice, first smudged and then rewritten more clearly
j   *Touker* deleted
k   *ad Se le Touker strete .14. gressus* deleted. The *Se* (beginning of *Seynt?*) has itself been deleted, before the whole phrase was crossed through
l   *continet* repeated

(60)

Via longitudo de Seynt leonardes yate vsque ad Ecclesiam sancte Werburge continet .120 gressus ad medium jntroitus Ecclesie sancte Werburge. Et sic continuando per altam crucem continue vsque eundo per officium domus de le Pyllorye continuando ad antiquissimam portam de le Oldgate muri ville ad viam siue venellam. eundo & retornando ad portam Ecclesie sancti Petri. vocate Castellstrete; jn qua via siue venella murus antiqus porte ville Bristollie scituabatur citra[a] tenementa patris mee quondam Agnete Randolf in quibus vnus aurifaber manet modo in anno christi .1480 & de nouo edificauit dicta duo tenementa in sinistra manu eundo ad portam nouam Newgate continet

p. 100

tota predicta via a porta sancti leonardi directe eundo per Cornstrete & per altam crucem ac per Ecclesias sancte Werburge & sancte trinitatis ac directe eundo per <u>Vinchstret ab antiquo vocatum Tourstret</u>, dimittendo murum antiquum ville ac antiquissimam porta ville citra pyttey yate aliter dicta ayllewardes yate. in sinistra manu dicta antiquissima porta scita in vico de Pyttey super montem de Pyttey prope vicum de Tourestrete eundo ad portam antiquissimam vocatam . ... .[b] prope cimiterium sancti Johannis baptiste Et sic[c] longitudo predicte longe vie a Porta sancti leonardi directa linea eundo per officium domus justitie de le Pyllorye vsque ad illam venellam qui ducit in eundo versus Ecclesiam sancti petri. in loco principij dicte vie siue loci erat antiquis temporibus. porta antiqua scita citra nouiorem portam de Newgate modo prostrata. ac murum antiquissimum Bristollie[d] que predicta via sic jncipiendo de porta sancti leonardi in occidente scita ad locum Porte antiquissime sic dirute in parte orientali prope Castrum ville continet in longitudine .580. gressus.[e]

(61)

Via vocata Irysh meede aliter Russh lane scita directe ad finem vie de Brode mede. in parte boriali[f] Ecclesie Fratrum predicatorum vocati[g] Castel frerys Et via maresshallestrete

---

a *de* deleted
b Blank in MS
c *Et sic* is smudged, and rewritten more clearly above the line
d *cu* deleted
e *q'* (for *questio* or *query*?) in margin opposite
f Followed by a thick vertical stroke
g Originally *vocate*, amended to *vocati*

(60)

The length of the road from St Leonard's Gate as far as St Werburgh's church measures 120 steps to the centre of the entrance of St Werburgh's church. And thus continuing past the High Cross, going on along past the public Pillory building, continuing to the oldest gate of the town wall, the Oldgate, to the road or lane called Castle Street [which] goes to and turns at the door of St Peter's church.

In which road or lane the old wall of the town gate of Bristol was situated, this side of the houses of my father's, formerly of Agnes Randolf, in which a goldsmith now lives in this year of Christ 1480; and he rebuilt the said two houses on the left-hand side going towards the new gate [of] Newgate.

p.100

The whole aforesaid road measures from St Leonard's Gate going straight along Corn Street and past the High Cross, and past the churches of St Werburgh and Holy Trinity,[1] and going straight along Winch Street, anciently called Tower Street, leaving the old town wall and the oldest town gate on this side of Pithay Gate, otherwise called Aylward's Gate, on the left-hand side. The said oldest gate [is] situated in Pithay Street, on Pithay Hill, next to the street of Tower Street, going towards the oldest gate called ... next to the churchyard of St John the Baptist.

And thus the length of the aforesaid long road from St Leonard's Gate going straight along past the public place of punishment at the Pillory as far as that lane which leads in the direction of St Peter's church, to the place at the beginning of the said road, or the spot [where] in ancient times the old gate (now thrown down) was situated, on this side of the newer gate of Newgate, and the oldest wall of Bristol: which aforesaid road thus beginning from St Leonard's Gate situated on the west, to the site of the oldest gate, now demolished, on the east side, near the Castle of the town, measures in length 580 steps.

(61)

The road called Irishmead, otherwise Rush Lane, [is] situated right at the end of the road of Broadmead, on the north side of the church of the Friars Preachers, called Castle Friars. And the Marshall Street road, coming from the Castle, crosses

---

1   Now Christ Church

(61) [continued]
veniente de Castro intersecat viam Brodemede & dictam viam
de Irysh mede. super quandam pontem lapideam. jn jncepcione
dicte vie. et longitudo eius[a] a principio vie de Brode mede
vsque ad quandam antiquam viam siue venellam scitam in[b]
orientali parte & boriali vltra Ecclesiam fratrum predicatorum
veniente ab antiquis temporibus per viam de kyngystrete de
campis borialibus ville Bristollie ex parte horfelde &
Rydelyngfelde ad antiquum mercatum ville Bristollie per
orientalem partem Chori dictorum fratrum vocatum Castell
frerys. aliter Frere prechours, Et in dicto[c] vico olim Coci &
venditores[d] victualium ibi manebant diebus antiquis. Et
longitudo dicte vie continet .370.[e] gressus vel circa.
latitudo predicte vie continet .14. gressus;

p. 101

(62)
De Voltis de archis de petra factis[f] et Cellarijs cum mearemio &
arbore coopertis. secundum jnformacionem Willemi Clerk de
vico seynt marye the Port strete; die sabbato ... [g] Septembris
anno christi .1480.

In hyghstrete sunt .19. Voolta archuata. et .12. cellaria de
voltis vero in toto .31.

In bradstrete vltra[h] .20. volta & Cellaria

memorandum[i]
In cornstrete sunt .20. cellaria & volta

In pyttey aliter Aylewardestrete sunt in occidentali parte[j] vie
alte vbi antiqua porta ville est edificata ∵ [k] prope vicum
strictum de Tourstrete eundo versus Ecclesiam sancti Johannis
per Blynde yate sunt .4. cellaria

In Wynchstrete. sunt .27. volta & Cellaria .3. in[l]

---

a   *continet* deleted
b   *bori* (for *boriali*) deleted
c   *dicta* corrected to *dicto*
d   *vicu* (error for *victualium*) deleted
e   *370* written again above
f   *de petra factis* written above the line, over *de archis*
g   Small blank space, sufficient for the insertion of one or two figures
h   *xx* deleted

(61) [continued]
the Broadmead road and the said road of Irishmead upon a
certain stone bridge, at the start of the said road. And its[1]
length from the beginning of the Broadmead road as far as a
certain old road or lane situated on the north–east side,
beyond the church of the Friars Preachers, coming since
ancient times by way of King Street from the northern fields
of the town of Bristol out by Horfield and 'Rydelyngfelde'[2] to
the old market of the town of Bristol, past the east side of the
chancel of the said Friars called Castle Friars otherwise Friars
Preachers. And cooks and sellers of provisions formerly lived
in the said street in the old days. And the length of the said
road measures 370 steps or thereabouts; the breadth of the
aforesaid road measures 14 steps.

p.101

(62)
Concerning the arched vaults made of stone, and the cellars
roofed with beams and timber, according to the information of
William Clerk of the street of St Mary le Port Street, on
Saturday ... September[3] in the year of Christ 1480.

In High Street are 19 arched vaults, and 12 cellars: so 31
vaults in all.

In Broad Street, more than 20 vaults and cellars.

Memorandum,
In Corn Street are 20 cellars and vaults.

In Pithay, otherwise Aylward Street, on the west side of the
upper road where the ancient gate of the town was built, next
to the narrow street of Tower Street, going towards St John's
church past Blind Gate, are 4 cellars.

In Wynch Street are 27 vaults and cellars, 3 in[4]

---

1   i.e. Irishmead
2   Perhaps Redland Field? cf. **(169)**, **(197)**
3   Possibly 23rd September: cf. **(66)**
4   See note 1 below

---

i   In the margin
j   *predicte* deleted
k   *prope ... 4 cellaria* is written in the margin, linked with ∴ symbol
l   *sic*, leaving sentence apparently unfinished for lack of space

(62) [continued]
In vico Shamelys[a] Volta quam lata longa & profunda continet quelibet volta longitudinis .12.[b] virge

In seynt maryeportstrete. in vtraque parte vici sunt .15.[c] volta et Cellaria

In Radclyff strete sunt plurima volta & Cellaria

In Shamelys quondam Worshypstrete sunt .12. volta & Cellaria jn vna parte kynges Shamelys;

In Seynt Collas strete sunt vltra .12. volta & Cellaria.

In Smalstrete sunt ... [d] volta et Cellaria circa .12. & vltra

In Hoorstrete aliter horstrete sunt vltra .6. solaria[e] seu volta

In vico Brodemede vna volta de petra[f] constructa de proprijs expensis Willelmi Botoner dictus W.Worcestre[g] in anno christi .1428.

---

(63)
GYSTON CLYFF
The halle of the Chapell of seynt Vyncent of Gyston Clyff ys .ix. yerdes long,
and the brede ys .3. yerdys
The[h] lenght of the[i] kechyn ys ... [j] yerdes
and the brede of the kechyn ys .3.[k] yerdes
and from the chapelle of seynt Vyncent ys[l] to the lower water .40. vethym[m]

---

a　*Cellarium* has been deleted and *Volta quam lata longa & profunda* then written above the line
b　*.12.* repeated above the line
c　*.15.* repeated
d　Blank in MS
e　*sic*, cf. possible confusion of *solaria* and *cellaria* in **(37)** n.3
f　*constru* deleted where Worcestre ran out of space at end of line
g　*W.Worcestre* underlined by Talbot with a note in the margin alongside:
　　　§ *ij names vide post iiij leaves*　(2 names see 3 pages later)
h　*brede* deleted

(62) [continued]
In the street of The Shambles, vaults which are wide and long and deep; each vault measures 12 yards in length.

In St Mary Port Street, on either side of the street, are 15 vaults and cellars.

In Redcliffe Street are many vaults and cellars.

In The Shambles, formerly Worship Street, are 12 vaults and cellars on one side of the King's Shambles.

In St Nicholas Street are more than 12 vaults and cellars.

In Small Street are ... vaults and cellars, about 12 or more.

In Horestreet otherwise Horse Street are more than 6 cellars or vaults.

In the way of Broadmead, one stone vault built at his own expense by William Botoner, called W.Worcestre,[1] in the year of Christ 1428.

---

(63)
GHYSTON CLIFF
The hall of St Vincent's chapel, of Ghyston Cliff, is 9 yards long.
And the width is 3 yards.
The length of the kitchen is ... yards.
And the width of the kitchen is 3 yards.
And from St Vincent's chapel to the low water mark is 40 fathoms.

---

1   Not the writer, who would only have been 13 in 1428; cf. **(205)**

---

i   *Chapelle* deleted; *kechyn* has been inserted above
j   Blank in MS
k   *.2.* altered to *.3.* or *vice versa*: unclear which amendment is later
l   *40 Fethymes* deleted
m   *vethym* has been underlined, probably by Talbot, and *fethem* written
    above in darker ink, in Talbot's hand

(63) [continued]

and from the ovyr part of the mayn grounde lond of[a] the seyd hygh rok downe to the seyd Chapelle of seynt Vyncent ben .xx.[b] vethym.[c] rekened and proved & so from the hygh mayn ferme lond of the seyd Rokk downe to the lowest water ground of the chanell of Avyn & frome water ys .60. vethym[d] lowest water ys .60. fethym & moch more proved by a yong man of smyth ys occupacion yn Radclyffstrete that seyd yt to me hath both decended from the hyghest of the Rok doune to the watersyde

(64)

Fons est ibidem circa bowshott apud le blak Rok in parte de Ghystonclyff in fundo aque et est jta calidus sicut[e] lac vel aqua Badonis[f]

Scarletwelle est fons preclarissimus emanens de alto rupe in parte oppositie aque in dominio de Lye. et est in altitudine in alciori parte de le Rok de parte ville de lye altitudinis .xij pedum

Rok brekefaucet per vnum iactum lapidis versus Bristolliam in parte Ghystonclyff

Foxhole est volta mirabiliter scita super in alto de Ghyston Clyff super ripam de le Rokk alciorem & valde periculosus locus ad jntrandam voltam. ne cadat in mari profunditatis .60. brachiorum & vlterius

p.102

(65)

De heremitagio[g] & Capella sancti Vincencij[h] in quadam Rupe altissimo siue[i] Scopula durissima & profunditatis vsque ad aquam venientem de Bristollia. videlicet

    latitudo aule heremitagij est .7. virgas.[j]

    longitudo vie ad Ecclesiam de aula in Rupe predicta

        fodiata .16. virgas[k]

---

a *of* repeated; the phrase *of the seyd hygh rok* is written in the margin, linked with ∴ symbol

b *20* written above at the same time

c ⊗ mark by Talbot in margin opposite

d The last phrase is cramped for lack of space, and the rest of this note is squeezed into the margin; this may explain the repetition of *.60. fethym*

e *aqua lactus* deleted

f This note is bracketed, with § in margin, probably by Talbot

(63) [continued]
And from the upper part of the actual ground surface above the said high rock, down to the said chapel of St Vincent, is 20 fathoms calculated and proved. And so, from the top actual solid ground above the said rock down to the lowest water mark of the channel of the rivers Avon and Frome is 60 fathoms. Lowest water is 60 fathoms and much more. Proved by a young man, working as a smith in Redcliffe Street, who told it me, he having descended right from the very top of the rock down to the waterside.

(64)
There is a spring about a bow-shot [distant] at the Black Rock, in the depth of the river on the Ghyston Cliff side, and it is as warm as milk or the water at Bath.

Scarlet Well is an extremely clear spring flowing out of a high rock on the opposite side of the river, in the lordship of Leigh. And it is high up in the upper part of the rock, on the Leigh village side, at a height of 12 feet.

Breke Faucet Rock [lies] a stone's throw towards Bristol on the Ghyston Cliff side.

Foxhole is a remarkable cave situated high up on Ghyston Cliff, upon a ledge of the highest rock; and [it is] an exceedingly dangerous spot for getting into the cave, lest one falls to the depths of the water 60 fathoms and more below.

p.102

(65)
Concerning the hermitage and the chapel of St Vincent, in a certain most high rock or grim crag, plunging down to the river flowing from Bristol, to wit:
> The width of the hall of the hermitage is 7 yards.
> The length of the way from the hall to the church dug into the aforesaid rock, 16 yards.

---

g   *sancti* deleted. There is a mark ⊗ by Talbot in the margin opposite
h   Faint smudged insertion, possibly beginning *in quadam*, breaks off at the end of the line
i   *Say* deleted
j   Repeated as *virge*
k   *de aula in Rupe predicta fodiata* inserted above the line

(65) [continued]

longitudo[a] Capelle sancti Vincencij 8. virgas
latitudo Capelle sancti Vincentij .3.[b] virgas,
longitudo domus Coquine .6. virge.

(66)

Vie ascensus de Capella in Rupe .20.[c] brachiorum circa
medietate Rupis Ghyston clyff ascendo ad terram altam ∴ [d] in
eundo & ascendendo per W.Botoner dictus Worcetre eundo &
numerando die dominica 26. die mensis Septembris in anno
christi 1480.   continet dicta altitudo ab Capella heremitagij
.124. gressus   Et sic patet quod quilibet ascensus[e] in eundo
contra aliquem montem semper secundum ratam altitudinis .20.
brachiorum anglice a vathym computabit in altitudine ascensus
.124. gressus vel circa

(67)

Vie de horstrete de porta Fromeyate[f] eundo per Ecclesiam
sancti Bertholomei ad eundo per figuram beate marie virginis in
muro hortis Carmelitarum. sic eundo vsque ad bakkam sancti
augustini. continet ad edificacionem dicte vie in parte sinistre
versus aquam de Frome .420. gressus.

(68)

longitudo trium domorum magnificarum & magne altitudinis
wocat le[g] seynt marye Port cum profunda volta de lapidibus
archuata in profunditate graduum quasi circa .40. gradus. jd
est Steppys. continens in longitudine a vico de lez Shambles
vsque jntrando in domibus tribus magnis predictis continet .18.
virgas.

(69)

longitudo Rupis Ghyston clyff est jncepcio per spacium[h]
duorum miliariorum ab hyghstret cruce Bristollie eundo per
villulam Clyffton cuius dominus ville est[i] N. ... [j] Broke vocatus
dominus Cobham

---

a   *Capelle* was written first, then deleted
b   *3* repeated, more clearly written
c   *.46.*, underlined as a deletion, with *.20* written above
d   The rest of this note is packed into the margin, linked by ∴ symbol
    and with *altam* repeated as a catch-word
e   *versus* deleted
f   *ad* deleted
g   *Port* deleted
h   *vnius miliaris* deleted

(65) [continued]
>The length of St Vincent's chapel, 8 yards.
>The width of St Vincent's chapel, 3 yards.
>The length of the kitchen, 6 yards.

(66)
The way upwards from the chapel in the rock: 20 fathoms [from] about the middle of Ghyston Cliff rock, climbing up to the high ground: as walked and climbed by W.Botoner called Worcestre, walking and counting, on Sunday 26th September in the year of Christ 1480,[1] the said height from the chapel of the hermitage measures 124 steps. And so it appears that any ascent, in going up any hillside, after the rate of 20 fathoms (in English 'a vathym') in height, [is] always reckoned in height as an ascent of 124 steps or thereabouts.

(67)
The road of Horestreet from the gate of Frome Gate, going past St Bartholomew's church, going by the statue of the Blessed Virgin Mary in the wall of the Carmelites' garden, [and] thus going as far as St Augustine's Back, measures 420 steps to the built-up [part] of the said road on the left-hand side, towards the river Frome.

(68)
The length in steps of the three fine halls, of great height, called the Saint Mary Port, with a deep cellar vaulted with stone down below, [is] in steps roundabout 40 steps (that is, 'steppys').[2] Measuring in length from the street of The Shambles as far as the entrance to the aforesaid three great halls measures 18 yards.

(69)
The length of Ghyston Cliff rock begins two miles away from the High Street cross of Bristol, going by the little village of Clifton, of which the Lord of the Manor is N ... Broke, called Lord Cobham.

---

1 *sic*, but 26th September was not a Sunday in 1480; possibly an error for Sunday 24th September; cf. **(62)** and his diary **(437)**
2 Worcestre has confused *gressus* (his own steps) and *gradus* (stairs) but presumably intended his own steps for a horizontal length measurement

---

i *Dominus* deleted
j Blank in MS

(69) [continued]

Breke[a] Faucet est quedam Rupis in Ghystonclyff locus periculosus pro obuiacione navium tempore introitus navium tam magnorum quam paruorum quorumcunque ponderum seu quantitatis fuerint. in fundo aque de Frome & avyn[b] veniencium de Bristollia. & morabitur navis supra dictum brekefaucet quousque fluxus marinus fluendo ad portum Bristollie accrescet, et distat a Rupe a capella sancti vincentij versus Bristolliam per spacium jactis sagitte

ledes[c] sunt Rupes fracte profundissime[d] in jnferiori parte aquarum de[e] Avyn & Frome[f] currente de Bristollia. Et[g] dicti Rupes fracti quando non fluit mare faciunt naves ex carente aqua subito decendere in jnfimum locum anglice dictum a Depe Falle[h] et dicti Rupes fracti continet[i] latitudinem tocius aque de le Chanelle a loco vocato le Ghyston Clyff[j] transmeando ad aliam partem Rupis alterius partis vocat Rupis in Dominio de ville de Ashton Lye.[k] de Comitatu Somerset directe in opposita parte Ghyston Clyff. vbi Portus de hungrode cum navibus magnis jntrant

p.103

(70)

<u>Via longa de Kyngystrete</u> apud Beggherwelle continuata que via venit de monkenbrygge jncipiendo dictam viam de kyngystrete ad Beggherwelle, continet … [l] gressus

Et sic a dicta via de Beggherwelle continuando viam directa via in sinistra manu de Erlesmede vsque ad finem occidentalem dicti prati continet longitudo a dicta fonte vocata Beggher welle .840. gressus[m]

---

a   O in darker ink in margin opposite by Talbot
b   *in fundo aque de Frome & avyn* underlined, with § in margin opposite by Talbot
c   *ledes* underlined and O in darker ink in margin opposite by Talbot
d   Worcestre originally wrote *ledes est vna profunda Rupis* (The Leads is a deep rock), then added *sunt Rupes fracte profundissime*, without any caret mark, above the line
e   *Fro* (for *Frome*?) deleted
f   *Avyn & Frome* underlined by Talbot
g   This sentence is written in the margin, opposite an isolated caret mark in the main text which suggests that it should be inserted as shown
h   *in jnfimum locum anglice dictum a Depe Falle* is underlined, with § in the margin opposite by Talbot

(69) [continued]
Breke Faucet is a certain rock at Ghyston Cliff, a dangerous place in the depths of the rivers Frome and Avon flowing from Bristol that obstructs incoming shipping, both great and small, of whatever weight or size they may be. And a ship shall wait at the said Breke Faucet every time the flood tide rises, flowing into the port of Bristol. And it lies distant from the rock at the chapel of St Vincent, towards Bristol, by the space of one arrow's flight.

The Leads are jagged rocks, very deep down in the bottom of the rivers Avon and Frome, flowing from Bristol. And the said jagged rocks, when the tide is not rising, cause ships, from lack of water, to fall suddenly into a deep place called (in English) 'a deep fall'. And the said jagged rocks extend the width of the whole river-channel, from the place called the Ghyston Cliff, zig-zagging across to the other side [to] the higher rock on [that] side called the Cliff in the Lordship of Ashton-Leigh in the county of Somerset: right opposite the Ghyston Cliff side, where [there is] the anchorage of Hungroad with the big ships coming in.

p.103

(70)
The long road of King Street, at Beggarwell, continued: which road comes from Monkenbridge, [and] from the beginning of the said road of King Street, to Beggarwell, measures ... steps.

And so continuing the said road from Beggarwell, straight along the road on the left-hand [side] of Earlsmead, as far as the western end of the said meadow, measures in length from the said well called Beggarwell, 840 steps.

---

i   Worcestre originally wrote *dicta Rupis continet*, then added *dicti Rupes fracti*, without any caret mark, above the line
j   *vsque* deleted
k   *Lye* underlined, perhaps by Talbot
l   Blank in MS
m   *q'* (for *questio* or *query*?) in margin; the figure has been added afterwards in different ink

(71)
VIA BORIALIS AD CAPUT IACENS AD CAPUT DE
ERLESMEDE

Via alia longa borialis jncipiendo a fine orientali de Erlesmede.[a]
et directe retornando ad pontem le lokbryg, citra molendinum
quondam diebus meis vocatum Bagpath mylle jn quo loco vt
aliqui dicunt libertas & Franchesie ville Bristollie extendit vsque
dictum pontum qui est pars orientalissima & finis orientalis
dicti pulcri prati per quam pontem aqua de Frome transit per
dictum pontem et sic continue transit per latus meridionale
dicti famosi prati & per Castrum ville per latus vici de la
Weer

Et sic longitudo retornacionis dicti prati ad caput finis
quadranguli per dictum pontem orientalem citra predictum
molendinum vocatum Bagpath mille continet in latitudine dicti
Erlesmedew[b] .300. gressus,[c]

p. 104   *[Blank]*

p. 105

(72)
FRATRES CARMELI[d]
Ecclesia Fratrum Carmelitarum viz Navis Ecclesie continet .45.
gressus siue ... [e]
latitudo eius continet .25. gressus
latitudo turris campanile continet .5. gressus[f]
altitudo turris ... [g]

(73)
Chorus Ecclesie fratrum predictorum[h] continet .45. gressus
Claustrum eorum ex omnibus .4. partibus continet .40.
gressus,

(74)
GAUNTES
Ecclesia Religionum vocata le Gauntes viz Navis Ecclesie
continet .43. gressus in longitudine
latitudo eius continet .26. gressus

---

a   Worcestre actually wrote *Erlesmedeme*, possibly intending *Erlesmedewe*
b   *continet* deleted
c   *q'* (for *questio* or *query*?) in margin opposite the end of this paragraph
d   *apud Bristowe* has been added to this heading by Talbot
e   Blank in MS
f   cf. **(338)**: a remarkably small, but consistent, measurement
g   Blank in MS

(71)
THE NORTHERN ROAD LYING AT THE HEAD OF EARLSMEAD
The other long northern road beginning at the east end of Earlsmead, and turning straight back to the Lokbridge on this side of a certain mill called, in my day, Bagpath Mill (to which spot, as some say, the liberties and franchises of the town of Bristol extend), as far as the said bridge, which is the easternmost side and eastern end of the said fair meadow. By which bridge the river Frome, flowing under the said bridge, and so continuing, flows along the southern edge of the said renowned meadow, and past the Castle of the town, beside the broad street of The Weir.

And thus the length of the return through the said meadow, at the square head end by the said eastern bridge, this side of the said mill called Bagpath Mill, measures for the width of the said Earlsmead, 300 steps.

p.104   *[Blank]*

p.105

(72)
THE CARMELITE FRIARS
The church of the Carmelite friars, to wit: the nave of the church measures 45 steps or ...
Its width measures 25 steps.
The width of the bell-tower measures 5 steps.
The height of the tower ...

(73)
The choir of the church of the aforesaid friars[1] measures 45 steps.
Their cloister measures 40 steps on all 4 sides.

(74)
THE GAUNTS
The church of the religious house called The Gaunts, to wit the nave of the church, measures 43 steps in length.
Its width measures 26 steps.

---

1 See note h below

---

h *predictorum* is blotted, and could perhaps be *predicatorum*, as Dallaway read it; but this would make **(73)** the Friars Preachers, which seems unlikely, between the Carmelite Friars and The Gaunts. The item has, however, been numbered separately because of this uncertainty

(75)
LONGITUDO SANCTUARIJ
Sanctuarium locum sancti augustini ab oriente vbi introitus sanctuarij est in occidens ad portam extremam ad intrandam Curiam abbatis de officijs domorum granariorum pistorum pandoxatorum stablaorum pro dominis &c continet .360. gressus directe eundo iuxta Ecclesiam sancti augustini

latitudo dicti sanctuarij a porta predicta ad venellam jntrantem vocatam Froglane continet 240. gressus

latitudo siue distancia loci ab occidentali parte porte de Gauntes ad portam jntroitus Ecclesie abbathie sancti augustini continet ex transverso .180. gressus

(76)
Froglane jncipiendo ad borialem finem Ecclesie de Gauntes retornando per orta & gardinam de lez Gauntes & per murum fratrum Carmelitarum vsque ad Stypstrete altitudinem vbi fons est de Frestone versus Ecclesiam sancti michaelis continet .660. gressus

(77)
PRYOUR YS LANE PROPE ECCLESIAM SANCTI JACOBI
Venella magna vocat le pryour ys lane sancti Jacobi qui jncipit apud le style in angulo cornerij de lewynesmede vsque ad murum extremum directum super montague hille eundo per murum fratrum sancti Francisci ex vna parte & murum monacorum ex orientali continet[a] vsque returnum ad montem sancti michaelis continet directa linea .360. gressus. scilicet sic retornando venellam ad Ecclesiam sancti michaelis[b] per continuacionem dicte venelle versus occidentem

venella a capite anguli muri fratrum minorum vocat le Pryour lane monachorum in parte occidentali sic eundo ad montem sancti michaelis versus eius Ecclesiam[c] vsque ad locum & montem vocat Stypstrete prope fontem de Frestone continet ...[d] gressus

---

a *preter* deleted
b Worcestre has put a mark + in margin opposite the phrase underlined
c *continet* deleted
d Blank in MS

(75)

THE LENGTH OF THE PRECINCT

The precinct area of St Augustine's, from the east where there is the entrance of the precinct, to the west at the furthest gateway leading into the Abbot's court of household buildings, granaries, bakehouses, brewhouses, stables for the gentry,[1] etc., measures 360 steps, going right next to St Augustine's church.[2]

The width of the said precinct from the aforesaid gateway to the entry [into] the lane called Frog Lane, measures 240 steps.

The width or distance of the area from the western side of the The Gaunts' gateway, to the entrance-door of the church of St Augustine's abbey, measures 180 steps across.

(76)

Frog Lane, beginning at the north boundary of The Gaunts' church, turning past the orchard and garden of The Gaunts and past the wall of the Carmelite Friars as far as upper Steep Street, where there is a well of freestone, towards St Michael's church, measures 660 steps.

(77)

PRIOR'S LANE, NEAR ST JAMES'S CHURCH

The big lane called The Prior's Lane, St James's, which begins at the stile at the angle of the corner of Lewinsmead, straight as far as the further wall upon Montague Hill (going past the wall of the Franciscan Friars on one side, and the monks' wall[3] on the east), measures 360 steps as far as the bend towards St Michael's Hill, measuring in a straight line, namely to [where] the lane thus bends towards St Michael's church along a continuation of the said lane towards the west.

The lane called the Prior's Lane (of the monks) from the top corner of the wall of the Friars Minor on the west side, thus going to St Michael's Hill [and] towards that church, as far as the place and hill called Steep Street, near the well of freestone, measures ... steps.

---

1   Or possibly 'for the canons'?
2   i.e. St Augustine the Less, as opposed to the abbey church
3   i.e. the monks of St James's priory

p.106

(78)[a]

[b]

Melchior Rex aubre adesto te poscentibus veniam Impetrare Baltazar non deneges cum Jasper egregie Regi nostro & nobis scitis coadiutor es primicie inter gentes Christi precamine;   Ora pro nobis vt infer cuius liberi[c] efficiamur gracias dei

[d]

Deus qui tres Reges orientales ex Balaham linea procreatos legittime Baltazar melchior & Jasper vt te misticis muneribus adorent ad tua cunabula sine jmpedimento Induxisti & absque periculo ad propria reduxisti concede propicius Regi nostro & nobis per eorum merita in labore & itinere quo iturus est & ituri sumus induci & reduci sine deuiacione dispendio a periculo ad loca destinata et affectata cum tranquillitate securitate & pace te vera luce & stella ducente saluatore mundi. Qui viuis & regnas deus per omnia secula seculorum amen,

Beati viri Brendani sancta preconia.   O inestimabilis dileccio caritatis qui dum seculi pompam contempsit eterne vita coniunctus es alleluia.   Ora pro nobis beate Brandane vt digni efficiamur &c

[e]

Deus qui beatum Brandanum confessorem tuum atque abbatem in terra & in mari virtutibus atque[f] miraculis decorasti da nobis ipsius precibus cunctorum malorum fluctus euadere & cum eo paradisum pariter introire per dominum nostrum Jhesum Christum filium tuum qui tecum[g]

(79)
SHAMELLYS
Vicus de Shamelys ab antiquo vocato Worshypstrete vbi portus[h] navium & lanarum existebat continet in longitudine a porta sancti Nicholai directe eundo ad quandam finem loci vie quadrate; continet .300. gressus.

---

a   Item **(78)** is included in Harvey, *Itineraries*, pp. 302-305, with some variations in transcription and translation.   The separate prayers appear to have been copied onto this page on different occasions, and the particularly difficult hand has posed some problems of interpretation

b   Heading *iij kynges off Coleyn* added by Talbot

c   *liberi* repeated

d   *oratio pro itinerantibus* (a prayer for pilgrims) in margin by Talbot, who has also drawn a vertical line down the left-hand side of this prayer

e   *S.Brandan* written in margin by Talbot

f   *atque abbatem ... virtutibus atque* underlined by Talbot

p.106

(78)
O Melchior, King of Araby, come to thy supplicants. Do not refuse, Balthazar, to ask pardon [for us]. While thou, illustrious Caspar, art the upholder of our King and our laws. First among the peoples of Christ through prayer: Pray for us, that by the grace of God we may be made free from hell.

O God, who led to thy cradle, without hindrance, the three Kings of the East duly born of the line of Balaam, Balthazar, Melchior, and Caspar, to thy cradle without hindrance so that they might adore thee with mystic gifts, and without danger took them back to their own country: Grant, through their merits in endurance and journeying, a propitious [outcome] to our King and to us, so that wheresoever he or we shall be sent, we may be led to the places intended and desired, and brought back, without straying, delay or danger, [and] in tranquillity, safety and peace, being led by thee the true light and guiding star, Saviour of the world, who lives and reigns God of all, world without end, Amen.

Holy eulogies in praise of the blessed man Brendan. O inestimable lover of charity, who, while scorning the pomp of the world, art united to eternal life, Alleluia. Pray for us, blessed Brendan, that we may be made worthy, etc.

O God, who has adorned the blessed Brendan, thy confessor and abbot, with virtues and miracles by land and sea, grant us by his prayers to avoid the tides of ill-fortunes and together with him to enter paradise, through our Lord Jesus Christ thy Son who with thee[1]

(79)
THE SHAMBLES
The street of The Shambles, anciently called Worship Street, where the harbour for shipping and the market for wool used to be, measures in length from St Nicholas's Gate, going straight to a certain end of a square area of the road: it measures 300 steps.

---

1 Sentence apparently unfinished

---

g Sentence apparently unfinished
h Worcestre, perhaps influenced by the proximity of St Mary le Port, has deftly used *portus* in its dual sense of a harbour for ships and a market-place for goods; cf. **(68)**

(80)

Vicus defensorius jncipiente ad finem de via vocata le Shamelys directe jncipiendo ad locum rectum quadrati per vicum de extransuerso de seyntpeterstrete coram nouo fonte facta de bonis Canynges de alto domo[a] de Frestone a exteriore[b] parte vie de Wynchstrete continet .135. gressus

(81)

IN ORIENTALI PARTE COLLEGIJ DE KALENDERS

Via parua quamuis lata in occidentali parte Ecclesie omnium sanctorum & Collegij kalendarij prope ibidem jntrando versus meridiem in parte iuxta cimiterium dicte Ecclesie continet .60. gressus

(82)

Collegium[c] presbiterorum vocatum le kalenders in occidentali parte Ecclesie omnium sanctorum in quo Collegio Thomas Botoner[d] avunculus meus fuit frater Collegij et sepelitur in meridionali noue Ele[e] Ecclesie omnium sanctorum ab antiquo fundatum diu ante conquestum Willelmi Conqquestoris; circa annum christi .700.[f]

Domus conducti aque pulcher sub domo kalendarij est scituata.

p.107

(83)

De capella sancte anne per duo miliaria de Bristollia.

Quidam[g] Dominus de le Warr Fundauit primo capellam sancte anne primo
Capella sancte anne continet in longitudine 19.[h] virgas
latitudo eius continet .5. virgas

---

a   *coram nouo … de alto domo* underlined by Talbot, who has drawn a vertical wavy line down the left-hand side of the paragraph, and added § *vid. post unum fo.* (see one page further on) in the margin. He has also written *Ca* over, and two dots .. for emphasis under, *Canynges*
b   *orientale* added above the line
c   *Collegium* has been underlined and *Collegium Brist'* written in the margin in a hand that is neither Worcestre nor Talbot, but possibly Aldrych
d   *Thomas Botoner* underlined by Talbot, and linked to a note by him at the foot of the page: *Botiner qui voc Worcestr*
e   *Ele* written a second time more clearly; cf. *ale* and *alam vel Elam* in **(201)**
f   The note *circa annum christi .700.* has been added by Worcestre in the margin alongside; cf. **(387)** and see N.Orme, 'The Guild of Kalendars, Bristol', *T.B.G.A.S.*, xcvi (1978), p. 33

(80)

The defensive street[1] beginning at the end of the road called The Shambles, starting right at the four-square place, along the street, crossing St Peter's Street in front of the new fountain made by the Canynges estate as a tall building of freestone, to the further side of the road of Wynch Street, measures 135 steps.

(81)

ON THE EASTERN SIDE OF THE COLLEGE OF KALENDARS

The small but broad road on the west side of All Saints' church and the nearby College of Kalendars, opening towards the south on the side next to the churchyard of the said church, measures 60 steps.

(82)

The College of Priests called The Kalendars [is] on the west side of All Saints' church; of which College my uncle Thomas Botoner was a brother. And he is buried on the south [side] of the new aisle of All Saints' church, anciently founded long before the conquest of William the Conqueror, about the year of Christ 700.

A fair water-conduit house is situated beneath the Kalendars' hall.

p.107

(83)

Concerning the chapel of Saint Anne, two miles
away from Bristol.

A certain Lord de le Warr first founded the chapel of Saint Anne.

The chapel of Saint Anne measures 19 yards in length.
Its width measures 5 yards.

---

1   So-called because it ran alongside the cross-wall that was an outwork of the castle; later Dolphin Lane

---

g   Worcestre originally wrote *Abbas de Abbathia de Keynysham ff*, deleted it, and inserted *Dominus de le Warr* above, partly in the margin. He also wrote *Anno christi* in the margin at the beginning of this note, but without any year.

h   *gressus* deleted

(83) |continued|

Et sunt de boterasses circa capellam .19.

Item sunt due ceree anglice quadrate vna de dono officij artis wevers. de terra ad coperturam archuati volti continet altitudo .80. pedes.

Et densitudo vnius cere quadrate[a] lez officium artis Corduanarij continet in latitudine .10. pollices fere vnius pedis

Et in Densitate .8. pollicium

Et cerea quadrata data par officium artis textorum anglice Wefers continet in longitudine ad voltam capelle .80. pedes[b]

latitudo .8. pollices

densitudo .7. pollices

Et quolibet anno dicte ceree sunt renouate erga diem pentacosten.

Et qualibet cera quadrata ex ponderibus cere & factura constabat .5. libras.

Et sic due predicte ceree constabant .10. libras.

Et sunt in dicta capella .32. naves & navicule ac de caracis navibus

Et sunt de navibus de argento formatis & factis .5. naves.

precium cuiuslibet navis .20. s.

Et[c] coram ymagine sancte anne sunt .13. ceree quadrate appreciate ad ... [d]

(84)

MURUS IN VNA PARTE DE ORTO PROPE RADCLYFF

In[e] orientali via de Radclyf chyrch[f] Capelle beate marie est murus longus versus pylehille fontem ad eundum ad sanctam annam continet dictus murus in longitudine .50. virgas siue .70. gressus per filium meum numeri virgarum numeratur ad jncepcionem muri prope orientalem partem Cimiterij dicte Ecclesie

---

a   *continet* deleted

b   *sic*, perhaps in error for 80 inches or even 8 feet (just credible for a major ceremonial candle), or perhaps confused by the 80 foot roof vault and the 8 inch thickness of the mortars, Worcestre has postulated a candle of impossible height; *ped* is written at the end of the line, with insufficient space, so *pedes* has been rewritten in full, without any deletion, followed by *in l* (for repetition of *in longitudine*) deleted. This lack of space and consequent muddle may explain a mistake in the figures. Worcestre may just have absent-mindedly repeated the vault measurement

c   *sunt* above line and deleted

d   Blank in MS

(83) [continued]

And there are 19 buttresses around the chapel.

Also, there are two square candles (in English),[1] one the gift of the Weavers' craft guild. From the ground to the arched roof of the vault measures 80 feet in height.

And the thickness of one of the square candles, [the gift] of the Cordwainers' craft guild, measures in width 10 inches or almost one foot,

And in thickness, 8 inches.

And the square candle given by the Weavers' craft guild (in English, "Wefers"), measures 80 feet in length to the chapel vault.[2]

Width 8 inches.

Thickness 7 inches.

And each year the said candles are renewed for Whit-Sunday. And each square candle, in weight of wax and [in] manufacture, costs £5.

And so the two aforesaid candles cost 10 pounds.

And there are in the said chapel 32 boats and little boats, and some carracks.[3]

And, of the boats fashioned and made out of silver, there are 5 boats, the value of each boat 20s.

And before the statue of Saint Anne there are 13 square candles, worth ...

(84)

THE WALL ON ONE SIDE OF THE GARDEN NEXT TO REDCLIFFE

In the eastern road from Redcliffe Church [by] the Lady chapel is a long wall towards Pylle Hill well, going to Saint Anne's. The said wall measures 50 yards or 70 steps in length (the number of yards was counted by my son) to the beginning of the wall next to the east side of the churchyard of the said church.

---

1   *sic*, with no English word. Worcestre perhaps intended 'mortars', thick, square candles

2   For possible explanations of this measurement, see note b opposite

3   While *naves & navicule* could be either boats or incense-boats, the reference to carracks seems to confirm that these were models of ships, votive offerings to St Anne, patron saint of sailors

---

e   *q'* (for *questio* or *query*?) in margin opposite this paragraph

f   *ma* (for *marie*?) deleted

(85)
OCCIDENTALIS PARS CIMITERIJ RADCLYFF
Et ab jncepcione dicti muri in orto claudati iuxta cimiterium orientalis partis muri predicti a dicto merestone in eadem parte eundo per cimiterium predictum iuxta Collegium capellanorum Willelmi Canyngys. ad[a] domum Camerarum dictorum capellanorum continet in latitudine .150. gressus.

latitudo vie de Radclyffhyll. de cameris presbiterorum predictorum. ad alteram parto[b] domorum operariorum de Frestone pro fundacione Ecclesie de Radclyff sunt .40. gressus

Et a loco Camerarum Willelmi Canyngys[c] jn fine occidentali Cimiterij predicti. vsque ad Radclyff yate continet circa .180. gressus

(86)
CIRCUMFERENCIA PRINCIPALIUM COLUMPNARUM
Columpna principalis quatuor Columpnarum qui portant turrim competentem coram hostium Chori occidentalis Ecclesie Radclyff continet .103. bowtells
Circumferencia principalium Columpnarum & quilibet eorum quatuor columpnarum continet .6. virgas

p.108
Radclyff
Circumferencia aiiorum[d] Columpnarum tocius Ecclesie continet .4. virgas.

(87)
latitudo vie de Radclyff stret coram Turrim Ecclesie de[e] Ratclyff continet .14. gressus et eadem latitudo durat jnfra Radclyff strete

---

a *Willelmi Canyngys. ad* underlined by Talbot, with § in margin opposite
b *sic*
c *quod* deleted. *Willelmi Canyngys* underlined, probably also by Talbot
d *sic*
e *de* repeated

(85)
THE WEST SIDE OF REDCLIFFE CHURCHYARD
And from the beginning of the said wall enclosing the garden next to the churchyard, on the east side of the aforesaid wall, from the said boundary stone[1] on that side, going along by the aforesaid churchyard, next to William Canynges's college of chaplains, to the hall of residence of the said chaplains, measures 150 steps in width.

The width of the road of Redcliffe Hill. From the chambers of the aforesaid priests to the other side of the stonemasons' workshops for the construction of Redcliffe church, is 40 steps.

And from the site of William Canynges's chambers on the west end of the aforesaid churchyard, as far as Redcliffe Gate, measures about 180 steps.

(86)
THE CIRCUMFERENCE OF THE MAIN PILLARS
The main pillar of the four pillars which support the fitting tower in front of the western door of the quire of Redcliffe church, contains 103 bowtels.[2]

The circumference of the main pillar, and each of these four pillars, measures 6 yards.

p.108

Redcliffe

The circumference of the other pillars throughout the church measures 4 yards.

(87)
The width of the road of Redcliffe Street in front of the tower of Redcliffe church measures 14 steps; and that width extends throughout Redcliffe Street.

---

1   *sic*, although there is no immediately preceding reference
2   *sic*, see glossary. Worcestre is describing the four larger pillars at the crossing and, viewing the fine crossing vault from below, makes what must be an inadvertent reference to it as a tower. He was keenly interested in the tower at the west end; any earlier central tower (M.Q.Smith, *St Mary Redcliffe* (1995) p. 79, citing Brakspear (1922)) had long gone. The triplet clusters of shafts (ibid., p. 84) on these pillars presumably account for Worcestre's extraordinary total

(88)
Via[a] jnfra Ratclyffstrete[b] per murum vocatum le toune walle eundo versus seynt Thomastrete cuius sinistra pars vie est bene edificata & altera pars dextra manu est murus vocatus le toune walle continet in longitudine[c] .152. gressus;
Latitudo dicte vie ... [d]

(89)
longitudo vie de le toune walle ad seynt Thomas strete de angulo ex parte [penticiorum?][e] de muro edificatorum[f] eundo ad vicum[g] ad pontem Bristollie continet[h]

(90)
BRODEMEDE
latitudo de Brodemede continet .28. gressus

(91)
VIA DE MONKENBRYGGE AD CRUCEM PROPE IBIDEM
latitudo[i] brevis vie de kyngystrete[j] a principio dicte vie prope turrim de monkynbrygge in quadam venella vsque le style ad eundum ad cimiterium sancti Jacobi, in parte anguli hospicij Willelmi Pownam. apud crucem & pontem eundo in dicta via per lez barrys et vsque Erles mede continet .100. gressus
Et a principio[k] cimiterij sancti Jacobi vsque eundo per lez barrys eundo ad pratum Erlysmede[l]

(92)
latitudo vie in principio de lewenysmede prope Ecclesiam sancti Jacobi .8. gressus, eundo vsque Fromeyate

(93)
Crux decens de Frestone erecta super arcum volte vnius gradus vie intrantis ad aquam de Frome anglice a Slypp in vico knyfesmythstrete aliter Cristmastrete

Venella brevis scita jn angulo vltra Crucem predictam ad quendam hostium, vsque aquam de Frome per prope Fromeyate in boriali parte predicte crucis continet in longitudine circa .60. gressus in fine Cristmassestrete,

---

a   *de* deleted; *q'* (for *questio* or *query?*) in the margin
b   *ad* deleted
c   *continet* repeated
d   Blank in MS
e   Uncertain reading of an illegible word
f   *ad* deleted
g   *de Radclyff* deleted
h   *.660.* deleted, but *660. gressus* written in the margin opposite
i   *sic*, error for *longitudo*
j   Originally *marchallstrete*, *marchall* deleted and *kyngystrete* inserted

(88)
The inner road from Redcliffe Street along by the wall called the town wall, going towards St Thomas Street (of which the left-hand side of the road is well built up, and the other side, on the right hand, is the wall called the town wall) measures in length 152 steps.
The width of the said road ...

(89)
The length of the road from the town wall to St Thomas Street at the corner on the pentices' end of the wall of buildings going to the street to Bristol Bridge, measures [660 steps].

(90)
BROADMEAD
The width of Broadmead measures 28 steps.

(91)
THE ROAD FROM MONKENBRIDGE TO THE CROSS NEAR THERE
The length of the short road of King Street, from the beginning of the said road in a certain lane near the tower of Monkenbridge as far as the stile going to St James's churchyard, alongside the corner of William Pownam's lodgings at the cross and bridge, going along the said road past The Bars and as far as Earlsmead measures 100 steps.
And from the beginning of St James's churchyard going past The Bars as far as the meadow of Earlsmead

(92)
The width of the road at the beginning of Lewinsmead, near St James's church, going as far as Fromegate: 8 steps

(93)
A fine cross of freestone [is] built upon the arch of a vault of one stairway leading to the river Frome (in English, 'a slip'), in the street [of] Knifesmith Street, otherwise Christmas Street.

A short lane situated on the corner beyond the aforesaid cross, at a certain doorway, as far as the river Frome close by Fromegate on the north side of the aforesaid cross, measures in length about 60 steps to the end of Christmas Street.

---

k   *de* deleted
l   *Erlys* at the end of the line with insufficient space, and *Erlysmede* rewritten in full above. The sentence appears unfinished

p.109

(94)[a]

Sciendum Crucis latitudo[b] de hyghstrete continet latitudo .2. virge

altitudo crucis continet ... [c]

(95)

De Cellarijs, &c

HYGHSTRETE

In alto vico hyghstrete[d] sunt in parte orientali of the hygh crosse de seynt Cholas yate .17.[e] Cellarij

Et in opposita & parte occidentali dicti hyghstrete sunt .12. cellarij

summa 29.

CORNSTRETE

Item in Cornstrete de cruce alta jn parte boriali vici[f] ad portam sancti leonardi per Ecclesiam sancte Werburge sunt .18. Cellarij computati

Item in parte meridionali vie de alta cruce eundo per Ecclesiam omnium sanctorum sunt .17. Cellaria

Venella paruissima de hyghstrete iuxta meridionalem[g] ∴ partem Ecclesie omnium sanctorum & officium cocorum continet .60. gressus

summa .35.

BRADSTRET

Item in vico Bradstrete eundo ab alta cruce ad partem orientalem de Bradstrete[h] per Ecclesiam sancte trinitatis. continet .15. Cellaria

Item eundo in parte occidentali dicte vie per tenementum magistri Willelmi Botener ac domum Gylhalde ac capellam sancti Georgij sunt .15. Cellaria

summa 30

---

a   Item **(94)** has been jotted at the top of p. 109 in the small space left after **(95)** had been written
b   *alta* deleted and *latitudo* inserted above
c   Blank in MS
d   Latin *alto vico* is written above English *hyghstrete*

p.109

(94)
Note: the width of the High Street cross: it measures in width 2 yards.
The height of the cross measures ...

(95)
Concerning cellars, etc.

HIGH STREET
In the high street ('High Street') there are on the east side of the High Cross, from St Nicholas Gate, 17 cellars.
And on the opposite and west side of the said High Street there are 12 cellars.
Total 29

CORN STREET
Also, in Corn Street, on the north side of the street from the High Cross to St Leonard's Gate, past the church of St Werburgh, 18 cellars have been counted.
Also, on the south side of the road from the High Cross going past the church of All Saints, there are 17 cellars.
A very small lane from High Street next to the south side of All Saints' church and the Cooks' hall measures 60 steps.
Total 35

BROAD STREET
Also, in the street of Broad Street: going from the High Cross to the east side of Broad Street past the church of the Holy Trinity, it contains 15 cellars.
Also, going on the west side of the said road past the house of Master William Botoner and the Guildhall building and the chapel of St George, there are 15 cellars.
Total 30

---

e   *.16.* has been deleted by underlining, and *.17.* written above
f   *sunt* deleted
g   This note continues in the margin, linked by ∴ symbol
h   *sunt .15. Cellarij* was originally written at this point, then the figures *.15.* (but not the words) were deleted, and the total given at the end to match the other sections of this item

(95) [continued]
WYNCHSTRETE

In Wynchstrete aliter Castelstrete[a] ab alta cruce[b] jn parte dextra siue meridionali dicte vie per le pyllory eundo ad portam Newgate sunt .21. cellarii bis numerate & probate[c]

Et a dicta cruce eundo in Wynchstrete[d] per latus borialis dicte vie[e] continue vsque ad portam Newgate 14 sunt cellarij et vlterius continuando ad finem orientalis vie de le Weere[f] per molendinum Castri. sunt 10[g] Cellaria.

summa .35.[h]

(96)
LE PYLLORYE OFFICIUM

[i] Domus justicie & officij Collistrigij scita circa medium de Wynchstrete[j] coram finem vie de Pyttey yate est rotundum constructum de opere Frestone decente tam amplitudinis quam altitudinis cum cameris. ac fenestris cum barris de ferro artificiose compactis continet in spacio circuitus domus dicti officij ... [k] gressus; Et desuper domus Collistrigij est jnstrumentum de arboribus opere carpentarij constructum. ad collistrendum infamos homines. vel homines[l] delinquentes in pistura granorum tortarum &c

(97)
PYTTEY

In Pytteystrete infra aylwardyate siue pyttey yate prope ibidem in magno spacio veluti locus trianguli est Fons ampla. & profunda cum Frestone bene circumdata[m] &[n] alta[o] pro hominibus hauriendo aquam fontanam. & dicta Fons bene tegulata desuper ad custodiendum homines aquam haurientes de pluuia seu procellis. et sunt in boriali parte vice pyttey .2. Cellaria;

summa 2

---

a   *a cru* (for *a cruce*) deleted
b   *ad* deleted
c   *bis numerate & probate* added later in different ink, presumably at the time of the second count
d   *per* smudged and re-written
e   *ad* deleted
f   *de le* deleted
g   Worcestre first wrote *24*, the combined total for the north side, then deleted it
h   Worcestre's final total comprises all the cellars in Wynch Street but excludes those beyond Newgate in The Weir

(95) [continued]
WYNCH STREET
In Wynch Street, otherwise Castle Street, on the right-hand or south side of the said road going from the high cross, past the pillory, to the gate of Newgate, there are 21 cellars, twice counted and proved.

And going from the said cross into Wynch Street along the northern edge of the said road, continuing as far as the gate of Newgate, there are 14 cellars, and continuing further to the east end of the road of The Weir, past the Castle mill, there are 10 cellars.

Total 35

(96)
THE PUBLIC PILLORY
The house of punishment and the public pillory, situated about the middle of Wynch Street, in front of the end of the road from Pithay Gate, is circular, constructed in fine freestone work, as broad as [it is] high, with cells and windows with close bars of wrought iron. A circuit of the said public building measures in length ... steps. And above the pillory building is the device of timber work, built by carpenters, to pillory wicked people or wrongdoers in baking of bread, tourtes[1] etc.

(97)
PITHAY
In Pithay Street, within Aylward Gate or Pithay Gate, in a big area like a triangle nearby, there is a large and deep well, beautifully surrounded and [built] up with freestone, for people drawing well-water. And the said well [is] neatly roofed over with tiles, to protect the people drawing water from rain or stormy weather. And on the north side of Pithay Street there are 2 cellars.

Total 2

---

1   Tourte was rough brown bread, containing husks, probably used for trenchers

---

i   Worcestre made a false start to this note, with *Ab alta cruce eundo in parte siue costera vie ex parte orientale* (From the high cross, going on the side or edge of the road on the east side) deleted
j   *ex o* (for *ex opposito*?) deleted
k   Blank in MS
l   Rewritten a second time more clearly
m   *Fons ibidem* written in the margin opposite this point
n   *&* deleted
o   *ad* deleted

(98)
DOMUS LATRINI
Officium domus latrine anglice a pryvey. tam pro mulieribus quam hominibus in latitudine meridionali spacij dicti trianguli

(99)
longitudo vie ab angulo principij[a] pontis ad portam sancti Nicholai[b] sunt .9. virge. idest spacium vie retornando ad le bake

(100)
longitudo[c] porte[d] sancti Nicholai; ... [e]
longitudo porte sancti Johannis .8. virge, baptiste[f]

p.110

(101)
SEYNT COLASTRET
In vico sancti Nicholai sunt .12. Cellarij de porta sancti Nicholai vsque portam sancti leonardi
summa .12.

(102)
In venella sancti leonardi per cimiterium eundo in Smalstrete[g] sunt plures volte siue cellarij de subterra. quia tota venella est & cimiterium est magne altitudinis respectu vie trianguli de le kay. quasi circa 10 pedum. subtus vie cimiterij eundo ad Smalstrete,

(103)
PYLLESTRET
In[h] parochia sancti Stephani,
Vicus pyllestret est via a Seyntleonard ys yate eundo ad triangulum venellarum ad orientalem fenestram altaris Ecclesie sancti[i] Stephani. viz. venella vna retro orientalem fenestram sancti[i] Stephani. venella alia apud le Style ecclesie sancti Stephani ad keyam dimittendo cimiterium in manu dextra. Et tercius vicus est longus jncipiente a Fine predicti Pyllestrete et eundo per merstrete[j] longa via ad Mershyate,

---

a *jnfra* deleted
b *portam sancti Nicholai* written again more clearly above
c *vie* deleted
d *sancti Johannis baptiste* deleted
e Blank in MS
f *baptiste* omitted and added afterwards
g Worcestre originally wrote *Smalstre*, then later added *Smalstrete* more clearly above

(98)
LATRINE BUILDING
The public latrine building (in English, 'a privy'), for women as well as men, [is] in the wide southern area of the said triangle.

(99)
The length of the road from the corner at the beginning of the bridge, to St Nicholas's Gate, is 9 yards: that is, the area of the road turning off to the Back.

(100)
The length of St Nicholas's Gate ...
The length of St John the Baptist's Gate is 8 yards.

p.110

(101)
ST NICHOLAS STREET
In St Nicholas's Street, from St Nicholas's Gate as far as St Leonard's Gate, there are 12 cellars.
Total 12

(102)
In St Leonard's Lane, going past the churchyard into Small Street, there are many vaults or cellars underground, because the whole lane is, and the churchyard is, of great height by comparision with the triangular roadway of The Key, which is about 10 feet below the churchyard road going to Small Street.

(103)
PILL STREET
In the parish of St Stephen.
The street of Pill Street is a road from St Leonard's Gate going to the triangle of lanes at the east window of the altar of St Stephen's church; to wit, one lane at the back of the east window of St Stephen's; another lane at the stile of St Stephen's church, to The Key, leaving the churchyard on the right hand; and the third street is a long one, beginning at the end of the aforesaid Pill Street and going along Marsh Street, a long road to Marsh Gate.

---

h   Worcestre wrote *In* in the margin, then the full heading centrally
i   *augustini* deleted, and the correct *Stephani* written above
j   *sic*

(104)

DOMUS CONDUCTI IN TRIANGULO LOCO DE LE KAY PRO
AQUA HABENDA

Apud le kay in spatio trianguli largi est in medio dicti trianguli
pucherima[a] Domus de Frestone Rotundus & altus de Frestone
erecta. sumptuouse operata. in qua est conductus[b] aquarum de
plumbo conducte de Fonte cuius principium fontis est apud

... [c]

(105)

Via alia de pylle stret[d] extendendo ad domum custume Regis
vbi vendunt salsas pisces continet ad principium trianguli .64.
gressus

(106)

Cristmasstrete vel knyfsmythstrete continet in latitudine .12.
gressus jdest ... [e] virgas

(107)

Vie interius latitudo ad le key de seynt Johnys yate continet .6.
gressus

(108)

Triangulus qui est magnum & amplum spacium apud le key vbi
domus conducti aque in[f] medio trianguli scituatur. continet ex[g]
tribus partibus de le customhous ad keyam. et de keya ad le
post [showtes?][h] ... [i]

(109)

FROMEYATE

Porta de Fromeyates due porte cum cathena ferri continent
cum vacuo spacio longitudinis dictarum portarum continet .22.
virgas. super archus & duas pontes edificatas

(110)

Cristmastrete

PONS CUM CRUCE IN VICO DE CRISTMAS STRET

Pons siue archus sub vna cruce decenti de Frestone desuper
erecta ad quendam angulum ad modum trianguli. super

---

a   *sic*
b   *fon* (for *fonte*?) deleted
c   Blank in MS
d   *ex* smudged and deleted
e   Blank in MS
f   *tria* deleted
g   This note is continued in the margin, with *ex* repeated as a catchword

(104)
THE CONDUIT HOUSE FOR HOLDING WATER, IN THE TRIANGULAR PLACE OF THE KEY
At The Key, in the large triangular space, there is in the middle of the said triangle a very beautiful freestone building, round and tall, built of richly worked freestone, in which is a water-conduit of lead leading from a spring of which the main source is at ...

(105)
Another road, where they sell salt fish, extending from Pill Street to the King's Customs House at the beginning of the triangle, measures 64 steps.

(106)
Christmas Street, or Knifesmith Street, measures in width 12 steps, that is ... yards.

(107)
The width of the inner road to The Key from St John's Gate measures 6 steps.

(108)
The triangle, which is a big, wide space at The Key, where the water-conduit house is situated in the middle of the triangle, measures along the three sides, from the Customs House to The Key, and from The Key to the 'post shutes'[1] ...

(109)
FROME GATE
The gate of Fromegate, two gates with an iron chain, built upon an arch and two piers, measure, together with the open space the length of[2] the said gates, 22 yards.

(110)
Christmas Street.
BRIDGE WITH CROSS IN THE STREET OF CHRISTMAS STREET
The bridge or arch below a fine freestone cross set thereon, at a certain corner of triangular shape, set up over the bridge-

---

1 It is unclear what Worcestre meant by this landmark
2 i.e. between the two gates

---

h A doubtful reading: *showtes* is cramped and unclear
i Blank in MS

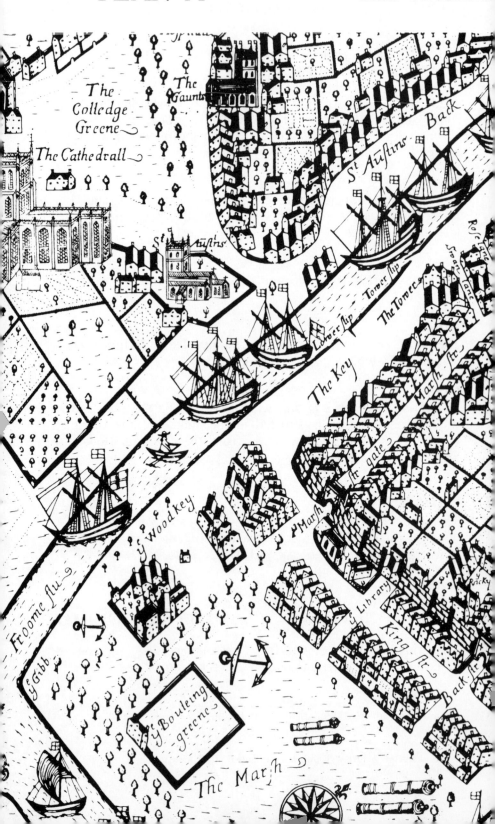

The Colledge Greene

The Gaunts

The Cathedrall

St Austins

St Austins Back

Roseane

Tower flip

Lower flip

The Tower

Store gate

The Key

Marsh ſtr

ytt gate

y Wood key

y Marſh

y Library

y Racky

Froome flu

King ſtr

Back ſtr

y Gibb

y Bouleing greene

The Marſh

BRISTOL IN 1673

Jacobus Millerd

(110) [continued]
pontem archus erecta^a in fine vice vocate, Cristmassestrete
aliter knyfesmythstrete prope Fromeyate continet ... ^b
gressus

LE SLEPE IN CRISTMASTRETE
<u>Gradus anglice</u> a slepe subtus archus & crucem ad eundem ad
aqua de Frome pro lotura vestimentorum lineorum seu
laneorum in fine de Cristmastrete continet circa ... ^c gressus,

latitudo vie de <u>Cristmastrete</u> jncipiendo apud portam sancti
Johannis continet .12. gressus.

p.111

(111)
Radcliff hylle vltra Ecclesiam
Via^d de Radclyffstrete jncipiente in parte meridionali ville
Bristollie vltra Ecclesia Radclyff apud angulum vie ducentis ad
trillyemyllys vsque ad vltimam portam prope conductum porte
de Radclyff. continet^e novies .60. gressus qui est .540.
gressus
latitudo vie maioris loci continet ex opposito turis^f campanile
Radclyff continet .12. gressus

(112)
Memorandum quod longitudo turris Campanile in volta nova
factus continet .24. pedes ab oriente in occidentem & .22.
pedes a boria in meridiem

Item^g basis quadrati fabricationis Spere de Radclyff qui est de
octo panis. primus cursus super locum quadrature spere
constat in densitudine^h lapidibus .duorum pedum ex duobus
petris cementatis quia durum contrehere vnam lapidem talis
densitudinis. & sic continuat minorando vsque ad certam
altitudinem, ac quatuor sconci de lapidibus ab vno quarterio
anguli. in proximum ad ligandam speram que quidem spera stat
modo vltraⁱ .100. pedes

---

a   *erecta continet in longitudine* [blank] *gressus,* deleted; *erecta* repeated,
    and a mark + in margin, perhaps a reminder to fill in the number
b   Blank in MS
c   Blank in MS, with + in margin opposite (cf. note a)
d   *jnci* (for *jncipiente*) deleted
e   *9* deleted
f   *sic*
g   *q'* (for *questio* or *query*?) in margin, and a marginal note by Worcestre
    in different ink: *nota exemplum pro spera Ecclesie norwici* (Note
    example for the spire of Norwich church)

(110) [continued]
arch at the end of the road called Christmas Street, otherwise
Knifesmith Street, near Fromegate, measures ... steps.

THE SLIP IN CHRISTMAS STREET
A stairway (in English, 'a slip') at the end of Christmas Street,
below the arch and cross, for going to the river Frome for the
washing-place of linen or woollen clothes, measures about ...
steps.

The width of the road of Christmas Street, beginning at St
John's Gate, measures 12 steps.

p.111

(111)
Redcliffe Hill beyond the church
The road of Redcliffe Street, beginning on the south side of the
town of Bristol, beyond Redcliffe church, at the corner of the
road leading to Treen Mills, as far as to the further gate, near
Redcliffe Gate conduit, measures nine times 60 steps, which is
540 steps.
The width of the road at the biggest point, opposite Redcliffe
bell-tower, measures 12 steps.

(112)
Memorandum, that the length of the bell-tower upon the
newly-built vault measures 24 feet from east to west, and 22
feet from north to south.

Also, of the square foundation of the construction of Redcliffe
spire, which is of eight panels: the first course of the spire,
upon the squared base, consists of a two-foot thickness of
stones, from two stones cemented together, because it is hard
to obtain a single stone of such thickness.   And so it
continues, diminishing up to a certain height; and there are
four corbels[1] of stone, at each of the four corners, to hold
together the spire; which same spire now stands more than
100 feet.

---

1   cf. Salzman, *Building in England* pp. 104-5: *sconchons*. These may have
    been splayed stones retaining the spire on the outside rather than
    corbels supporting it (cf. 'sconces') on the inside

---

h   *ex* deleted
i   *100* smudged and deleted

(113)

ā

Item domus longitudo presbiterorum Canynges jn longitudine 20 virgarum vel .19. virgarum cum .4. baywyndowes de Frestone pro cameris .4. presbiterorum

(114)[a]
COLLEGIUM SANCTI JOHANNIS

ā   dedicacio Ecclesie sancti Johannis baptiste Bristollie die .17. Jullij .b.[b]

ā   translacio sancti[c] Wlstani Episcopi .7. die Junij

ā   translacio sancti Edmundi archiepiscopi .9. die Junij & confessoris .f. littera

ā   translacio sancti Ricardi Episcopi & confessoris .16. die Junij .f littera

ā   translacio sancti Eduuardi Regis & martiris .20. die Junij .C. littera

Ista cronica jnueni in libro portiferij Ecclesie sancti Johannis prope Radcliff chyrch[d]

---

(115)[e]

Ab Adam ad diluuium .2242.

A diluuio ad Abraham .942

Ab Abraham vsque ad natiuitatem Christi .2015

Et sic anni ab Adam ad natiuitatem Christi .5189.

A natiuitate christi vsque ad pasca quod fuit .7. kalendas
      Aprilis littera dominicalis A. litter tabularis ... [f]

Ciclus solaris .28. ciclus lunaris .16. annus .3.[us] a bisexto concurrentes .6. 1307.

ā Et sic fuerunt anni mundi vsque ad predictam Pascha[g]
     .6406

---

(116)
ECCLESIA SANCTI JOHANNIS BAPTISTE

longitudo Ecclesie sancti Johanni baptiste .21. virge latitudo eius .8. virge,

---

a   Item **(114)** was included in Harvey, *Itineraries*, pp. 304-5, with some variations in transcription and translation

b   *littera* has been omitted

c   *Du* (possibly for *Dunstani*?) deleted, and *sancti* repeated

d   This note has been added by Worcestre in different ink

e   Item **(115)** was included in Harvey, *Itineraries*, pp. 304-7, with some variations in transcription and translation

(113)
Also, the length of the house of the Canynges priests [is] 19 or 20 yards in length, with 4 bay-windows of freestone, for the rooms of the 4 priests.

(114)
THE COLLEGE OF ST JOHN
The dedication of the church of St John the Baptist at Bristol:
       17th day of July. [Letter] B
The translation of St Wulstan the Bishop: 7th day of June.
The translation of St Edmund, Archbishop and Confessor: 9th
       day of June. Letter F
The translation of St Richard, Bishop and Confessor: 16th day
       of June. Letter F
The translation of St Edward King and Martyr: 20th day of
       June. Letter C
This chronicle I found in a portable breviary book in the church of St John near Redcliffe church.

---

(115)
From Adam to the Flood, 2242
From the Flood to Abraham, 942
From Abraham up to the birth of Christ, 2015
And so the years from Adam to the birth of Christ, 5189[1]
From the birth of Christ up to the Easter which was the 7th
      kalends of April,[2] Dominical letter A, tabular letter ...,
      solar cycle 28, lunar cycle 16, the third year from leap
      year, concurrents 6, 1307
And thus there have been years of the world, up to the
      aforesaid Easter, 6406[3]

---

(116)
THE CHURCH OF ST JOHN THE BAPTIST
The length of the church of St John the Baptist: 21 yards.
Its width: 8 yards.

---

1   Error for 5199
2   26th March, which was Easter Day in the year 1307
3   Error for 6506

---

f   Blank in MS
g   *60 .646. 646. anni* deleted

(117)
RADCLIF STRETE
Via vocata Radclyfstrete jncipiendo a porta de Radclyff
continuando viam vsque principium pontis Bristollie continet
.710. gressus
latitudo vie continet .12. gressus

(118)
DE PONTE BRISTOLLIE
ā
spacium tenementorum mansionum ex quolibet latere pontis
Bristollie .10. virgas continet

Item[a] spacium interceptum in loco latrinarum officij super
pontem ad jncepcionem mansionum prime partis pontis de
Radclyff strete. vere jncepcionis pontis continet .18. virgas

p. 112[b]

(119)
Memorandum tempore eclipsis generalis apud Damsk monachi
de Rolieff veniebant apud Damsk ad succurrendum preter vnum
monachum. Et homines lollardi de patria prage cum .xviij.
milia hominum[c] & cum Rege de Pollarland, ceperunt abbathiam
de Rolieff et ceperunt dictum monachum et super
haynesburghille prope dimidium miliare[d] sicut Brandescombe
extra Bristollie fecerunt poni contra ignem in veru de vno
fyrre tre fecerunt rostrari per ketyrs gentes de praga, jta quod
homines de Damsk possunt videre ipsum monachum ad veru
positum

Et in redeundo quod dicti homines de praga redeundo de
obsidione ciuitatis Damsk occiderunt ipsos ad numerum .xviij.
milia hominum sicut Imperator scripsit magno mastro[e] de
spruce,

---

a   *a le A le* deleted
b   This page of miscellaneous notes was written at a different time from
    pages 111 and 113. Items **(119)**, **(120)** were included in Harvey,
    Itineraries, pp. 306-7, while **(121)**, **(122)** on the same page were
    included in Harvey, *Itineraries,* pp. 366-7, both with some variations in
    transcription and translation.
c   *lollardi de patria prage cum .xviij* underlined, probably by Talbot, who
    has also drawn a vertical wavy line down the left-hand side, with § in
    the margin
d   *de* deleted
e   *sic*

(117)
REDCLIFFE STREET
The road called Redcliffe Street, beginning at Redcliffe Gate, continuing [along] the way as far as the beginning of Bristol Bridge, measures 710 steps.
The width of the road measures 12 steps.

(118)
CONCERNING BRISTOL BRIDGE
The depth of the dwelling houses on either side of Bristol Bridge measures 10 yards.

Also, the intervening space on the site of the public latrines upon the bridge, from Redcliffe Street to the beginning of the dwelling houses on the first side of the bridge, at the true start of the bridge, measures 18 yards.

P.112

(119)
Memorandum: at the time of the general eclipse[1] at Danzig,[2] the monks of Rolieff[3] came to Danzig to help, except one monk.   And the Lollards of the country of Prague, with 18,000 men and with the King of Poland[4] took the Abbey of Rolieff, and they took the said monk, and on Haynesburg Hill[5] nearby, half a mile [away] like Brandon Hill outside Bristol, they set [him] against a fire impaled upon a spit made of a fir-tree by the Cathars,[6] people of Prague, so that the men of Danzig could see that monk fixed on the spit.

And that, in returning from the siege of the city of Danzig, the said men of Prague were themselves slain to the number of 18,000 men, as the Emperor[7] wrote to the Grand Master of Prussia.

---

1   The total eclipse of 17 June 1433: cf. **(50)** and **(120)**.   John Sherp was mayor from Michaelmas 1432-1433, so that Worcestre's previous date of 17 June 1432 **(50)** for the eclipse may be an error for 1433
2   Now Gdansk
3   Probably Oliwa Cathedral, on the outskirts of Gdansk, and originally a Cistercian monastery
4   King Wladislaus II (1350-86; d.1434). Harvey, *Itineraries*, p. 306 n.2 summarises the background to this episode.   The 'Lollards' are presumably the Hussites of Bohemia whom King Wladislaus II supported in their opposition to the Emperor Sigismund
5   Harvey suggested that this is Hagelsberg
6   i.e. heretics
7   The Emperor Sigismund (1368-1437).   The Grand Master of the Teutonic Order 1422-41 was Paul von Russdorf (Harvey, *Itineraries*, p. 307 n.4)

(120)

Et[a] dicto anno Sherp junior fuit primo vice maior Bristollie tempore generalis Eclipsis

(121)

Walterus Grymstede	Isti .4. parochie sancti
Johannes Swayn	Jacobi contra Thomam
Nicholaus dant lawyer	Watkyns,
Ricardus Clayfeld	

(122)

Memorandum Richardus Corleonis[b] fecit Castrum de Almade in Portugalia ex opposito Lysbon;

p.113

(123)

<u>le Bakk Bristollie,</u>

longitudo[c] via vocata le Bak vbi naues Wallie jntrant & continet a principio domus conducte prope pontem vsque ad Portam extremam vocatam mershyate continet in longitudine .3030[d] gressus per aquam Avone[e]

latitudo dicte vie vocate le bak ad proiciendum bosca & alias mercandizas. continet secundum maius & minus .30. gressus

altitudo[f] maris avone.[g] quando nouus Refluxus maris est in prima die[h] commutacionis lune vt vidi & audivi in lunacione proxima ante jntroitum solis in libram est .7. vel .8. brachia apud le bak anglice vathym[i] et brachium continet .6. pedes

(124)

BAFFTSTRET

Via longitudo vocata Baftstret, jncipiente ex opposito crucis in Baldwynestrete vsque murum ville[j] ex opposito de le Mersh. continet a retro capelle de le bak in occidentali parte dicte capelle continet .240. gressus

---

a　Unclear part word, possibly *eod* (for *eodem*?), smudged and deleted
b　*cour de lion rex Anglie* added above by Talbot, who has also underlined
　　Corleonis, de Almade and *Lysbon*, and added *vlissipponis* after *Lysbon*
c　*longitudo* has been added afterwards, which explains clumsy phrasing
d　*sic*, clear but very compressed; perhaps an error for *.330.*?
e　*Avone* underlined by Talbot, who has written *avone* again after it
f　*q'* (for *questio* or *query*?) in margin opposite beginning of the paragraph
g　*avone* underlined by Talbot, linked with a line to *Avone*: see note (e)
h　*et* deleted

(120)

And in the said year Sherp the younger[1] was mayor of Bristol for the first time, at the time of the general eclipse.

(121)

Walter Grymstede	These four of St James's
John Swayn	parish against Thomas
Nicholas Dant, lawyer	Watkyns
Richard Clayfeld	

(122)

Memorandum: Richard Cœur de Lion built the castle of Almada[2] in Portugal, opposite Lisbon.

p.113

(123)

The Back of Bristol.

The length [of] the road called The Back, where the Welsh ships come in, and it measures beginning from the conduit house near the bridge, as far as the further gate called Marsh Gate: it measures 3030 steps[3] in length, along by the river Avon.

The width of the said road called The Back, to the heaps of wood and other goods, measures more or less 30 steps.

The height of the tide of the Avon, when there is a new spring tide, on the first day of the change of the moon, as I have seen and heard, in the lunar cycle immediately before the entry of the sun into Libra,[4] is 7 or 8 fathoms (in English, a 'vathym') at The Back, and a fathom measures 6 feet.

(124)

BACK STREET

The length [of] the road called Back Street, beginning opposite the cross in Baldwin Street, as far as the town wall opposite the Marsh, at the back of the Chapel on The Back, on the west side of the said Chapel, measures 240 steps.

---

1   John Sharpe was Mayor of Bristol 1432-3, and again in 1439-40; the eclipse was on 17th June 1433: cf. **(50)**, **(119)**
2   Almada lies on the south side of the mouth of the Tagus estuary
3   Error, perhaps, for 330 steps: cf. note e opposite
4   Autumn equinox, 22/23 September 1480

---

i   *vathym* underlined by Talbot with a marginal note: *fathoms*
j   *cl* deleted

(124) [continued]
latitudo dicte vie ad spacium longitudinis .180. gressuum.
continet .20. gressus sed in prima jncepcione vie apud crucem
in Baldewynestrete per spacium longitudinis .60. gressuum eius
latitudo est stricta via. nisi latitudinis <u>trium virgarum</u>[a]

(125)
Vie .4. ex omni latere in occidentali parte capelle de le Bakk in[b]
Edificacione quadrata per A B – facta continent ex qualibet .4.
lateribus ... [c] gressus

(126)
Porta sancti Nicholai continet a boria in meridiem in longitudine
.7. virgas
latitudo dicte porte continet ... [c]

latitudo vie de hyghstrete finiente ad dictam portam continet
.20. gressus

(127)
Porta sancti[d] leonardi continet ex parte orientali in longitudine
.7. virgas & ex parte occidentali ... [e] virgas
latitudo porte continet ... [e] virgas
altitudo porte cum campanile continet per estimacionem ... [e]

latitudo vie vocate Smalstrete ad finem porte sancti leonardi[f]
continet 30. gressus[g]

(128)
Porta sancti Johannis baptiste continet in longitudine a boria in
meridiem versus bradstrete, .7. virgas & ab oriente in
occidente versus le kay latitudo vie de Bradstrete ad finem
dicte porte continet .18. gressus.

(129)
latitudo vie vocate seynt laurens lane continet .6. gressus

---

a   Worcestre wrote *.3.* above *trium*, then underlined *trium virgarum* and
    added *.3. virgarum* again in different ink
b   *vt* or *vi* deleted
c   Blank in MS
d   *Nicholai* deleted
e   Blank in MS

(124) [continued]
The width of the said road, for a distance of 180 steps in length, measures 20 steps; but at the starting-point of the road, at the cross in Baldwin Street, for a distance of 60 steps in length, its width is a narrow way, less than three yards wide.

(125)
The 4 roads, on every side, on the west side of the chapel on The Back (in the square building put up by A.B.[1]) measure, on each of the 4 sides, ... steps.

(126)
St Nicholas's Gate measures in length from north to south 7 yards.
The width of the said gate measures ...

The width of the road of High Street, ending at the said gate, measures 20 steps.

(127)
St Leonard's Gate, on the east side, measures 7 yards in length, and on the west side ... yards.
The width of the gate measures ... yards.
The height of the gate with the bell-tower measures by estimation ...

The width of the road called Small Street at the St Leonard's Gate[2] end measures 30 steps.

(128)
St John the Baptist's Gate measures in length from north to south, towards Broad Street, 7 yards, and [the same] from east to west, towards The Key; the width of the road of Broad Street at the end of the said gate, measures 18 steps.

(129)
The width of the road called St Lawrence Lane measures 6 steps.

---

1   Thomas Knapp: cf. **(219)**, **(220)**, **(252)**, **(342)**
2   See note f below

---

f   *sic*, but either Small Street is an error for Corn Street, or St Leonard's Gate is an error for St Giles's Gate
g   *prova* (check) in margin

(130)
Porte due super pontem de Fromeyate[a] continent in longitudine
... [b] virgas[c] vel .34. gressus
latitudo duarum portarum continent ... [d] virgas
Pons duorum archuum per[e] aquam de Frome transeuntem
continet[f] in longitudine. ... [g] virgas vel ... [g] gressus
latitudo dictarum pontem continet, ... [g] vel ... [g] gressus

p.114

(131)[h]
Obijt Johannes Barstable Burgensis ville Bristollie[i] anno Domini
.1411. .m[l] iiij[c] xj. quinto decimo kalends Octobris & habuit
Nicholaum Barstable presbiterum magistrum Capelle sancte
trinitatis

(132)
Ecclesia sancte Werburge continet in latitudine .19. virgas vel
34. gressus
longitudine dicte Ecclesie continet ... [j]
Turris quadratus dicte Ecclesie continet ex omni parte quatuor
costarum .5. virgarum[k]

(133)
Tourstrete longitudo vie de Wynchstrete apud le pyllorye
continuans per cimiterium sancti Johannis prope blynde yate
vsque Bradstrete continet .370. gressus
latitudo dicte vie continet ad minus .2. virgas sed a orientali
parte Ecclesie sancti Johannis baptiste continet .3. virgas

(134)
Porta vocata Blyndeyate continet in latitudine .9 pedes & in
latitudine vie .3. virgas id est 9 pedes desuper edificate,[l]

---

a   *pontem de Fromeyate* underlined by Talbot, with § in margin opposite
b   Blank in MS
c   *et* deleted
d   Blank in MS
e   *porta* deleted
f   *continet* repeated
g   Blank in MS
h   This item was added at the top of the page in different ink
i   *anno* deleted

(130)
The two gates upon the bridge of Fromegate measure in length
... yards or 34 steps.
The width of the two gates measures ... yards.
The two-arched bridge crossing over the river Frome
measures in length ... yards or ... steps.
The width of the said bridge measures ... yards or ... steps.

p.114

(131)
John Barstable, burgess of the town of Bristol, died A.D.
1411, on the fifteenth kalends of October,[1] and he had
Nicholas Barstable master of the priests of the chapel of the
Holy Trinity.

(132)
The church of St Werburgh measures 19 yards or 34 steps in
width.
The length of the said church measures ...
The square tower of the said church measures 5 yards on each
of the four sides.

(133)
Tower Street: the length of the road from Wynch Street, at
the pillory, going past St John's churchyard, near Blind Gate,
as far as Broad Street, measures 370 steps.
The width of the said road measures less than 2 yards, except
at the east end of St John the Baptist church [where] it
measures 3 yards.

(134)
The gate called Blind Gate measures 9 feet in width, and the
road 3 yards in width – that is, 9 feet above[2] the building.

---

1   17th September 1411
2   i.e. on the uphill side of the gate

---

j   Blank in MS
k   *sic*
l   Between **(134)** and **(135)** is the start of another item, *latitudo porte sancti
    Johannis a*, (the width of St John's Gate from) deleted

(135)
longitudo Ecclesie sancte Werburge continet in longitudine .21. virgas
latitudo eius .19. virge;
Turris Ecclesie quadrate continet .5. virge ex omni latere
Columpne archus .6. Fenestre .6. in vna parte & in qualibet Fenestra .5. panelle & totidem columpne & archus in alia parte
Fenestre vna in orientali & alia in occidentrali,

(136)
Venella vie a vico de smalstrete per Ecclesiam sancte Werburge ad jntroitum vie. vocate Seynt Colastrete continet .145. gressus; ex opposito venelle vie per spacium .32. graduum ad Baldwynestrete

(137)
Venella vie ad Baldwynestrete ex opposito superscripte eundo per certos gradus inferiores ad numerum[a] .32. & ... [b] gressuum ad vicum Baldwynestrete ex opposito crucis lapidee, continet cum dictis .32.[c] gradibus gressuum, et ... [d] gressibus

(138)
Via[e] ab Ecclesia sancti Nicholai cum .5. gressibus aree dicte Ecclesie ad jntroitum Ecclesie volte vocate le Crowd cum spacio latitudinis volte de dicta Ecclesia arcus.[f] ac spacio[g] latitudine .20. gressibus ad decensum volte de le croude continet vltra dictos 20. gressus. preter .2. virgas ... [h]

tamen latitudo tocius volte, cum duobus alis ex numero .5. pyllerys;[i] archuatis continet .12. vyrgas,
Et .5. magne columpne ac .5. archus sunt in dicta crippa siue volta,
Item turris quadratus Campanile ecclesie predicte continet .5. virgas ex omni parte,

---

a　*30* deleted
b　Blank in MS
c　*gres* deleted. Worcestre himself is clearly confused between his own [foot]step (*gressus*) and a stair-step (*gradus*)
d　Blank in MS
e　*a* deleted
f　*continet* deleted

(135)
The length of the church of St Werburgh: it measures 21 yards in length.
Its width, 19 yards.
The square tower of the church measures 5 yards on each side.
6 arched pillars, 6 windows on one side, and 5 lights in each window; and as many pillars and arches on the other side.
One window at the east [end], and another at the west [end].

(136)
The alley-way from the street of Small Street by St Werburgh's church, to the entry to the road called St Nicholas Street, measures 145 steps.   [It is] opposite an alley-way extending [down] 32 stairs to Baldwin Street.

(137)
The alley-way to Baldwin Street, opposite the above-written [one], going by certain lower stairs, to the number of 32, and ... steps, to the street of Baldwin Street opposite the stone cross, measures both the said 32 stair-steps and ... [foot]steps.

(138)
The way from St Nicholas's church, with 5 steps of open area [around] the said church, to the entrance of the church crypt called The Crowde, together with a space the width of the arched vault of the said church, and also a space 20 steps wide at the entry down to the crypt of The Crowde, measures apart from the said 20 steps, scarcely 2 yards ... [1]

However, the width of the whole crypt, with two aisles numbering 5 arched pillars, measures 12 yards.
And there are 5 great pillars and 5 arches in the said crypt or vault.
Also, the square bell-tower of the aforesaid church measures 5 yards on every side.

---

1   This note appears to be incomplete

---

g   Worcestre first wrote *20*, deleted it, and then wrote *spacio* above
h   Blank in MS
i   *continet* deleted

p.115

(139)

Ad ecclesiam Sancti Michaelis,

Via in occidentali parte Ecclesie sancti Bertholomei Bristollie eundo ad Ecclesiam sancti Michaelis, super altissimum montem,

STYPSTRETE,

a via vocata le stypestrete jncipiendo est[a] a collegij sancti[b] Bertholomei semper ascendendo ad quandam fontem & crucem lapidis in monte sancti michaelis sic eundo vsque Ecclesiam Religionum beate marie[c] magdalene pauperis Religio trium monacharum continet .360. gressus

(140)

MONASTERIUM   SANCTARAM[d]   VIRGINIS   MARIE MAGDALENE

Et a dicta Ecclesia Religiosa siue Ecclesia parochialis sancti michaelis vsque ad lapidem altum assignatum pro limite Franchesie ville Bristollie prope crucem & locum furcarum pro justicia legis pro traditoribus & latronibus suspendendis & execucione mortis 420 gressus assendendo semper ad montem. Sed a dicta petra que est finis Franchesie Bristollie plage meridionalis ab alta cruce ad locum justiciee exequendum continet in toto cum .120. gressibus .540. gressus

(141)

THYRDAMDOWNE

Capella sancte crucis super Thyrdam doune versus Collegium de Westberye continet in longitudine[e] .9.[f] virgas latitudo eius continet .5. virgas. et habet mantellum[g]

(142)

COLLEGIUM DE WESTBERY

Ecclesia Collegij diaconatus de Westbery continet in longitudine .42. virgas vel .lx. 50 gressus.[h] latitudo eius continet .24. virgas vel .25.

---

a *sic*, probably in error for *et*
b *Nicholai* deleted
c *mag(dalene)* incomplete for lack of space, rewritten in full on next line
d *sic*
e *.8.* deleted
f *gressus* deleted
g *mantellum* is followed by an illegible word or words, ?..*m..retac*...?
h *la* incomplete at end of line, and *latitudine* rewritten in full on next line

p.115

(139)

To the church of St Michael.

The road on the west side of the church of St Bartholomew of Bristol, going to St Michael's church, upon the highest hill.

STEEP STREET
Beginning at the road called the Steep Street, and from the College of St Bartholomew climbing upwards all the time to a certain well and stone cross on St Michael's Hill, thus going as far as the church of the religious house of Blessed Mary Magdalene, a community of three poor nuns,[1] measures 360 steps.

(140)
THE NUNNERY OF THE HOLY VIRGIN MARY MAGDALENE
And from the said church of the community, or the parish church of St Michael, as far as the tall stone appointed as the boundary of the franchise of the town of Bristol, near the cross and the site of the gallows for the legal punishment, by hanging and putting to death, for traitors and thieves: 420 steps, climbing all the time up the hill. But to the said stone, which is the end of the franchise of the county of Bristol from the high cross on the south,[2] [and on] to the place of executing punishment, measures in all, with 120 [more] steps, 540 steps.

(141)
DURDHAM DOWN
The chapel of the Holy Cross upon Durdham Down, towards the College of Westbury, measures 9 yards in length.
Its width measures 5 yards, and it has a cloth[3]

(142)
WESTBURY COLLEGE
The church of the College of Deacons at Westbury measures 42 yards or 60 50[4] steps in length.
Its width measures 24 or 25 yards.

---

1 Despite his confused case-endings, it seems probable that this is Worcestre's meaning: cf. **(408)**. By the time of its dissolution in 1536, there were only two nuns
2 The high cross marked the official centre of the county of Bristol
3 Or napkin, or cloak? Followed by an illegible word: see note g opposite
4 It is unclear whether Worcestre intended 60 or 50 steps, having apparently confused his Roman and arabic numbers

(143)[a]
STURMYN MERCATOR
1447　Memorandum quod Navis Roberti Sturmy in primo viagio suo veniendo de Jerusalem fuit submersus prope Modon jnsula[b] ex fortuna casu in nocte, accidente & .37. homines Bristollie sue navis vocate le[c] Gog Anne[d]
Et ipsi .37. homines sepulti apud Modon et Episcopus patrie fecit capellam nouam ad orandum pro animabus eorum

---

(144)

Toukerstrete
de[e] ponte Bristollie .90.
TOKERSTRETE
1. Venella prima in Toukerstrete continet .90. gressus ad aquam Avone,

Stallage cros .100.
2. Venella secunda versus Stallage cros continet .100. gressus ad aquam de Avyn. et ista venella est apud Stallage cros ex opposito
latitudo dicte venelle est .4. gressus.

(145)
IN PARTE BORIALI DE TEMPLESTRET
Via in fine Tokerstrete jncipiente a retro de Templest[rete][f] vltra magnum fontem prope magnum & profundum gradum anglice a slepe in fine de Touker strete & eundo[g] coram aquam de avyn per prata. in boria[li][h] parte aque. continet ad retornam venelle in Templestrete[i] ad le pyllory continet .420. gressus et dicta via est edificata nisi vna parte versus dexteram manum. et alia pars vie est cursus aque de avyn,
latitudo dicte vie est vltra circa .8. gressus. et aliquando .20. gressus[j]

(146)
Venella[k] .2.[da] existens coram aquam avyn in dicta via retornando versus & ad templestrete continet[l] .90. gressus

---

a　Item **(143)** was included in Harvey, *Itineraries*, pp. 306-7, with some variations in translation; cf. **(248)**
b　*Modon jnsula* underlined, probably by Talbot
c　*Go* deleted
d　*pylgrymes* written in margin by Talbot
e　Deletion, probably of *Avone*
f　Edge of page torn away
g　*ad* deleted
h　Edge of page torn away
i　*.420. gressus* in margin opposite

(143)
STURMY, A MERCHANT
1447 Memorandum that the ship of Robert Sturmy, coming
on his first voyage from Jerusalem, was sunk near the island
of Modon,[1] by a stroke of fate in the night, together with 37
Bristol men of his ship, called the *Cog Anne*.
And these 37 men were buried at Modon, and the bishop of
the country built a new chapel to pray for their souls.

---

(144)

Tucker Street
from Bristol Bridge: 90
TUCKER STREET
1. The first lane in Tucker Street measures 90 steps to the
river Avon.

Stallage Cross: 100
2. The second lane, towards Stallage Cross, measures 100
steps to the river Avon; and this lane is right opposite Stallage
Cross.
The width of the said lane is 4 steps.

(145)
ON THE NORTH SIDE OF TEMPLE STREET
The road at the end of Tucker Street, beginning behind Temple
Street beyond the great well, near the great and deep stairway
(in English, a 'slip') at the end of Tucker Street, and going
alongside the river Avon, by the meadows on the north side of
the river, measures 420 steps to the turning of the lane to
Temple Street at the pillory. And the said road is built up[2]
only on one side, towards the right hand; and the other side of
the road is the course of the river Avon.
The width of the said road is more than about 8 steps, and
sometimes 20 steps.

(146)
There is a second lane fronting the river Avon, turning off the
said road, towards and to Temple Street; it measures 90
steps.

---

1 Probably present-day Methoni, near the tip of Cape Akrita, westernmost
  of the three Peleponnese capes, with islands immediately offshore
2 Probably 'built up with houses', as **(88)**, **(197)**; but could be 'paved', cf.
  (188), **(189)**

---

j + mark in margin opposite
k *prima* deleted
l The contraction for *con* is written twice

(147)
Venella secunda in dicta via coram aquam de avyn continet
circa .90. gressus et transcit in retorno de quadam peruisina[a]
ponte arboris quod equus non transciet ad prata coram aquam
avyn & sic retornando in templestrete ex opposito le pyllory
prope Ecclesiam templi continet vt super .90. gressus
latitudo dicte venelle continet .4. virgas

p.116

(148)

Ecclesia Templi sancte crucis

ECCLESIA TEMPLI
longitudo Ecclesie de Templo sancte crucis continet .57. virgas
& circa .100. gressus per estimacionem
latitudo eius continet[b] .42. gressus[c]
Turris nouus Ecclesie campanilis continet .5. virgas ex omni
parte quadrate
altitudo eius continet . ... .[d] & renouatum in edificijs circa
annum christi .1460.

(149)
Via[e] subtus le tounewallys jncipiendo a porta templest[ret]e[f] et
eundo infra murum & iuxta murum intrando per via vocata
seynt Thomas strete continet ... [g] gressus

(150)
Venella in templestrete vltra Ecclesiam templi ex parte
meridionali de templestrete idest in parte opposita Ecclesie.
versus portam templi qui est .2.[da] venella a cruce de Stallage
cros continet in longitudine versus & ad Radclyfstrete eundo
...[g] gressus
latitudo dicte venelle ... [g]

---

a The word appears to read *peruisina* but could perhaps be intended for
   parviculina (very small)
b *.38.* deleted
c *vel .57. virgas* deleted
d Blank in MS
e *Via* repeated

(147)

The second lane in the said road fronting the river Avon measures about 90 steps; and it goes along to turn off by a certain local[1] wooden bridge, which a horse cannot cross, to the meadows alongside the river Avon; and so returning to Temple Street opposite the pillory near Temple church, it measures as above 90 steps.

The width of the said lane measures 4 yards.

p.116

(148)

The church of Holy Cross, Temple

TEMPLE CHURCH

The length of the church of Holy Cross, Temple measures 57 yards, and by estimation about 100 steps.

Its width measures 42 steps.

The new bell-tower of the church measures 5 yards on each side of the square.

Its height measures ... and the structure was rebuilt about the year of Christ 1460.

(149)

The road under the town walls, beginning at Temple Street Gate and going inside the wall, and alongside the wall, passing across the road called St Thomas Street, measures ... steps.

(150)

The lane in Temple Street beyond Temple church, at the southern end[2] of Temple Street (that is, on the side opposite the church, towards Temple Gate) which is the second lane from the cross of Stallage Cross, measures ... steps in length towards and going to Redcliffe Street.

The width of the said lane ...

---

1   See note a opposite; this could perhaps mean 'a certain very small bridge'
2   *parte* here has the English sense of 'part' or 'end' rather than the more usual Latin 'side', since the street runs north-south

---

f   *sic,* for *templestrete*
g   Blank in MS

(151)

DE MURO VILLE [IN][a] PARTE MERIDIONALI DE TEMPLESTRETE

longitudo muri ville Bristollie transceundo per[b] ortas Templeyate sed jncipiendo vltra orientalem partem cancelle fratrum Augustiniensum super borduram aque de Avyn continuando vsque templeyate continet .600. gressus. Et iter sic continuando a porta templeyate per muros ville vsque ad primam portam de Radclyffstrete qui est finis dicte vie de Radclyffstrete continet .435. gressus

Et in toto[c] ab aqua Avene predictus murus continet vsque ad portam primam de Radclyfyate sic in toto .1035.[d] gressus[e]

Muri densitudo. super viam quam homines ambulant .2. virge Spissituodo[f] tocius muri continet .2. virgas & duas pedes

(152)

DE VENELLA IN PARTE ORIENTALI DE RADCLYFFSTRETE VSQUE SEYNT THOMAS STRETE

Venella in Radclyfstrete a prima[g] porta Radclyff vocata hounden lane. continet a via Radclyf vsque seynt Thomasstret continet in longitudine circa[h] .170. gressus

latitudo dicte venelle continet .2. virgas

(153)

Venella ex parte meridionali Ecclesie sancti Thome eundo iuxta Ecclesiam continet in longitudine .170. gressus

latitudo eius continet ... [i]

Venella in parte boriali Ecclesie sancti Thome[j] prope Ecclesiam transceundo per cimiterium continet ... [k]

(154)

ECCLESIA SANCTI THOME

Ecclesia sancti Thome cum choro continet in longitudine .80. gressus vel ... [k] virgas

latitudo eius continet .35. gressus, vel ... [k] virgas

altitudo Campanile ... [k]

---

a Edge of page worn away
b *per* repeated
c *toto* written again above
d *.1035.* seems to have been added afterwards
e *q'* (for *questio* or *query*?) in margin opposite this total, presumably for the insertion of the figures (note d above)
f *sic*
g *a* repeated
h *.2* deleted

(151)
OF THE TOWN WALL AT THE SOUTH END[1] OF TEMPLE
STREET
The length of the town wall of Bristol going past the Temple
Gate gardens, but beginning beyond the east end of the chancel
of the Augustinian Friars, upon the banks of the river Avon,
continuing as far as Temple Gate, measures 600 steps. And
thus continuing the way from the gate of Temple Gate along
by the town walls as far as to the first gate of Redcliffe Street,
which is the end of the said road of Redcliffe Street, measures
435 steps.
And the aforesaid wall measures in all, from the river Avon as
far as to the first gate of Redcliffe Gate, thus in all 1035
steps.

Thickness of the wall–walk upon which people stroll: 2 yards.
Thickness of the whole wall measures 2 yards and 2 feet.

(152)
OF THE LANE ON THE EAST SIDE OF REDCLIFFE STREET
AS FAR AS ST THOMAS STREET
The lane in Redcliffe Street from the first Redcliffe Gate, called
Hound Lane, measures about 170 steps in length from the
Redcliffe road as far as St Thomas Street.
The width of the said lane measures 2 yards.

(153)
The lane on the south side of St Thomas's church, going close
by the church, measures 170 steps in length.
Its width measures ...

The lane on the north side of St Thomas's church, next to the
church [and] going past the churchyard, measures ...

(154)
ST THOMAS'S CHURCH
St Thomas's church, including the quire, measures 80 steps or
... yards in length.
Its width measures 35 steps or ... yards.
The height of the bell–tower: ...

---

1   *parte* here has the English sense of 'part' or 'end' rather than the
    more usual Latin 'side', since the road runs north–south

---

i   Blank in MS
j   *continet* deleted
k   Blank in MS

(155)
MURUS VILLE BRISTOLLIE TRANSCEINDO[a] PER LE BAKE[b]
DE FROME YATE VSQUE PYTTEY YATE
Muri longitudo ex parte orientali ville prope Pyttey yate
jncipiente in meridionali de Pyttey yate vsque viam ducentem ad
portam vocatam le blynde yate[c] continet .170. gressus versus
monkenbrygge & continuando vsque Fromeyate sic continet
vlterius ... [d]

(156)
Muri ville Bristollie. videlicet. a principio[e] de Fromeyate & sic
returnando vsque per lewelynsmede[f] & retornando[g] per
seyntjamysbak. & brodemede ac le bak parum vsque pyttey
yate. continet dictus murus per aquam de Frome girando[h]
.1000. gressus;

p.117

(157)[i]
Asshton. Burton, Yatton. manet apud le Court

(158)
FINE DE SEYNT THOMAS STRETE
Via de fine Seynt Thomas strete jncipiente apud le toune walle
continuando sub le tounewall ad portam primam de
Radclyffyate qui est finis longe vie de Radclyffstrete continet
.170. gressus edificatus jn parte orientali[j] de le tounewalle
latitudo dicte vie continet .8. gressus

(159)
Via jncipiente apud occidentalem finem de cimiterio de
Radclyffchyrch sic transceundo per viam ducentem ad
trenemyllys & continuando vsque domum hospitalis beate marie
magdalene in dextra manu eundo versus pontem de Bryghtbow
continet ad crucem & capellam dicti hospitalis continet .300.

---

a *sic*, presumably error for *transceundo*
b *parochialis sancti Jacobi* deleted
c *veniente* deleted
d Blank in MS
e *de pytteyate returnando* deleted
f *vsque* deleted
g *sic*, two spellings of *returnando/retornando* in the same sentence
h Unclear, very faint word, possibly *quamlibet*, followed by *.1000. gressus* deleted
i A note written across the top of the page, unrelated to the rest. It was included in Harvey, *Itineraries*, pp. 312-3, with some variations in transcription and translation

(155)
THE WALL OF THE TOWN OF BRISTOL GOING ALONG
FROM FROME GATE AS FAR AS PITHAY GATE
The length of the wall on the east side of the town near Pithay
Gate, beginning on the south of Pithay Gate, as far as the road
leading to the gate called the Blind Gate, measures 170 steps;
[going] towards Monkenbridge and continuing thus as far as
Frome Gate, measures a further ...

(156)
The walls of the town of Bristol, to wit, beginning from Frome
Gate and thus bending round as far as Lewinsmead, and
turning off by St James Back and Broadmead and also the
Little Back, as far as Pithay Gate: the said wall, winding all
about[1] along by the river Frome, measures 1000 steps.

p.117

(157)
Ashton, Bourton, Yatton; he lives at The Court.[2]

(158)
THE END OF ST THOMAS STREET
The road from the end of St Thomas Street, beginning at the
town wall, continuing under the town wall to the first gate of
Redcliffe Gate, which is the end of the long road of Redcliffe
Street, measures 170 steps; [it is] built up on the east side of
the town wall.[3]
The width of the said road measures 8 steps.

(159)
The road beginning at the west end of the churchyard of
Redcliffe church, thus going past the road leading to Treen
Mills, and continuing as far as the hospital of the Blessed Mary
Magdalene, on the right hand going towards the bridge of
Brightbow, measures 300 steps to the cross and chapel of the

---

1 See note h opposite
2 This jotting appears to refer to [Long] Ashton, [Flax] Bourton and Yatton,
   south-west of Bristol, and to Sir John Newton (d.1488) of Court de
   Wyck. The medieval manor house at Court de Wyck burned down in
   the early 19th century
3 As the wall itself ran north-west to south-east, Worcestre is presumably
   referring to buildings on the inside (north-east) of the wall

---

j *de e* deleted

(159) [continued]
gressus.   Et a dicta domo hospitalis vsque pontem de
Bryghtbow continet .230. gressus[a] vbi libertas ville Bristollie
extendit.   sic in tot[b] .530. gressus[c]

(160)
[d] pons aque de Bryghtbow versus Ecclesiam hospitalis sancte
Katerine continet[e] .24.[f] gressus in longitudine

(161)
HOSPITALE SANCTE KATERINE
Via predicta continuando a ponte de Bryghtbow versus
Bedmynster[g] vsque ad capellam liberam hospitalis sancte
Katerine continet .170. gressus,

(162)
Via de hospitali Ecclesie sancte Katerine vsque pontem[h]
vocatem Bryghtbow eundo versus Ecclesiam de Radclyff[i]
continet in longitudine, .240 gressus

(163)
Pons vocat Bryghtbowe[j] vbi extrema pars libertatis ville
Bristollie e[x]istens[k] versus occidentem eundo vsque Wellys
per Bedmynster. continet .17. virgas longitudinis. siue[l] 36
gressus
latitudo dicti pontis continet .5. virgas

(164)
DE PONTE BRYGHTBOW AD PORTAM VLTIMAM DE FINE
RADCLYFFSTRETE,
Vie longitudo de porta vocata Radclyff yate versus Bedmynster
et transceundo per Ecclesiam Radclyff & domum[m] mansionis
presbiterorum Canyngys vsque pontem vocatum Bryghtbow vbi
ad dictum pontem libertas & Franchesia ville Bristollie extendit
in occidentali parte ville Bristollie continet .1200. gressus
ā [n]

---

a   + mark in margin opposite
b   *sic,* for *toto*
c   *q'* (for *questio* or *query*?) in margin opposite
d   *via de* deleted
e   *.170. gressus* deleted: cf. **(161)**
f   *24.* written again above
g   *ad* deleted
h   *de* deleted
i   *per alium domum hospitalis* (past the other hospital), i.e. St Mary
       Magdalene, deleted

(159) [continued]
said hospital. And from the said hospital as far as Brightbow bridge, [to] where the liberty of the town of Bristol extends, measures 230 steps; thus 530 steps in all.

(160)
Brightbow bridge over the river, towards St Katherine's hospital, measures 24 steps in length.

(161)
ST KATHERINE'S HOSPITAL
The aforesaid road, continuing from Brightbow bridge towards Bedminster, measures 170 steps as far as to the free chapel of St Katherine's hospital.

(162)
The road from the church of St Katherine's hospital as far as the bridge called Brightbow, going towards Redcliffe church, measures 240 steps in length.

(163)
The bridge called Brightbow, where the furthest western extent of the liberty of the town of Bristol is, going through Bedminster towards Wells, measures 17 yards, or 36 steps, in length.
The width of the said bridge measures 5 yards.

(164)
FROM BRIGHTBOW BRIDGE TO THE FURTHEST GATE AT THE END OF REDCLIFFE STREET
The length of the road from the gate called Redcliffe Gate towards Bedminster, and going past Redcliffe church and the dwelling house of the Canynges priests, as far as the bridge called Brightbow, where (at the said bridge) the liberty and franchise of the town of Bristol extends on the west side of the town of Bristol, measures 1200 steps.

---

j   Worcestre made several false starts, writing *Bryght* (left unfinished) and then *be be bow*, all deleted, before finally writing *Bryghtbowe*
k   Worcestre actually wrote *eistens*
l   *36* smudged and deleted, then rewritten
m   *capelle* deleted; *capelli hospitali* above the line also deleted
n   In margin with *q'* (for *questio* or *query*?), both perhaps relating to the figure *.1200.*, which appears to have been added afterwards

(165)

Portarum duarum predictarum in fine Radclyffstrete continet
spacium longitudinis inter dictas duas portas continet .36.
gressus;

(166)

Capella sancti[a] marie magdalene ab antiquo[b] fundata cum
hospitali[c] gencium leprosorum scita est in parte boriali versus
pontem de Bryghtbow vltra domum capellanorum Willelmi
Canyngys que capella scita est vltra viam ducentem ad[d]
molendinam vocatam tremyllys in altera parte cimiterij de
Westmynster[e]

p. 118   *[Blank]* [f]

p. 119[g]

(167)[h]

        De vico fratrum predicatorum vocate Marchalstrete[i]
Memorandum quod vicus vocata Iryshmede[j] jn orientali parte
de marshall strete continet in longitudine prope pontem lapidis
iuxta murum Fratrum predicatorum ... [k] gressus

(168)

sancta Cuthburga virgo die vltimum augusti non martiris
sancta Keneburga virgo 25. die Junij .A. littera,

---

(169)

Via vocata le Marchallstrete jncipit ab anguli principij vie de le
Weer[l] eundo directe per fratres predicatores ad le barres per
tenementa patris me W.Worcestre & eundo continue per[m]
horrea prioratus sancti Jacobi ad quen[dam][n] metum de

---

a   *sic*
b   *sancti marie magdalene* in fact inserted, with caret mark, at this point
c   Worcestre wrote *hospitaleate*, deleted ...*leate* and wrote *li* above
d   Worcestre wrote *mo* at the end of the line and then, lacking space,
    molendinam in full on the next line
e   Underlined by Talbot, who has written *in bristow - a Westmynster* at
    the foot of the page
f   Except for a note by Talbot, *Nomen patris ei[u]s qui hunc librum scripsit
    W.Worcestr.* (The name of the father of he who wrote this book: W.
    Worcestre.), referring to **(169)** on p.119 opposite, with a line linking
    the two
g   p.119 is a mixture of entries apparently made at different times
h   **(167)** has been added in the margin afterwards

(165)
Of the aforesaid two gates at the end of Redcliffe Street, the space between the said two gates measures 36 steps in length.

(166)
The chapel of St Mary Magdalene, founded long ago with a hospital for leprous people, is situated beyond the house of William Canynges' chaplains, on the north side, towards Brightbow bridge; which chapel is situated beyond the road leading to the mill called Treen Mills, on the other side of Westminster[1] churchyard.

p.118   *[Blank]* [2]

p.119

(167)
Of the street of the Friars Preachers called Marshall Street.
Memorandum, that the street called Irishmead, on the east side of Marshall Street, measures ... steps in length by the stone bridge next to the wall of the Friars Preachers.

(168)
St Cuthburga the Virgin: the last day of August; not [feast] of a martyr
St Cyneburga the Virgin: 25th day of June, letter A.

---

(169)
The road called the Marshall Street starts from the corner at the beginning of the road of The Weir, going straight past the Friars Preachers to The Bars, past the house of my father W. Worcestre; and continuing along past the barns of St James's

---

1   Presumably referring to London, in error for Redcliffe rather than
    Bedminster
2   See note f opposite

---

i   *q'* (for *questio* or *query*?) written twice in margin opposite
j   *vocat* deleted
k   Blank in MS
l   *vie de le Weer* underlined by Talbot and linked by a single diagonal
    line to *Domini de le Warre* in the middle of **(177)**, associating
    (incorrectly) the two names
m   *quia* deleted
n   Edge of page missing

(169) [continued]
exteriori lapide libertatis ville Bristollie eundo ex parte boriali
ad Redlyng Felde & Westbery[a] versus[b] Gloucestriam continet
.1020. gressus

(170)
MARCHALLE STRET
Ecclesia Fratrum predicatorum in Marshall strete.

Memorandum lez barrys comyn women ibi[c]
ā[d]

Via predicta[e] vocata Marchallstrete jncipiendo directa linea de
muro principij de vie vocate le Were prope angulum domus
Bagpathe. ex opposito[f] duorum molendinorum ville prope
Castrum ville & eundo per fratres predicatores & transceundo
per lez barres directa per horrea prioris sancti Jacobi eundo
per Redelond vsque Collegium Westbery. & per villam
Tokyngton versus Austclyff ad Severnwater & Gloucestriam,
continet 1020. gressus bina vice probatus per meos gressus.
et dicta via de Marchall strete[g] habet finem vltra horrea
prioratus sancti Jacobi ad quemdam Frestone longitudinis vnius
virge stantem que est meta & finis libertatis Bristollie. in parte
boriali eiusdem

(171)
PORTA VOCATA NEWYATE
longitudo portarum vocatarum Newyate. continet .20. gressus

(172)
longitudo Ecclesie sancti petri continet .54. gressus
latitudo eius continet. ... [h]

(173)
NORTON YS PLACE
longitudo edificacionis a retro Ecclesie predicte sancti petri a
via sancti petri. ex orientali parte retornando versus le aquam
de Avyn continet .75. gressus. et consimili modo in retorno
per dictum cimiterium. ab orientali Ecclesie sancti petri ad
occidentalem partem dicte Ecclesie de Edificacione magnifica
hospicij et tenementorum ... [h] Nortons continet .75. gressus,

---

a   *ad* deleted
b   *Gloucestriam* badly smudged, deleted and then rewritten
c   In margin opposite *lez barres* below
d   *q'* (for *questio* or *query*?) in margin opposite
e   *de* deleted
f   *m* deleted

(169) [continued]
priory to a certain stone boundary-mark of the outer limit of
the liberty of the town of Bristol, going northwards to
'Redlyng Felde'[1] and Westbury, towards Gloucester, it
measures 1020 steps

(170)
MARSHALL STREET
The church of the Friars Preachers in Marshall Street.

Memorandum: The Bars - common women here.

The aforesaid road called Marshall Street, beginning in a
straight line from the wall at the start of the road called The
Weir, near the corner of Bagpath's house, opposite the two
town mills near the Castle of the town, and going by the Friars
Preachers, and going past The Bars, straight past the barns of
the Prior of St James (going by Redland as far as Westbury
College, and by the village of Tockington, towards Aust Cliff,
to the Severn estuary and Gloucester) measures 1020 steps,
tested twice over by my own steps. And the said road of
Marshall Street ends beyond the barns of St James's priory at
a certain freestone standing one yard high, which is the marker
and limit of the liberty of Bristol on its north side.

(171)
THE GATE CALLED NEWGATE
The length of the gates called Newgate measures 20 steps.

(172)
The length of St Peter's church measures 54 steps.
Its width measures ...

(173)
NORTON'S PLACE
The length of the building at the back of the aforesaid church
of St Peter, from St Peter's Street on the east side, turning
off towards the river Avon, measures 75 steps; and likewise
on the return past the said churchyard. From the east of St
Peter's church to the west side of the said church, [the length]
of the splendid structure of ... Norton's residence and houses,
measures 75 steps.

---

1   Perhaps Redland Field? cf. **(61)**, **(197)**

---

g   *finit* deleted
h   Blank in MS

(174)

Venella^a longitudo de Wynchstrete ex opposito le pyllery eundo
per caput vie de pyttey directe ad portam sancti Johannis per
cimiterium sancti Johannis baptiste continet .410. gressus ad
portam sancti Johannis baptiste transceundo
latitudo dicte venelle^b continet^c duas virgas jd est .6. pedes,

(175)

.b.
Ecclesia sancte marie de Poort continet cum campanule eius
longitudo .60. gressus.

(176)

.a.
Porta sancti Johannis baptiste super quam edificatur tam turris
quadratus quam vna spera desuper de Frestone cum duobus
batillementis^d super turrim. continet in longitudine .17.
gressus. et de nouo edificata fuit cum Ecclesia sancti Johannis
per Walterum Frampton nobile[m]^e mercatorem ville Bristollie

(177)

Ecclesia^f sancti Bertholomei quondam prioratus canonicorum
regularium. per antecessores Domini de le Warre fundata.^g et
modo hospitale pauperum annui valoris ... ^h est scita prope &
extra portas vocatas Fromeyate in boriali parte ville
Bristollie;

(178)

latitudo dicte porte sancti Johannis baptiste continet ... ^h
virgas.

p.120

(179)

DE PORTA JNTROITUS AD TURRIM BRISTOLLIE
Via a Porta jntroitus ad Castellum Bristollie prope Ecclesiam
orientalem sancti Petri & sic eundo & girando per murum fossi
murorum Castri per Portam Newgate & per vicum vocatum le

---

a   *vicus* deleted, and *Venella* written in front of it afterwards
b   *vie* deleted, and *venelle* written above and in front of it afterwards
c   *.2.* inserted above and in front; also written over *duas* but deleted
d   Worcestre first wrote *batillementes*, then added correct ending *...is*
e   Edge of page worn. The rest of the sentence is added in the margin
f   *quo* (for *quondam*) deleted
g   Linked by Talbot to *vie de le Weer*, **(169)** note d

(174)

In length, the lane from Wynch Street going from opposite the pillory, past the top of the Pithay road straight to St John's Gate, past St John the Baptist's churchyard, going along to St John the Baptist's Gate, measures 410 steps.

The width of the said lane measures 2 yards, that is, 6 feet.

(175)

(b)

The church of St Mary le Port, with its bell-tower, measures 60 steps in length.

(176)

(a)

St John the Baptist's Gate (upon which is built not only a square tower but also a spire above, of freestone, with two battlements[1] upon the tower) measures 17 steps in length, and was built anew, together with St John's church, by Walter Frampton, a worthy merchant of the town of Bristol.

(177)

The church of St Bartholomew, formerly a priory of regular canons founded by the ancestors of Lord De La Warr, and now a hospital for the poor of the annual value of ... , is sited just outside the gates called Fromegate, on the north side of the town of Bristol.

(178)

The width of the said gate of St John the Baptist measures ... yards.

p.120

(179)

OF THE ENTRANCE GATE TO BRISTOL KEEP

The road from the entrance gate into Bristol Castle near the eastern church of St Peter,[2] and thus going and winding along the bank of the ditch of the Castle walls, through the gate of Newgate, and along the street called The Weir, and over the

---

1   Perhaps the two levels of battlemented parapets, one over the gate and
     one around the top of the tower
2   As opposed to St Mary le Port, the western church of the pair

---

h   Blank in MS

(179) [continued]
Weere & per pontem de le Were[a] dimittendo le Wateryngplace
in manu sinistra. ac girando per dictum murum fossi versus
meridiem[b] prope crucem de le market sic continuando usque
magnam petram de Frestone vnius virge erectam ad extremam
libertatis Franchesie ville Bristollie in altera parte gardinorum
Willemi Worcestre.[c] ad portam primi introitus Castri ex parte
occidentali Ecclesie sancti Philippi, que est ad finem venelle
retro vie mercati. continet in circuitu vnius partis Turris &
murorum Castri .420. gressus.

(180)
TRIANGULUS
Via quasi trianguli ab origine[d] anguli pontis Bristollie in
opposita parte porte sancti Nicholai ad principium de le Bake
vbi vn[us][e] domus aque conductus .9. pedum longitudinis.
scituatur. continet .30. gressus et a predicto angulo pontis
Bristollie ad principium porte sancti Nicholai que est pars dicte
vie[f] triangularis continet .14. gressus. et a domo conducti de
Frestone que est conductus aquarum in principio de le bakk
eundo per Ecclesiam de le Crowd sancti Nicholai ad portam
sancti Nicholai.[g]

(181)
BAK
Via a dicti domus aque conductus eundo per le bakke coram
aquam de Avyn vsque ad portam de Meshyate[h] par le Crane &
per orientalem partem Capelle continet .270. gressus

(182)
SUPER PONTEM BRISTOLLIE
Porte due[i] cum archu desuper super extremam occidentalem[i]
Capelle sancte Marie pontis Bristollie continet longitudo inter
primum[j] murum archuatus dicto muro archus computato cum
vacua placea coram hostium capelle ad alteram portam peti
archuati cum muro dicti archuati computato continet .9. virgas.
siue[k] .16. gressus

a   *vicum vocatum ... de le Were* underlined by Talbot, who has written
    in the margin opposite, *an m de nomen dominis de la Weer* (a memo. of
    the name of Lord De La Warr), making an incorrect association between
    The Weir and the De La Warr family; cf. **(169)**, **(177)**
b   *ad* deleted
c   *Willelmi Worcestre* underlined by Talbot, who has written in the margin
    opposite, *patris .viz. huius authoris* (To wit, the father of this writer)
d   *pont* (for *pontis*) deleted
e   Ending unclear
f   *tri* (for *triangularis*) smudged and deleted
g   Sentence left unfinished, with no space for completion

(179) [continued]
bridge of The Weir, leaving the watering-place on the left
hand; and winding southwards along the said bank of the ditch,
near the market cross; thus continuing as far as the great
stone of freestone one yard [high], set up at the furthest
[limit] of the liberty [and] franchise of the town of Bristol, on
the other side of William Worcestre's gardens, to the main
entrance gate of the Castle on the west side of St Philip's
church, which is at the end of the lane at the back of Market
Street.   The circuit of one side of the Keep and walls of the
Castle measures 420 steps.

(180)
THE TRIANGLE
A kind of triangular roadway, beginning at the corner of
Bristol Bridge, on the side opposite St Nicholas's Gate, to the
beginning of The Back, where the water-conduit house 9 feet
in length is situated, measures 30 steps.   And from the
aforesaid corner of Bristol Bridge to the beginning of St
Nicholas's Gate, which is a side of the said triangular roadway,
measures 14 steps.   And from the freestone conduit house,
which is the water-conduit at the beginnning of The Back,
going past The Crowde of St Nicholas's church to St Nicholas's
Gate[1]

(181)
THE BACK
The road from the said water-conduit house, going along The
Back alongside the river Avon as far as the gate of Marsh
Gate, past the crane and past the east side of the chapel,
measures 270 steps.

(182)
UPON BRISTOL BRIDGE
Two gates with an arch above, upon the western end of the
chapel of St Mary on Bristol Bridge: the length between the
first wall of the arch (counting the said arch wall together with
the open space in front of the door of the chapel) to the other
gateway of the smaller arch (counting in the wall of the said
arch) measures 9 yards or 16 steps.

---

1   Sentence left unfinished; see note g opposite

---

h   *sic*
i   *de* deleted
j   *arc* (for *archuatus*?) deleted
k   *siue* appears to be written over *et*

(182) [continued]
PONS
latituto^a tocius pontis vt potest probari per spacium vie^b pontis
latitudinis inter dictos duas portas continet .5. virgas

(183)
latitudo vie ad finem meridonalem^c pontis ad primum jntroitum
longe vie de Radclyffstrete continet .5. virgas siue .8.
gressus

p.121-122   *[Blank]*

p.123

(184)

Marketplace

VIA LONGA IN POSTERIORI PARTE A RETRO VIE DE OLD
MARKET
vsque Laffordysyate.^c
via^d posterior ex parte meridionali a retro de antiquo market
jncipiendo a porta prima Castri Bristollie et transceundo per
tria gardina Willelmi Worcestre^e in meridionali de le crosse in
mercato predicto sic transciens per longam viam iuxta
Cimiterium & Ecclesiam sancti Philippi vbi quondam Ecclesia
Religiosorum monachorum & prioratus in orientali parte
Ecclesie sancti Philippi scituatur. et sic continue eundo a retro
gardina tenementorum in mercato antiquo, vsque ad murum
Ecclesie occidentalem Ecclesie hospitalis sancte trinitatis per
venerabilissimum mercatorem quondam ville Bristollie. ad
dictam Ecclesiam sancte trinitatis per ... ^f Barstaple fundatum
& edificatum pro xiij. hominibus pauperibus. continet in
longitudine .660. gressus^g

hospitale domus cum capella in veteris^h mercato prope
laffordysyate cum capella condecente per dicti ... ⁱ Barstaple
est fundata & erecta

---

a   *sic*
b   *v* of *vie* appears to be written over *a*
c   Worcestre originally wrote *Laffordsyate* over a now illegible word in
    fainter ink, then inserted *vsque* in front and the first *y* above
d   *v* of *via* is written over a faint *d*
e   Underlined, probably by Talbot
f   The space left for a first name has subsequently been filled in, in error,
    with the figures *.660.*, in the same darker ink as the closing phrase (see
    note g); cf. **(186)** note e

(182) |continued|
THE BRIDGE
The width of the whole bridge, as I was able to prove by the extent of the road the width of the bridge between the said two gates, measures 5 yards.

(183)
The width of the road at the south end of the bridge, at the very start of the long road of Redcliffe Street, measures 5 yards or 8 steps.

p.121–122 *[Blank]*

p.123

(184)

The Market Place
THE LONG ROAD AT THE BACK SIDE BEHIND THE ROAD OF OLD MARKET
as far as Lawford's Gate.
The back road on the south side behind Old Market, beginning from the main gate of Bristol Castle and going past the three gardens of William Worcestre on the south of the cross in the aforesaid market, thus passing along the long road next to the churchyard and church of St Philip (where formerly the church of a community of monks and a priory was sited, on the east side of St Philip's church); and so continuing along behind the gardens of the houses in Old Market, as far as to the west church wall of the church of the hospital of Holy Trinity, [founded] by a most highly respected merchant formerly of the town of Bristol – to the said church of the Holy Trinity, founded and built by ... Barstaple, for 13 poor men, measures 660 steps in length.

The hospital building and chapel, in Old Market next to Lawford's Gate, with a fitting chapel, was founded and built by the said ... Barstaple.

---

g *continet in longitudine .660. gressus* is in darker ink, presumably added later. In the margin, in the original ink, is *880.* (deleted) *660 gressus*
h *veteris*, badly written, has been rewritten above, without any deletion
i The space originally left for a first name has been filled in with *dicti*

(185)

Porta laffordysyate per dictum Walterum Barstaple de nouo[a]
fundata et composita tempore Regis Edwardi tercij vel[a] Ricardi
Regis secundi vbi Finis libertas & Franchesie ville Bristollie in
hoc termino occidentali extendit ad quendam petram altitudinis
vnius virge extra laffordysyate erectam in parte boriali dicte
porte per me visam & palpatam
continet dicta porta in longitudine . ... .[b] pedes
latitudo dicte porte ...   [b]
altitudo dicte porte super pulcram mansionem desuper
edificatum ...   [b]

(186)
VIA EXTRA LAFFORDYATE
Vie longitudo[c] ab exteriori parte laffordysyate continuando
vsque ad Ecclesiam & domum ac hospitale pertinenti dicte
Ecclesie continet in longitudine in Comitatu Gloucestrie
jncipiente. et[d] versus viagium ad Civitatem londoniarum
transceuncium per Forestam de kyngyswod[d] jnicipiente apud
laffordysyate. continet vsque dictum hospitalem sancti laurencii
per ... [e] fundatam quamuis modo pertinet tempore Edwardi
Regis quarti Collegio & Ecclesie de Westbery .1200.[f] gressus
per W.Worcestre[g] mensuratis,

(187)
DUA VIE JN PARTE BORIALI PROPE LAFFORDYS YATE
Via magna prope laffordysyate in parte boriali dicte porte iuxta
le meerestone finis libertatis Bristollie ac Via magna in parte
boriali similiter non multum longe qua itur & reuertitur in
parte & clima boriali extra laffordisyate eundo & equitando. per
... .[h] ad villam Gloucetyr per villas Wynterborn, Tyderynton
Newport ... [h] usque Gloucestre per spacium[i] .30.[j] miliariorum
distans a Bristollia;

---

a   Two phrases, each underlined and linked by X in the margin, probably
    by Talbot.
b   Blank in MS
c   *ab* smudged and deleted
d   Faintly underlined in same ink as (a)
e   The space left for a name has subsequently been filled in, in error (cf.
    note a), with *1200. gressus*, in the same ink as the figures below (note
    f). In the margin opposite, *q'* (for *questio* or *query*?) was presumably
    written before the figures were added
f   A space left, with *vacat* written above and another *q'* (for *questio* or
    query?) in margin opposite, has subsequently been filled in with *1200*
    in the same ink as the figures added at (e) above

(185)

The gate of Lawford's Gate, founded and constructed anew by
the said Walter Barstaple in the time of King Edward III or
King Richard II, where the limit of the liberty and franchise of
the town of Bristol extends at this western limit, at a certain
stone one yard high set up outside Lawford's Gate, on the
north side of the said gate, seen and touched by me.
The said gate measures ... feet in length.
The width of the said gate: ...
The height of the said gate above [which] a fair dwelling]is]
built: ...

(186)

THE ROAD OUTSIDE LAWFORD'S GATE

The length of the road from the outer side of Lawford's Gate,
continuing as far as to the church, and the house and hospital
attached to the said church: measures in length (beginning in
the county of Gloucester and going on the way to the city of
London across the Forest of Kingswood) starting at Lawford's
Gate: it measures 1200 steps as far as the said hospital of St
Lawrence (founded by ... , although now, in the time of King
Edward IV, it belongs to the College and church of Westbury),
measured by W. Worcestre.

(187)

TWO ROADS ON THE NORTH SIDE NEAR LAWFORD'S
GATE

The highway near Lawford's Gate, on the north side of the
said gate next to the merestone at the limit of the liberty of
Bristol (and also the similar highway on the north side [but]
not so long), which leads and turns on the north side and area
outside Lawford's Gate, for going and riding past ... to the
town of Gloucester, through the villages of Winterbourne,
Tytherington and Newport[1] ... as far as Gloucester, 30 miles
distant from Bristol.

---

1   Newport lies on the main road (now A38) southeast of Berkeley

---

g   Underlined, probably by Talbot, who has written *authorem* in margin
    opposite
h   Blank in MS
i   *villam Gloucetyr ... spacium* underlined, probably by Talbot
j   *30* also in margin, probably by Talbot

p.124

(188)

le Markett Weyes versus laffordyate,

Via longa^a non edificata in^b altera parte boriali
de le Market place in parochia sancti Philippi^c

Via longa jncipiente ad finem vie de le Weere ex altera parte
vie vbi equi Bristollie consueuerunt bibere^d in angulo cornerij
meridionali dicti wateryng place. & sic continuando viam vsque
domum hospitalis sancte trinitatis fundatum per Walterum^e
Barstaple prope laffordysyate Et ex transuerso vie veniente de
le veyle Market vsque aquam ad Erlesmedew per le graunt
Orchard markis William quondam Walteri Carillton. continet in
longitudine^f cum via returne versus & prope hospitalem sancte
trinitatis ad viam de Markett prope laffordysyate continet .569.
gressus

latitudo dicte vie per maiori partem continet .... ^{g} gressus per
estimacionem sed non est edificata nisi per longitudinem ... ^{g}
gressuum citra le Wateryng place de le Weer.^{h} sed in latitudine
circa ... ^{i} gressus^j

(189)
Venella prope Ecclesiam sancti Philippi ducens de le style
cimiterij dicte Ecclesie directe per le travers de dicti Market
continet .77. gressus
latitudo eiusdem venelle de petra non edificata continet .7.
virgas^k

(190)
Venella alia ducens directe de illa priori venella. ex transuerso
de le Market. transciens ad borialem viam siue partem per le
magnum gardinum & Orchard. markyswilliam maioris quondam

---

a   *longa* added above the line in different ink
b   *parte* deleted
c   This whole sentence has been inserted, probably as an afterthought
d   *finem vie ... bibere* underlined in darker ink, probably by Talbot
e   *Walterum* inserted later, into space left for it, in darker ink
f   *101 gressus* deleted, and the remainder of the sentence including the
     overall total of steps, *cum via retorne ... .569. gressus* inserted in
     darker ink (cf. e,j), with difficulty, around the deletion and into the
     small space between *in longitudine* and the next sentence.
g   Blank in MS
h   *le Wateryng place de le Weer* underlined as in note d above
i   Blank in MS

p.124

(188)

The market-roads towards Lawford's Gate.

A long road, not paved,[1] on the other[2] side, to the north
of the market place, in the parish of St Philip's.

The long road, beginning at the end of the road from The
Weir, on the other side of the road, where the horses of
Bristol are usually watered, at the angle of the southern corner
of the said watering-place; and thus continuing the road as far
as the hospital of Holy Trinity, founded by Walter Barstaple
near Lawford's Gate, and across the road coming from The
Old Market, as far as the river at Earlsmead by the great
orchard of Mark William, formerly of Walter Carlton.   It
measures in length, including the road turning off towards and
near the hospital of Holy Trinity, to the market-road near
Lawford's Gate: it measures 569 steps.

The width of the said road for the most part measures ...
steps by estimation, but it is not paved[3] except for a length of
... steps this side of the watering-place at The Weir; but in
width about ... steps.

(189)
The lane near St Philip's church, leading from the churchyard
stile of the said church, straight across to the said market,
measures 77 steps.
The width of the same lane, not paved[4] in stone, measures 7
yards.

(190)
Another lane leading straight from that previous lane across
The Market, going along to the northern road or side, past the
great garden and orchard of Mark William, formerly mayor

---

1 Or possibly 'not built up with houses': cf. **(88)**, **(145)**, **(189)**, **(197)**
2 If this heading is, as appears, an insert, the 'other' side is probably to
   locate the road in relation to Worcestre's perambulations on the south
   side of Old Market, e.g. **(184)**
3 As note 1 above
4 *de petra non edificata* here clearly indicates 'not paved': cf. note 1
   above

---

j The whole phrase *per estimacionem ... gressus* has been added
   subsequently, in same ink as the other inserts noted (e, f opposite)
k *latitudo eiusdam...continet .7. virgas* appears to have been inserted later,
   cf. **(188)** notes e.f.i

(190) [continued]
ville Bristollie[a] ad aquam de Frome vltra[b] le wateryng de le
Weere[c] versus Erlysmede
continet; .136. gressus,

(191)
MARKET
Via lapidea longa & lata vocata le veile Market a principio alte
crucis prope fossam Castri Bristollie directe eundo per quatuor
tenementa Willelmi Worcestre[d] ad laffordesyate scita[e] vt media
& principalis via duarum aliarum longarum viarum vna ex parte
meridionali & alia via ex parte boriali continet .660. gressus
latitudo dicte vie continet .54. gressus

(192)
∵ Via[f] eundo[g] prioratum montis acuti sancti Jacobi[h] per le
justyng place ab antiquis diebus

Via in parochiam sancti Jacobi jn occidentali parte Ecclesie
sancti Jacobi prope[i] portam principalem jntroitus ad prioratum
sancti Jacobi & partem muri orientalem fratrum sancti
Francisci

Via longa siue venella de fine vie lewenysmede ex opposito
cimiterij sancti Jacobi, eundo per hostium prioris[j] Religionum
dicte Ecclesie; et sic continuando ad extremam partem dicte vie
siue venelle per muros gardinorum fratrum sancti Francisci ad
quendam montem acutum in boriali parte dicte vie extremi &
retornando per aliud Retornum vie ducentis versus montem
Ecclesie[k] sancti Michelis,[l] continet dicta via siue venella erecta.
continet .300. gressus.   Et returnum dicte vie ad partem
orientalem per murum dictorum fratrum minorum vsque ad
venellam eundo ad Ecclesiam sancti Michelis et sic continuando
directe orientaliter vsque ad altam crucem petri erecti de
Frestone cum Fonte clausa de Frestone. ad altiorem finem vie
veniente de Ecclesia hospitalis sancti Bertholomei vocatum
Stypestrete.   continet .600 gressus

---

a   *magnum gardinum ... ville Bristollie* underlined, probably by Talbot
b   *le aquam* partially deleted
c   *le wateryng de le Weere* underlined, probably by Talbot
d   *Willelmi Worcestre* underlined, probably by Talbot
e   *inter* deleted
f   *Via* preceded by Worcestres's link symbol ∵ and followed by *a* deleted
g   *ad* deleted
h   *prioratum montis acuti sancti Jacobi* underlined, probably by Talbot

(190) [continued]
of the town of Bristol, to the river Frome beyond the watering–[place] at The Weir, towards Earlsmead.
It measures 136 steps.

(191)
THE MARKET
The long and broad stone-paved road, called The Old Market, from the beginning at the tall cross near the ditch of Bristol Castle, going straight past the four houses of William Worcestre to Lawford's Gate, lies as the central and main road [between] two other long roads, one on the south side and the other road on the north side. It measures 660 steps.
The width of the said road measures 54 steps.

(192)
The road going [up] the steep hill of St James's priory past the jousting-place of olden days.

The road in the parish of St James, on the west side of St James' church, next to the main entrance gate into St James's priory, and the east side of the wall of the Franciscan Friars.

A long road or lane from the end of the Lewinsmead road opposite St James's churchyard, going past the gate of the prior of the monks of the said church, and thus continuing to the further end of the said road or lane, past the walls of the gardens of the Franciscan Friars, to a certain steep hill on the northern side of the said far end of the road; and turning along another road that turns off, leading towards the hill of St Michael's church. The said road or lane upwards measures 300 steps. And the turning off from the said road at the east end, past the wall of the said Friars Minor, as far as the lane going to St Michael's church, and thus continuing due eastwards as far as a tall stone cross, set up in freestone, with a well walled with freestone, at the upper end of the road coming from the church of St Bartholomew's hospital, called Steep Street, measures 600 steps.

---

i   *jntroitum* deleted
j   *dicte* deleted
k   *Ecclesie* has been added above the line
l   *montem Ecclesie sancti Michelis* underlined, probably by Talbot

(193)

Memorandum[a] quod ad dictam crucem obviant .3. vie quarum vna vocatur ∴ Stanley[b] ducens ad villam Clyffton vel ad viam ducentam vsque Ghystonclyf

(194)

longitudo Porte sancti Johannis continet .17. gressus[c]
latitudo eius continet .4. virgas. prope conductorium pulcrum de Frestone in meridionali parte dicte porte scituate

p.125

(195)[d]

Notule de prima fundacione ordinis Sancti Johannis in Jerusalem, modo apud jnsulam Rodes custodita. & est in Anglia apud Clerkynwelle Londonijs vt scripsi extra tabulam pendentem in Ecclesia templi Bristollie.

Johannes baptista fuit Jerosolomitanus & patronus fratrum sancti[e] domus hospitalis Jerusalem. Et deuenit de grecis ad Latinos, ad Gerardum seruum Dei quando Godefridus de Buyllon conquisiuit Jerusalem & qualiter Raimundus de Perodis fuit primus frater professus in dicte ordinis[e] et fecit ordinem & regulam dicte ordinis a sede apostolica optinuit & intitulatur Beati Johannis baptiste Religio & ante Aduentum Christi primo tempore Samuelis prophete & consequenti tempore Alexandri magni diuino oraculo reuelatur de thesauro de Dauid abscondito per Melchiarem sacerdotem de[f] dicti Imperatoris in excellenti edificij magnitudine & plenitudine in Jerusalem esset fabricata in monte Syon vbi est Cenaculum se[d][g] consequenter propter peregrinos prope Sanctum Sepulcrum fuit per Latinos translata hec est illa sancta domus ad quam misit Judas Machabeus duodecim milia dragmas argenti offerri ibi pro peccatis mortuorum & est dicta sancta domus vbi Christus manducauit pascha agnum pascalem secundum ritum legis, et lauit[h] pedes discipulorum[i] jn die Jovis cena domini. & [insuper?][j] Zacarias

---

a *Memorandum* written again in margin opposite
b *Stanley ... Ghystonclyf* continued in margin, linked by ∴ symbol
c *la* (for *latitudo*) started but left unfinished
d This item was included in Harvey, *Itineraries*, pp. 312-3, with some variations in transcription and translation
e *sic*
f *de* has been written over *in*
g Worcestre actually wrote *se*
h The phrase *agnum pascalem secundum ritum legis* has been added later, with a caret mark after *lavit*, where it does not make sense

(193)

Memorandum, that 3 roads meet at the said cross, of which the one called Stonelea leads to the village of Clifton or to the road leading as far as Ghyston Cliff.

(194)

The length of St John's Gate measures 17 steps.
Its width measures 4 yards, near the fair conduit of freestone situated on the south side of the said gate.

p.125

(195)

Notes of the first foundation of the Order of St John in Jerusalem, now preserved at the island of Rhodes, and [which] is in England at Clerkenwell in London,[1] as I have copied down from a board hanging in Temple church, Bristol.

John the Baptist was a Jerusalem man, and the patron of the brothers of the hospital at Jerusalem. And it passed from the Greeks to the Latins, and to Gerard[2] the servant of God, when Godfrey de Bouillon conquered Jerusalem; and likewise Raymond de Puy was the first brother professed in the said order, and set up the order, and obtained the rule of the said order from the Apostolic See. It is called the Order of the Blessed John the Baptist. And before the time of Christ, first in the time of the Prophet Samuel and later in the time of Alexander the Great it was revealed by a divine oracle that the treasure of David had been hidden by the priest Melchiar from the said Emperor in a fine building of great size, [which] was built on Mount Sion in Jerusalem, where the Cenacle now is. But later, because of the pilgrims, it was moved by the Latins near to the Holy Sepulchre. This is the holy house to which Judas Maccabeus sent 12,000 drachmae of silver to be offered there for the sins of the dead; and it is the said holy house where Christ ate the Passover (the Paschal Lamb according to the rite of the Law) and washed the feet of the disciples, on Thursday of the Lord's Supper; and [moreover?] Zachariah the

---

1   Harvey noted that the London Temple was founded c.1144
2   Gerard, supposedly of Martigues in Provence, was administrator of the original hospital at the time of the First Crusade and the siege of Jerusalem in 1099

---

i   *lavit* repeated
j   *insuper*: uncertain reading

(195) [continued]
propheta fuit custos & electus dicte sancte domus.   Quidam
sancti Nicholaite beatum Stephanum prothomartyrem & alios
religiosos viros & mulieres in dicta domo statuerunt ad opera
misericordie & pietatis complenda circa pauperes & infirmos
qui professi dicte religionis promittunt se esse seruos in sui
voti ingressu, tradentes dictis religiosis pro habitu signum
sancte crucis quorum Paulus actuum apostolorum lucas
Euangelista conscripta perfecerunt   sanctum   Johannem
baptistam precursorem domini & antique legis vltimum
martirem pro patrono,

p. 126

(196)
JN PAROCHIA SANCTI JACOBI
Via vocata Marchallestrete in parochia sancti Jacobi viz a fine
vie Brodemede prope pontem muri fratrum predicatorum eundo
versus cimiterium sancti Jacobi per lez barrys vbi mulieres
fatuate morantur vsque ad angulum Cornerij, jntrando ad
prioratum horrei sancti Jacobi per vnum Mulberytree continet
.191. gressus
latitudo dicte vie per tenementa mea Willelmi Worcestre ... ᵃ

(197)
Via proxima sequente videlicet ab angulo Cornerij eundo versus
Redelyngonᵇ per le mulbery tree superius nominatum & sic
eundo versus Cimiterium sancti Jacobi vsque ad introitum
primum Ecclesie predicte continet .155. gressus.   Et sic
continuando per costeram Cimiterij sancti Jacobi vsque crucem
& pontem occidentalem dicte vie. ad returnum vie vocate le
bake.   ad finem occidentalem cimiterij predicti vbi vna porta
cum vno stilo petri scituatur.   continet 240 gressus & sic in
totoᶜ longitudo dicte vie continet .395 gressus
+ latitudo dicte vie ex vna parte edificate continet ... ᵈ
gressus

---

a   Blank in MS, with *Willelmi Worcestre* underlined by Talbot, who has
    written *mea* (for *memoria*?) in margin opposite
b   *sic*
c   *dicte* deleted
d   *395* written in error, smudged and deleted, and real figure omitted

(195) [continued]
prophet was warden and elect of the said holy house. Certain
holy Nicholaites set the Blessed Stephen protomartyr and other
religious men and women in the said house to carry out works
of mercy and piety for the poor and infirm. Those who are
professed of this Order promise, in their vow of entry, that
they will be servants, and the sign of the Holy Cross is given
to the said religious upon their habit. In whom [the words of]
Paul, in the Acts of the Apostles written by Luke the
Evangelist, are fulfilled, [by having] St John the Baptist, the
Lord's forerunner and the last martyr of the Old Law, for
[their] patron.

p.126

(196)
IN THE PARISH OF ST JAMES
The road called Marshall Street in the parish of St James, to
wit from the end of the Broadmead road near the bridge [at]
the wall of the Friars Preachers, going towards St James's
churchyard, past The Bars where the wanton women dwell, as
far as to the angle of the corner going into St James's priory,
by a mulberry tree, measures 191 steps.
The width of the said road by the houses of me William
Worcestre: ...

(197)
The next road along, to wit from the angle of the corner,
going past the above-mentioned mulberry tree towards
'Redelyngon',[1] and thus going towards St James's churchyard
as far as to the main entrance of the aforesaid church,
measures 155 steps. And thus continuing along by the side of
St James's churchyard as far as the western cross and bridge
of the said road, to the road turning off called The Back, at
the western end of the aforesaid churchyard, where a gate with
a stone stile is situated, measures 240 steps; and thus, in all,
the length of the said road measures 395 steps.
The width of the said road, built up[2] on one side, measures
... steps.

---

1 Probably Redland? cf. **(61)**, **(169)**
2 Or perhaps 'paved'? cf. **(88)**, **(145)**, **(188)**, **(189)**

(198)
JN PAROCHIA SANCTI NICHOLAI
latitudo vie de le bak in parochia sancti Nicholai continet 34.
gressus

latitudo secunde vie gradus vocate Anglice le slep qui est
proximior ad introitum Baldwynstrete. continet .4. virgas
longitudo dicte Slepe a primo ingressus ad fundum aque de
Avyn continet. ... [a]

(199)
Volta archus sancte crucis & Ecclesie sancti Johannis continet
in longitudine circa .60. gressus siue to[b] ... [c] virgas
latitudo dicte volte siue archus .13. gressus siue ... [c] virgas

---

(200)
KEY
Key longitudo a prima jncepcione coram muro templi judeorum
prope Portam petram jntroitus Smalstrete vsque. angulum
domus de petri muro fortisimo edificato. ex opposito Abbathie
sancti Augustini. continet. per aquam de Frome. & calcetum de
le key .480. gressus bene computatus.

(201)
ECCLESIA SANCTI EWEN.
longitudine Ecclesie Seynt Ewen. jdest sancti Adoen continet
.22. virgas.
latitudo dicte Ecclesie cuius orientalis pars[d] altaris est directe
ex opposit[e] Ecclesie. sancte trinitatis. prope crucem Bristollie
continet .15. virgas per mensuratas vel .30. gressus,
Et habet vnam nauem ecclesie. ex parte boriali ale & vnam alam
vel Elam que est capella sancti Johannis baptiste &
fraternitatem

---

a   Blank in MS
b   *sic*, probably for *tot*
c   Blank in MS
d   *est* deleted
e   *sic*

(198)
IN THE PARISH OF ST NICHOLAS
The width of the road of The Back in St Nicholas's parish
measures 34 steps.

The width of the second road, a stairway (called in English 'the
slip') which is nearer to the entry of Baldwin Street, measures
4 yards.
The length of the said slip from first entry to the bottom of
the river Avon measures ...

(199)
The vaulted crypt of Holy Cross and the church of St John
measure about 60 steps or the equivalent ... yards in length.
The width of the said crypt or vault is 13 steps or ... yards.

---

(200)
THE KEY
The Key: length from its very start alongside the wall of the
Jewish synagogue near the stone entry gate to Small Street, as
far as the corner of the stone house with the very strongly
built wall, opposite St Augustine's abbey, measures along the
river Frome and the pathway of The Key, 480 steps, carefully
counted.

(201)
THE CHURCH OF ST EWEN.
In length, the church of St Ewen, that is 'St Adoen',[1] measures
22 yards.
The width of the said church, of which the end east of the altar
is right opposite the church of Holy Trinity near the Bristol
cross, measures 15 yards by measurement, or 30 steps.
And it has the nave of the church on the north side of the
aisle, and one aisle (or 'Ile'), which is the chapel of St John the
Baptist, and [of that] Fraternity.[2]

---

1   The Latin version of St Ewen or Ouen is *Audoenus*
2   The Fraternity of Merchant Taylors, whose patron saint was St John the
    Baptist

(202)
ECCLESIA OMNIUM SANCTORUM
Ecclesia longitudo omnium sanctorum directe ex opposito[a]
Ecclesie omnium sanctorum[b] continet ... [c] gressus vel tot ... [d]
virgas
latitudo dicte Ecclesie continet .20. virgas; siue .34. gressus

p.127
Bristoll

(203)
ECCLESIA SANCTE TRINITATIS
longitudo Ecclesie predicte sancte trinitatis .22. virge
latitudo Ecclesie sancte trinitatis .35. gressus

(204)
latitudo vie hyghstrete ad altam crucem .24. gressus
latitudo vie de Wynchstrete ad altam viam[e] .16. gressus
.b. latitudo vie de Bradstrete ad altam crucem .14. gressus[f]
Sed eius latitudo in medio vie Bradstrete .24. gressus[g]
latitudo vie de Cornerstrete ad altam crucem .14. gressus
.a. longitudo vie vocate Bradstrete continet .328. gressus[h]

(205)
latitudo[i] domus Willelmi Botoner[j] .15. gressus

(206)
latitudo domus Gylhalde. cum capella sancti Georgij .40.
gressus

(207)
VOLTA,
ā
longitudine volte sancti Johannis constat ex sex archuatis cum
.6. fenestris in vna costera versus boriam & duobus fenestris
versus meridiem, frette vowted,
volta sancti Johannis baptiste est in alto .16. steppys siue
gradus & quelibet gradus continet[k] .8. pollices,

---

a   *crucis* deleted.   Worcestre is muddled, with three adjoining churches
b   *sic*, error for St Ewen's
c   Blank in MS
d   *.22.* deleted and total left incomplete
e   *sic*, error for *altam crucem*
f   Worcestre intended this note marked *.b.* to be preceded by *.a.* below
g   This note is an afterthought, cramped between the adjacent lines
h   marked *.a.* by Worcestre to indicate that it should precede *.b.* above
i   *q'* (for *questio* or *query*?) in margin opposite
j   *Willelmi Botoner* underlined, probably by Talbot
k   *10* deleted

(202)
ALL SAINTS' CHURCH
The church of All Saints, right opposite the church of All Saints,[1] measures ... steps in length, or the equivalent yards. The width of the said church measures 20 yards, or 34 steps.

p.127
Bristol

(203)
HOLY TRINITY CHURCH
The length of the aforesaid church of Holy Trinity: 22 yards. The width of the church of Holy Trinity: 35 steps.

(204)
The width of the High Street road at the High Cross: 24 steps
The width of the road of Wynch Street at the High road:[2] 16 steps
(b) The width of the road of Broad Street at the High Cross: 14 steps
But its width at the middle of the Broad Street road: 24 steps
The width of the road of Corn Street at the High Cross: 14 steps
(a) The length of the road called Broad Street measures 328 steps.

(205)
The width of the house of William Botoner: 15 steps.[3]

(206)
The width of the Guildhall, together with the chapel of St George: 40 steps.

(207)
THE CRYPT
In length, St John's crypt consists of six arches, with 6 windows on one side towards the north, and two windows towards the south, fan vaulted.[4]
The crypt of St John the Baptist is 16 steps or stairs in height, and each stair measures 8 inches.

---

1   Error for St Ewen
2   *sic*, error for High Cross
3   William Botoner: cf. **(62)**; the house adjoining Guildhall: cf. **(33)**, **(95)**
4   cf. Dallaway, pp. 97-8 'with recessed arches, richly pannelled'

(208)
VENELLA
Via vocata le through hows. in meridionali vie de Wynchstrete
per haddon tanerie ad vicum seynt mary port strete. continet
in longitudine .90. gressus
latitudo eius continet .4. gressus in medio vie,

(209)
VENELLA
Venella apud signum le swan in Wynchstrete transciens ad
vicum vocatum seynt mary port, continet circa .90. gressus;

(210)
WYNCH STRETE
latitudo vie Wynchstret in medium continet .22. gressus.

(211)
Vicus transciens de Wynchstrete ad vicum vocatum
seyntpeterstrete ex opposito Fontis de Frestone prope
Ecclesiam sancti petri continet .80. gressus

(212)
LE WEERE
Via de Newgate ad ponte de le Weere prope le[a] wateryng place
ad quendam petram magnam pro[p]e[b] murum de Dyke continet.
.360. gressus

(213)
Via proxima continua de predicta ponte in fine de Weere[c] &[d]
petri magne ad altam crucem de le market transeundo ex
opposito tenementorum Willelmi Worcestre continet 300.
gressus

(214)
MARKET
Via longa a dicta cruce ad portas. laffordesyate continet .600.
gressus vocata le Market per Ecclesiam hospitalis Barstaple
fundatam in honore sancte trinitatis
latitudo dicte vie de Mercato continet ... [e]

---

a   *ad ponte de le Weere prope le* underlined, probably by Talbot
b   Worcestre actually wrote *proe*
c   *in fine de Weere* has been inserted in different ink

(208)
A LANE
The road called The Through-House, on the south side of the road of Wynch Street past Haddon tannery to the street of St Mary le Port Street, measures 90 steps in length.
Its width in the middle of the road measures 4 steps.

(209)
A LANE
The lane at the sign of The Swan in Wynch Street, going across to the street called St Mary le Port, measures about 90 steps.

(210)
WYNCH STREET
The width of the road of Wynch Street, in the middle, measures 22 steps.

(211)
The street going across from Wynch Street to the street called St Peter Street, opposite the freestone fountain near St Peter's church, measures 80 steps.

(212)
THE WEIR
The road from Newgate to the bridge at The Weir, near the watering-place, to a certain great stone by the wall of the ditch, measures 360 steps.

(213)
The next road along from the aforesaid bridge at the end of The Weir, and the great stone, to the tall cross of The Market, going along opposite the houses of William Worcestre, measures 300 steps.

(214)
THE MARKET
The long road called The Market from the said cross to the gates of Lawford's Gate, past the church of the hospital founded by Barstaple in honour of the Holy Trinity, measures 600 steps.
The width of the said Market road measures ...

---

d   *pede*, perhaps in error for *petri*, deleted
e   Blank in MS

(215)

Castri orientalis partis muri profundi fossi a porta & angulo orientali a porta prope finem meridionalem[a] cimiterij[b] Ecclesie sancti Philippi continuando per fossam muri usque ad angulum orientalem pontis de Were & sic girando per pontem molendinorum prope Newgate & transceundo per[c] Portam Newgate vsque ad jntroitum porte fossi profundi fossi[d] ad valuas jntroitus Castri continet .sepcies .300.[e] gressus. qui faciunt circa .2100.[f] gressus

p.128

(216)

<u>Avyn Mersh</u>

Circumferentia Marisci .xjj[C]. brachia ut[g] relatum michi per vnum Ropemaker,

(217)

LE SLYPP SUPER LE BAK

longitudo de le Slip anglice a steyre de lapidibus ad[h] fundum aque de le bake idest a summitate vie desuper le bak vsque ad vltimum gradum continet in descensu .920.[i] gressus
latitudo dicte gradus. ad fundum aque continet 10 virgas jdest .30. pedes
altitudo de fundo aque Avone ad finem dicte gradus anglice a steyr continet circa .7. brachia vel .6. brachia

(218)

[j]

latitudo vie vocate Cornerstrete ad finem porte sancti[k] Leonardi .24. gressus vel ... [l]

---

a Worcestre first wrote *occidentalem*, deleted it, then wrote *meridionalem* above and in front

b *de* or *dicte*, smudged and deleted

c *por* (possibly for *portam*) smudged and written afresh on next line

d *fossi* repeated thus

e *.300.* probably an error for *.30.* Worcestre smudged and rewrote the *0* of *.30.* so that the figures look like *.300.*, giving the impossibly long total of *.2100.* steps

f Consequent error for *.210.*: see note i above; the *circa* perhaps reflects Worcestre's own doubts at this conclusion

g *ut* obscured by being written over an earlier error

h *le* deleted

(215)

The wall of the deep ditch, on the east side of the castle, from the eastern gate and angle (from the gate next to the southern end of the churchyard of St Philip's church) continuing along by the ditch of the wall as far as to the eastern angle of The Weir bridge, and thus winding past the bridge of the mills near Newgate and going past by the gate of Newgate, as far as to the entrance-gates of the deep ditch, to the entry-doors of the Castle: measures seven times 300[1] steps, which makes about 2100[2] steps.

p.128

(216)

Avon Marsh

The circumference of the marsh is 1200 fathoms, as told to me by a ropemaker.

(217)

THE SLIP UPON THE BACK

The length of The Slip (in English, a 'stair') of stones to the bottom of the river at The Back, that is, from the top at the road above The Back as far as to the last stair, measures downwards 920[3] steps.

The width of the said stairway to the bottom of the river measures 10 yards, that is, 30 feet.

The height from the bottom of the river Avon at the end of the said stairway (in English, a 'stair') measures about 6 or 7 fathoms.

(218)

The width of the road called Corn Street at the St Leonard's Gate end: 24 steps or ...

---

1   Probably an error for 30: see note e opposite
2   Consequent error for 210: see note f opposite
3   Probably an error for 92: see note i below

---

i   Worcestre first wrote *.90.*, deleted it, and then wrote *.920.*, which is impossibly long and probably intended for *.92.*
j   *Vie vocate Cornerstrete ad finem* written immediately at the end of **(217)**, then deleted and started afresh, with *latitudo*, on a new line
k   *porte sancti* repeated and deleted
l   Blank in MS

(219)

<u>RAKHYTH</u>

Eidificacio[a] quadrata vocata le Rakhyth. jn occidentali parte capelle. Thome knap super le bake scite vnum quadratum a borea in meridiem .50. gressus. Et ab oriente in occidens .40. gressus

(220)

Via siue venella[b] que ducit ab hostio de Rakhyth[c] ad le bake per meridionalem partem cimiterij capelle T. knapp continet circa .80. gressus

(221)

Via siue venella que jncipit in parte boriali Ecclesie sancti Nicholai de le porta eius siue de fine hyghstrete[d] ducens ad viam siue venellam decensus gradus .30. ad Baldewynestrete ex opposito crucis. continet ad principium dicti gradus .124. gressus.
Et sic continuando dictam[e] vsque portam sancti leonardi continet circa[f] .300. gressus

(222)

longitudine navis Ecclesie sancti leonardi continet .12. virgas,[g] cum choro .7. virge, .19. virge circa 30 gressus[h]
latitudo eius continet .10. virgas[i]

(223)

Vie latitudo a fine venelle ducente de[j] porta sancti leonardi viz a principis domus de le customhous usque venellam ab hospicio ... [k] Shyppard ad introitum venelle eundo ad occidentalem partem Campanile sancti Stephani continet .70. gressus ... [k] de ... [k]

Venella parua supranominata. eundo ad Ecclesiam sancti Stephani per[l] orientalem partem Ecclesie sancti Stephani altaris principalis Ecclesie predicte continet .80. gressus

---

a   *sic*
b   Worcestre actually wrote *Vnenella*
c   *Rakhyth* written faintly at end of line, then more clearly on next line
d   *ad* deleted
e   *sic*, omitting *viam*
f   + in margin opposite

(219)
RACKHAY
The square building called The Rackhay, on the west side of T[homas] Knapp's chapel situated upon The Back: a square, 50 steps from north to south, and 40 steps from east to west.

(220)
The road or lane, which leads from the door of The Rackhay to The Back, past the south side of the churchyard of T[homas] Knapp's chapel,[1] measures about 80 steps.

(221)
The road or lane which begins on the north side of St Nicholas's church, from its door or from the end of High Street, leading to the road or lane going down 30 stairs to Baldwin Street, opposite the cross, measures 124 steps to the start of the said stairway.
And thus going on along the said [road] as far as St Leonard's Gate measures about 300 steps.

(222)
The length of the nave of St Leonard's church measures 12 yards, with a quire of 7 yards: 19 yards, about 30 steps.
Its width measures 10 yards.

(223)
The width of the road from the end of the lane leading from St Leonard's Gate, to wit from the beginning of the Customs House building, as far as the lane from the residence of ... Shipward, to the entrance of the lane going to the west side of St Stephen's bell-tower, measures 70 steps ... from ...

The small lane above-mentioned, going to St Stephen's church past the east end of St Stephen's church [and] the high altar of the aforesaid church, measures 80 steps.

---

1 In fact, St Nicholas's churchyard

---

g *de* deleted
h *.19. gressus* added at end: perhaps a jotting, in error, for *.19. virge*
i + originally written above a small space into which Worcestre wrote *10*, roughly; *.10. virgas* then rewritten a second time, more neatly
j *de* repeated
k Blank in MS
l Worcestre first wrote *per turri Ecclesie predicte continet .80. gressus*, deleted *turri* and inserted *orientalem partem...altaris principalis*

(223) [continued]
VIA LATITUDO PARTE DE LE KEY
∴ latitudo partis de le Key vbi vnus condyt scituatur

latitudo vie de le key ex parte de le customhous vsque directe eundo ad quandam venellam jncipiendo a retro domus Shyppard. eundo ad portam ocidentalem[a] Ecclesie sancti Stephani .34. gressus. versus locum apertum partis de le key vbi in medio. vnus conductus aque de petra frestone scituatur

VENELLA EX PARTE MERIDIONALI & OCCIDENTALI PARTE ECCLESIE SANCTI STEPHANI
Venella proxima adiuncta eundo per le stile[b] per cimiterium[b] jncipiendo ab orientali parte Ecclesie sancti Stephani et sic directe eundo[b] per meridionalem partem cimiterij dicte Ecclesie usque le key. continet cum .30 gressibus per cimiterium predictum & tunc directe transceundo per occidentalem partem Ecclesie predicte ad locum vocatum le key continet .90. gressus (sed equi hauers non transceunt per dictam venellam)

p.129

(224)[c]
Duplicacio scaccarij[d] habetur in quodam libello existente in[e] Ecclesie sancti Stephani Bristollie in ala meridionali,[f]

     primus punctus scaccarij .j. granum
     .15.us punctus .j. quarter .17. galon
     .20.us punctus .j. busshel
     .23. .j. quarter
     .33. .1024. .j. perch
     .35. vnum hundred
     .39. vna baronia
     .42. vnus Comitatus
     .47. vnum regnum
     .64. .131072. / .262143. /
     Summa totalis de Regnis[g]
     .18446744073709551615[h]

---

a *sic*
b *ad* deleted
c This item was included in Harvey, *Itineraries*, pp. 314-5, with minor variations in transcription and translation
d *?Incipit* (uncertain reading) deleted
e *quodam libello* repeated

(223) [continued]
ROAD WIDTH BESIDE THE KEY
Width beside The Key where the conduit is situated.

The width of the road from The Key on the Customs House side, going straight as far as to a certain lane, beginning from the back of Shipward's house, going to the west door of St Stephen's church, [is] 34 steps, in the direction of the open space beside The Key where, in the middle, a water-conduit of freestone is situated.

LANE ON THE SOUTH AND WEST SIDE OF ST STEPHEN'S CHURCH
The next adjoining lane, going by the stile through the churchyard, beginning from the east side of St Stephen's church and thus going straight past by the south side of the churchyard of the said church as far as The Key, measures – including 30 steps through the aforesaid churchyard and then going straight past the west end of the aforesaid church to the place called The Key – measures 90 steps (but draught horses do not go through the said lane).

p.129

(224)
The duplication of the exchequer found in a certain little book kept in St Stephen's church, Bristol, in the south aisle.

	The first point of the exchequer: 1 grain
15th point	1 quarter 17 gallons
20th point	1 bushel
23rd	1 quarter
33	1024 1 perch
35	one hundred
39	one barony
42	one county
47	one kingdom
64	131072 262143

Grand total of Kingdoms:
18,446,744,073,709,551,615

---

f   The heading *Duplicacio ... meridionali,* has been added in different ink. This list occupies the left-hand side of the page, which Worcestre has divided with a vertical line.   Talbot has written *quere quid hoc.* (Query: what [is] this?) in the margin
g   *Summa totalis de regnis* repeated
h   cf. **(452)**

(225)^a

sancti Stephani Ecclesia

De operacione artificiosa porticus bor[ialis]^b Ecclesie sancti Stephani de opere manuali Benet le Fremason^c

> a cors wythoute
> a casement
> a bowtelle
> a felet
> a double ressaunt
> a boutel
> a felet
> a ressant
> a felet
> a casement with levys
> a felet
> a boutel
> a felet
> a ressant
> a felet
> a casement with trayles of le[vys]^d
> a felet
> a boutell
> a filet
> a casement
> a felet
> a casement
> a felet
> yn the myddes of the dore a boutelle

[Below this list, sideways on, is a sectional drawing of the mouldings as shown, much reduced, opposite. In one moulding, as shown, Worcestre has written Casement*]*

Thys^e ys the jamemoold of the Porche dore yn the southsyde of the chyrch of Seynt Stevyn

---

a　This item was included in Harvey, *Itineraries*, pp. 314-7, with some variations in transcription and translation. The drawing is reproduced by kind permission of Eleanour Harvey on behalf of the Harvey family

b　*bor[ialis]* error for *meridionalis*; the word is lost off edge of page

c　Heading, as (224), is in different ink, suggesting both lists were written on the spot, and headings added later. This list occupies the right-hand side of divided page

(225)
Saint Stephen's church
Of the ingenious workmanship of the north[1] porch of St
Stephen's church, of the handiwork of Benet the freemason.[2]

A course outside; a casement, a bowtel, a fillet,
a double ogee, a bowtel, a fillet, an ogee, a
fillet, a casement with leaves, a fillet, a bowtel,
a fillet, an ogee, a fillet, a casement with trails
of leaves, a fillet, a bowtel, a fillet, a casement,
a fillet, a casement, a fillet; in the middle of
the doorway, a bowtel.[3]

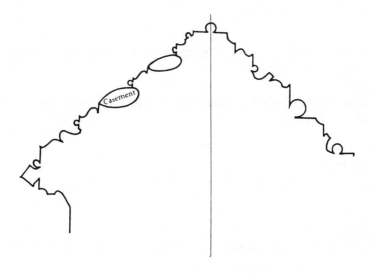

This is the jamb moulding of the porch door
on the south side of St Stephen's church

---

1   Error for south, noted correctly below the drawing
2   The professional expertise of the drawing suggests that it, as well as the
    carving, was the work of Benet the freemason – Benedict Crosse **(228)**
3   For terms, see glossary

---

d   Word is lost off edge of page
e   Worcestre started to write *T* underneath the drawing, but then wrote his
    note in the middle of it where there is more space

p.130

(226)

Turris de Radclyff

Turris Ecclesie Radclyff in longitudine continet .23. pedes dimidium

Et in latitudine .24. pedes[a]

Altitudo turris continet .120.[b] pedes[c] & altitudo de le spere sicut modo fractum continet .200. pedes[d]

Et diameter in superiori fracture continet .16. pedes

Et habet .8.[to] panas

Et quilibet lapis jn jncepcione spere continet in densitate duas pedes.[e]　Et apud le topp in altiori parte vbi crux scituatur continet densitudo .4. pollices.　Et quilibet lapis in fractione est .8. pedes[f] latitudine[g] in densitudine, Et latitudo de le Garlond continet .xj. pedes

(227)[h]

Memorandum ad jnquirendum de Roberto Euerard de norwico. questionem. anglicis verbis

QUESTIO.

How many onche doth the spere of trinite chyrch of norwich bater yn .vj. feete,[i]

(228)[j]

FREMASONS

Benet crosse.　Johannes norton　Fremasons Bristollie,

(229)

RADCLIFF

Densitudo Murorum turris de Radclyf in fundamento .7. pedes

Et in altitudine .120. pedum continet murus .5. pedes,

---

a　*Memorandum quadrata* (Memorandum, a square) in margin opposite
b　*.18.* deleted
c　*.120. pedes* written again in margin
d　*E* (for *Et*), not deleted, at end of line.　Sentence re-started below
e　*pedes* repeated
f　*sic,* error for *pollices?*
g　Illegible deletion, with *alti* written below and *latitudine* above the line
h　Items **(227)** and **(228)** were included in Harvey, *Itineraries,* pp. 366–7 with minor variations in transcription and translation

p.130

(226)

The tower of Redcliffe

The tower of Redcliffe Church measures 23½ feet in length.
And 24 feet in width.
The height of the tower measures 120 feet, and the height of
the spire as now broken [off] measures 200 feet.
And the diameter at the top of the break measures 16 feet.
And it has 8 panels.
And each stone at the beginning of the spire measures two feet
in thickness; and at the top, on the higher side where the cross
is fixed, it measures 4 inches in thickness. And each stone at
the break is 8 feet[1] wide in thickness, and the width of the
garland measures 11 feet.

(227)
Memorandum, to enquire of Robert Everard of Norwich:[2]
A question, in English words:
QUESTION:
How many inches does the spire of Trinity church, Norwich,[3]
batter in 6 feet?

(228)
FREEMASONS:
Benet Crosse, John Norton, freemasons of Bristol.[4]

(229)
REDCLIFFE
The thickness of the walls of Redcliffe tower at the base: 7
feet.
And at the height of 120 feet, the wall measures 5 feet.

---

1   *sic*, error for inches?
2   See John Harvey, *English Mediæval Architects* (1954), p. 102
3   i.e. Norwich Cathedral, the spire of which had, like that of St Mary
    Redcliffe earlier – cf. **(447)** – been destroyed in a storm in 1463
4   *Ibid*, pp. 79, 197

---

i   § in margin by Talbot
j   See note h

(230)
CAPELLA SANCTE MARIE PRINCIPALIS
longitudo prime[a] partis porticus Ecclesie beate marie continet
.7. virgas & capella continuata ad portam introitus porte
Ecclesie principalis continet .6. virgas
latitudo prime rotunditatis predictis[b] partis dicte capelle
continet[c] .5. virgas[d]
latitudo 2[da] principalis partis dicte capelle continet ... [e]

(231)
TURRIS ECCLESIE SANCTI JACOBI
Turris Campanarum. Ecclesie sancti Jacobi. ab[f] boriali et in[g]
meridiem continet .6. virgas
Et ab oriente in occidentem .5. virgas;

(232)
Ecclesie sancti Audoeni in latitudine .14. virgas
longitudo Ecclesie sancti Audoeni. ... [h]

(233)
latitudo Ecclesie sancte trinitatis continet .32 gressus, siue ... [h]
longitudo Ecclesie sancte trinitatis continet .22. virgas

(234)
latitudo Ecclesie sancte Werburge continet ... [h]

(235)
Ecclesia sancti Petri continet in longitudine preter chorum .54.
gressus
latitudo eius continet[i] .30. gresssus

(236)
Ecclesia sancte marie de la Port continet .preter chorum. in
longitudine .27. gressus
latitudo eius continet ... [j]

---

a   *prime* written again more clearly above
b   *rotunditatis predictis* is an uncertain readng of two unclear words
c   Illegible number, possibly *4*, deleted
d   *virgas* badly written, then rewritten more clearly above
e   Blank in MS
f   *orientale* deleted
g   *occidentem* deleted
h   Blank in MS
i   Illegible number, possibly *2*, deleted
j   Blank in MS

(230)
THE MAIN CHAPEL OF ST MARY[1]
The length of the first part[2] of the porch of St Mary's church measures 7 yards, and the chapel going on to the door of the main church entrance measures 6 yards.
The width of the first circuit[3] aforesaid of the part of the said chapel measures 5 yards.
The width of the second main part[4] of the said chapel measures ...

(231)
THE TOWER OF ST JAMES'S CHURCH
The bell-tower of St James's church measures 6 yards from north to south.
And from east to west, 5 yards.

(232)
St Ewen's church: in width, 14 yards
The length of St Ewen's church: ...

(233)
The width of Holy Trinity church measures 32 steps or ...
The length of Holy Trinity church measures 22 yards.

(234)
The width of St Werburgh's church measures ...

(235)
St Peter's church measures 54 steps in length, except for the quire.
Its width measures 30 steps.

(236)
The church of St Mary le Port measures 27 steps in length, except for the quire.
Its width measures ...

---

1 The north porch, the magnificent pilgrim entrance chapel, as opposed to the Lady Chapel at the east end
2 *parte* has the English sense of a part or section of the whole porch, the first part being the polygonal outer porch, and the second part the earlier inner porch; cf. *parte* in **(150)**, **(151)**
3 See note b opposite. Worcestre may be trying to convey its polygonal shape
4 See note 2 above

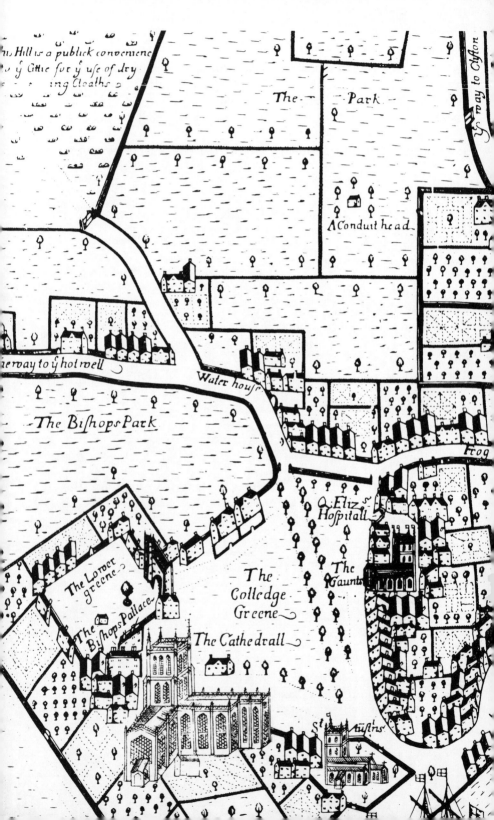

Hill is a publick convenience
y Cittie for y use of dry
ing Cloaths

The   Park

y way to Clifton

A Conduit head

he way to y hot well

Water house

The Bishops Park

Frog

Eliz
Hospitall

The
Lower
greene

The
Gaunts

The
Colledge
Greene

The Bishops Pallace

The Cathedrall

St Austins

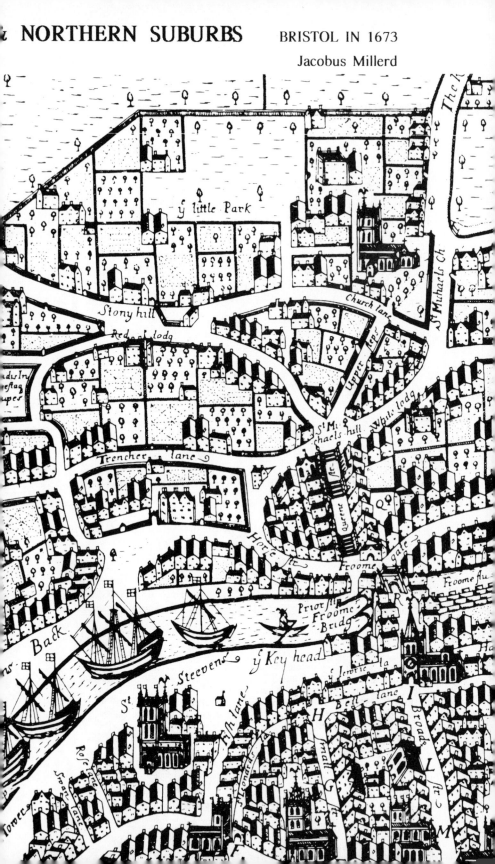

BRISTOL IN 1673

Jacobus Millerd

ẙ little Park

Stony hill

Red. lodg

Church lane

St Michaels Ch

Upper

Whit lodg

St Michaels hill

Trencher lane

Queene

Horse

Froome gate

Froome flu

Priory
Froome
Brid

Back

ẙ Key head

Froome

Steevens

Jenric la

Fish lane

Bell lane

Broad

St

H

Tower lane

Smale

J
G

(237)
MEMORANDUM .1469.
Master Robertus Lond obijt gramaticus ville Bristollie die .23.[a]
Februarij

---

(238)
RADCLYFF
ARCHUS & FENESTRE ECCLESIE DE LE OVYRSTORYE
longitudo navis Ecclesie de Radclyf continet .13. archus altos
cum .13. fenestris desuper le ovyrstorye. Et quelibet fenestra
habet .5. panes. altitudinis .12. pedum & latitudinis .4.[b]
virgarum vitreatarum sic in toto Et quilibet fenestra continet
.4. virgas latitudinis & habet .5. panys vitreatas quelibet
fenestra. sed in duobus alis Ecclesie. quelibet fenestra non
habet[c] nisi .4. panellas[d] vitreatas.

p.131
     [Notes written in 1480 about Oxford colleges] [e]

p.132

(239)[f]
INSULE IRLANDIE,
Arnys Insule tres[g] hibernie iacent vltra Blasquey Iland.
Slygh[h]

Et comprehendit .3. jnsulas Magnas.   et sunt infra dictas
jnsulas circa numerum vt dicitur .368. jnsulas
Et dicta .insula. est talis nature quod homines manentes in
dicta jnsula non possunt mori sed quando volunt ex nimia etate
mori debent ex eorum desiderio portari extra jnsulam & ibi
moriuntur, et continet in circuitu .24. miliaria.

---

a   *.23.* written again above
b   *.4.* appears to be written over *.5.*
c   *v* (for *vitreatas?*) deleted
d   *panellas* smudged, deleted, rewritten above and then repeated
e   Included in Harvey, *Itineraries*, pp. 276–9.
f   Item **(239)** was included in Harvey, *Itineraries*, pp. 308–9, with some
    variations in transcription and translation. It is included here because
    it relates indirectly to Bristol both in content and, possibly, in origin:
    cf. **(241)**, **(418)**
g   *.3.* written above
h   Ending unclear, read by Harvey as *Slygo*; cf. note 2 opposite

---

5   Worcestre further confuses his islands. Harvey suggested this may refer
    to Achill Island; or it might be Inishmore, largest of the Aran Islands

(237)
MEMORANDUM: 1469
Master Robert Londe, grammar-master of the town of Bristol, died the 23rd day of February.[1]

---

(238)
REDCLIFFE
THE ARCHES AND WINDOWS OF THE CLERESTORY OF THE CHURCH
The length of the nave of Redcliffe church contains 13 lofty arches, with 13 windows up above in the clerestory; and each window has 5 lights, 12 feet high, and 4 yards wide, glazed throughout. And each window measures 4 yards in width, and each window has 5 glazed lights. But in the two aisles of the church, each window has only 4 glazed lights.

p.131

[Notes written in 1480 about Oxford colleges]

p.132

(239)
THE ISLANDS OF IRELAND
The three Aran Islands, in Ireland, lie beyond Blasket Island. Slea [Head].[2]

And they comprise three large islands. And further along from the said islands there are, it is said, about 368 islands in number.[3] And [one] said 'island' has such a property, that the men living on the said island cannot die; but when on account of great age they wish to die, they are at their own request carried away from the island, and there die.[4] And it measures 24 miles in circumference.[5]

---

1 i.e. 23rd February 1470 New Style; cf. **(50)**
2 Harvey (note f opposite) read *Slygh* as *Slygo* and commented that this must be an error, Sligo lying as it does on the northwest coast of Ireland. It seems much more likely that the Aran Islands are 'beyond' the Blasket Islands, sailing clockwise around the coast, and that *Slygh* is Slea Head, the south-west point of Ireland off which the Blaskets lie
3 Worcestre has run together various traditions about different Irish islands. Harvey noted that Clew Bay, County Mayo, traditionally had as many islets as days of the year
4 Harvey noted the sources of this legend, said to refer to Monaincha, near Roscrea

(239) |continued|

Blasquey Iland prope Dengle

continet in circuitu ... ^a et qui voluerit velare ad jnsulam
Brasyle^b debet accipere cursum

Kelleques jland

MEMORANDUM DE GALEWAY^c

---

(240)

<u>Gyston Clyff</u>

APUD GYSTON CLYFF

Brekefaucet est subtus Gyston clyff. apud lymotes sub valle
Brandonhille^d

ā

Fons^e Calidus emanet de profundo aque Avyn.^f sicut est
Bathonie. in le Roke de Gyston clyff in eadem parte in le
sholeplace

ā

Scarlet Welle est directe on parte opposita. in alta parte de
hungrode emanente de Rupe

<u>Ledes</u>^g est vnus Rokk vnder Gystonclyff a danger si venit &
jntrat Bristollie id est nimis tempestiue. ovyrstone. & si diu
tardat. fluxum maris est periculosus ad velandum pro rupibus
iacentibus in fundo maris cursus de Gystonclyff

(241)^h

<u>HIBERNIA</u>

Brandon hylleⁱ in hibernia scita est altissimus mons tocius
hibernie. vltra blasquey.ⁱ in occidentalissima parte tocius
hibernie. Et ibi sunt lapides vocates Cristalle stonysⁱ

---

a   Blank in MS
b   *ad jnsulam Brasyle* underlined by Talbot, with § in margin opposite
c   Marginal heading with nothing further written alongside
d   :- by Talbot, with O in margin opposite
e   *Fons Calidus* has O by Talbot in margin opposite; *Calidus* has been
    smudged, deleted and rewritten
f   *Avyn* underlined, probably by Talbot
g   O in margin opposite by Talbot, who has also underlined *Ledes*, already
    underlined by Worcestre
h   Item **(241)** was included in Harvey, *Itineraries*, pp. 308-9, with minor
    variations in transcription and translation; through the association with
    Brandon Hill, it relates indirectly to Bristol

(239) [continued]
Blasket Island near Dingle.
It measures ... in circumference, and he who wishes to sail to
the island of Brazil ought to pick up the course [there].

Skellig island.[1]

MEMORANDUM OF GALWAY

---

(240)

Ghyston Cliff

AT GHYSTON CLIFF
Breke Faucet is below Ghyston Cliff, at the Bounds below the
hillside of Brandon Hill.

A hot spring rises out of the depths of the river Avon, just as
at Bath, in the rock of Ghyston Cliff, on the same side, at The
Shoal Place.

Scarlet Well is directly on the opposite side, on the higher side
of Hungroad, issuing out of a rock.

The Leads is a rock under Ghyston Cliff, a danger if, that is,
one comes into Bristol too early over the rocks; and if one
delays too long, the falling tide is dangerous for sailing,
because of the rocks lying in the depths of the seaway at
Ghyston Cliff.

(241)
IRELAND
Brandon Hill, situated in Ireland, is the highest mountain of all
Ireland;[2] [it is] beyond the Blasket in the westernmost part of
all Ireland. And there are stones there called crystals.

---

1 Probably the Skellig Rocks, off the southwest extremity of Ireland south
   of the Blasket Islands. Great Skellig was a considerable religious and
   pilgrim centre
2 Harvey notes that Brandon Hill, or Mount Brandon, on the peninsula
   immediately north of the Blasket Islands, is in fact the second highest
   mountain in Ireland

---

i *Brandon hylle, blasquey,* and *Cristalle stonys* underlined by Talbot, who
   has written *cristallus* in the margin

(242)[a]

a porta sancti leonardi fine vie de Baldwinstret vsque le Custom hous.[b]

latitudo vie ibidem .5. virge ad angulum trianguli de le Customhous jncipiente

(243)[a]

Cornerstrete; continet .17. cellaria in parte omnium sanctorum

(244)[a]

via[c] de[d] hyghstrete in parte posteriori Ecclesie omnium sanctorum continet .60. gressus

latitudo dicte vie. continet .vnam virgam.

(245)[a]

latitudo parue vie omnium sanctorum a retro occidentalis Ecclesie .5. virge,

in via predicto paruo est vnum Cellarium pro vino

p.133

(246)

> Naves Bristollie pertinentes in anno christi .1480
> > Mary grace .300. doliata[e]
> > le Trinite[f] .360. doliata
> > George .200. doliata
> > Kateryn .180. doliata
> > Mary bryd .100. doliata
> > Cristofer .90. doliata
> > Mary Sherman .54. doliata
> > leonard .50. Tontyghe
> > Mary of Bristow ... lex tonne[g]
> > le Gorge qui quere Ilanes[h] .511. tonne
> > ... [i] navis qui dispositus est ad mare
> > Johannes Godeman habet navium ... [i]
> > Thomas Straunge ... [i]

---

a Items **(242)**–**(245)** are written upside-down at the bottom of p.132, all crossed through with one large **X**, and *vacat* (cancelled) in the margin
b Worn edge of page: figures unclear, possibly *53*, while *gressus* or *virgas* has been lost completely
c *in* written first, then *de* written over it
d Faint letters, possibly *Ecc* (for *Ecclesie*) deleted
e Jotted above *doliata* but not necessarily related to it, is *m 17 score* (memorandum 340) or possibly (1340)
f *300* deleted
g *sic*, with a small blank space which may not be intended; perhaps an error for *lx tonne*?

(242)
From St Leonard's Gate at the end of the road of Baldwin Street as far as The Customs House: [53 steps?][1]
The width of the road there: 5 yards to the angle at the start of The Customs House triangle.

(243)
Corn Street contains 17 cellars on the All Saints side.

(244)
The road from High Street on the rearward side of the church of All Saints measures 60 steps.
The width of the said road measures 1 yard.

(245)
The width of the little road of All Saints behind the west [end] of the church: 5 yards.
In the aforesaid little road is a wine-cellar.

p.133

(246)
　　Ships belonging to Bristol in the year of Christ 1480:
　　　　Mary Grace 300 tons
　　　　The Trinity 360 tons
　　　　George 200 tons
　　　　Katherine 180 tons
　　　　Mary Bride 100 tons
　　　　Christopher 90 tons
　　　　Mary Sherman 54 tons
　　　　Leonard 50 'Tontyghe'[2]
　　　　Mary of Bristol ... statute ton[3]
　　　　The George which seeks 'Ilanes' 511 tons[4]
　　　　... ships which are dispersed at sea
　　　　John Goodman has, of ships, ...
　　　　Thomas Strange ...

1　The same route, continuing to the conduit, was 90-100 steps **(5)**, **(32)**
2　Meaning unclear; a type of small boat, or a variant on *tonne*, below?
3　Or perhaps an error for 60 tons?
4　Meaning unclear: *The George* which seeks 'Ilanes'/?the islands 511 tons
　　or: *The George* – who to ask – *[The] Elaine/Ellen* 511 tons
　　or: *The George* – about which ask 'Ilanes' – 511 tons
　　The size given is huge, cf. **(441)**, and might be an error for 51 tons, the lower end of tonnages as listed. This cannot be John Jay's un-named boat seeking the islands of Brazil **(418)**, because that was only 80 tons.

---

h　Uncertain reading: see note 4 above
i　Blank in MS. Talbot has added *circiter xij*. The rest of p. 133 is blank

p.134 *[Blank]*

p.135

(247)

Pons Bristollie

PONS BRISTOLLIE[a]

altitudo Turris quadratus Campanile in sinistra capelle edificate de petra. ab area continet ad cameram campanarum .15. brachia. et per cordas campanarum[b] mensuratas et altissima Camera continet in altitudine circa[c] tria brachia. sic in tota altitudine. circa .18. brachia

longitudo pontis predicte continet .94.[d] gressus

Memorandum quod helyas Spelly burgensis ville Bristollie est & fuit cum . ...[e] majores benefactores Capelle predicte vt patet in fenestris vitreatis cum figura eorum & uxorum suarum in dictis fenestris, videlicet helyas Spelly ... [f]

---

(248)[g]

JNCEPCIO VIAGIJ ROBERTI STURMY AD JERUSALEM .1446.

1446. Memorandum quod mense jullij ante festum sancti Jacobi. Robertus Sturmyn mercator ville Bristollie jncepit viagium suum de porta Bristollie[h] a Kyngrode ad Jerusalem cum circa .160. peregrinis. et nauigando per Cyville. eundo ad portam Jaff,[i] et ad Jerusalem.[j] et in redeundo versus Angliam per Modon jnsulam.[k] ex subito procello[l] et forti vento. orto in atra & obscura nocte 23. die decembris incaute ex jnprouiso navis eius vocata le Cogg Anne ad rupem & terram prostrata fuit & .37. homines & marinarij submersi[m] fuerunt in maximum[n] dolorem amicorum eorum bristollie & eorum vxorum

---

a   O by Talbot in margin opposite
b   *edificata* deleted
c   *.18.* deleted
d   *brach* (for *brachia*) deleted; this deletion was made, and *gressus* added, in different ink at a different time
e   A complete line has been left blank for the addition of other names; O by Talbot in margin opposite
f   A small space for names left at the end
g   Item (248) was included in Harvey, *Itineraries*, pp. 306-7, with some variations in transcription and translation. It is a fuller and more polished version of (143)
h   *ad* deleted
i   *ad portam Jaff* underlined, probably by Talbot

p.134 *[Blank]*

p.135

(247)

Bristol Bridge

BRISTOL BRIDGE

The height of the square bell-tower built of stone on the left of the chapel measures 15 fathoms from ground level to the bell-chamber, measured by the bell-ropes; and the highest chamber measures about three fathoms in height; thus about 18 fathoms in height altogether.

The length of the aforesaid bridge measures 94 steps.

Memorandum, that Elias Spelly is a burgess of the town of Bristol, and was, with ... ..., leading benefactors of the aforesaid chapel, as appears in the glass windows,[1] with the figures of them and their wives in the said windows, to wit Elias Spelly ...

---

(248)

THE BEGINNING OF THE VOYAGE OF ROBERT STURMY TO JERUSALEM, 1446.

1446.   Memorandum, that in the month of July, before the feast of St James, Robert Sturmy, merchant of the town of Bristol, began his voyage from the port of Bristol, from Kingroad, to Jerusalem, with about 160 pilgrims; and sailing by Seville, going to the port of Jaffa[2] and to Jerusalem.   And on returning towards England by the island of Modon,[3] [caught] unexpectedly off-guard by a sudden tempest and strong wind springing up in the black and murky night on the 23rd day of December, his ship called the *Cog Anne* was driven aground on a rock, and 37 men and seamen were drowned, to the great sorrow of their friends at Bristol, and of their wives.

---

1   This window depicting 15th century Bristol merchants must have been particularly spectacular; it is the only stained glass in Bristol of which Worcestre gives any details
2   Ancient Joppa, modern Yafa or Tel-Aviv
3   Probaby Methoni, in the Peleponnese: see **(143)**

---

j   *peregrini ad Jherusalem* written by Talbot in margin opposite
k   *Modon jnsulam* underlined, probably by Talbot
l   *sic*
m   *submersi* written by Talbot in margin opposite
n   From this point to the end of this item, Talbot has drawn a vertical line down the left-hand side of the text, with § in margin alongside

(248) [continued]
Sed quidam deuotus Episcopus de Modon in Grecia fecit
corpora mortuorum .37. predictorum honorifice sepeliri et
fundauit sanctam Capellam de nouo ibidem ad orandum pro
animabus eorum et omnium fidelium defunctorum,

(249)
BAKKE
latitudo siue spacium vie apud le bake in parochia sancti
Nicholai erga capellam de le Bakke continet .50 gressus prope
Crane;

---

(250)
SLYPP SUPER LE BAK
Gradus primus anglice. a Slypp super le Bak de aqua Avyn;
proxima vico vocato Baldewynstrete. anglice a Slepe continet in
longitudine ad[a] fundum aque Auene. continet in longitudine
ascendendo ad altum vicum de le bake 80.[b] gradus anglice
steyres[c]

SLYPP
Gradus .2.[us] secundus[d] anglice a Slypp proxime sequens in
dicto vico de le bake propinquia. capelle sancti Johannis
Euangeliste. continet in longitudine, circa .80. gressus.[e]

latitudo duorum longarum graduum. de le bake usque fundum
aque de Avyn vbi mulieres lauant pannos laneos[f] aliquando .12.
mulieres simul ad pedem aque de Avyn lauantes

p.136

Aqua de Avyn in le bakke[g]

pannos[h] lineos[i] & alia necessaria vidi vt Mulieres honeste sic
ibidem quando fluxus maris returnat versus mare ita quod aqua
Avyn veniente de ponte Bristollie sit clara et pura; sic lauant
certis temporibus die

---

a   *aqu* (for *aque*) deleted
b   *gressus.* deleted
c   *steyrys* repeated, because writing smudged first time
d   repeated thus
e   *gressus* has been smudged and deleted, but not replaced with *gradus* as
    presumably intended
f   *de Avyn ... pannos laneos* underlined, probably by Talbot
g   Heading added later; text continues from p. 135

(248) [continued]
But a certain devout bishop of Modon in Greece caused the bodies of the 37 aforesaid dead men to be honourably buried, and he newly founded a holy chapel there, to pray for their souls and [those] of all the faithful departed.

(249)
THE BACK
The width or extent of the road at The Back in the parish of St Nicholas over against the chapel of The Back, near the crane, measures 50 steps.

---

(250)
THE SLIP UPON THE BACK
The first stairway (in English 'a Slip') upon The Back of the river Avon, next to the street called Baldwin Street, measures in length from the depths of the river Avon rising up to the upper street of The Back, 80 stairs (in English 'steyres').[1]

THE SLIP
The second stairway (in English 'a Slip') next along in the said street of The Back, close to the chapel of St John the Evangelist, measures about 80 steps[2] in length.

The width of the two long stairways from The Back to the depths of the river Avon, where women wash woollen cloths: sometimes I have seen 12 women at a time at the foot [of the slip] at the river Avon, washing

p.136
The river Avon on The Back

woollen cloths[3] and other household items. For the goodwives, when the tide there flows back towards the sea, so that the river Avon coming from Bristol Bridge shall be clear and fresh, so then they do their washing at [those] particular times of the day.

1   Worcestre's repetitions in this item are omitted in translation
2   Presumably an error for 'stairs', as above (cf. note e opposite)
3   Probably cloth rather than clothes, and woollen rather than linen, given the previouse reference, the importance of clothmaking in Bristol and the proximity of the Rackhay, originally for cloth-drying (cf. note i below)

h   Worcestre actually wrote *panns*
i   *pannos lineos* (*sic*: linen cloths) probably in error for *pannos laneos* as above

(251)

Naves navicule. et cimbe. ac navicule vocate anglice wodbushys Cachchys[a] pycardes venientes de portubus villarum Wallie sunt de villis & havyns de[b] Tynby. Myllford.havyn.[c] West herford[d] lawgher. havyn. lanstefan havyn. Kedwelly havyn Swaynsey havyn. Neth havyn. Kerdyff havyn. Newport havyn. Wsque havyn. Kerlyon havyn.[e] Tyntern monasterium super Flumen de Wye. Chepstow havyn. Betysley[f] water super aquam de Wy. & alie Portus siue hauiones[g] de Comitatibus[h] & portubus Cornuallie[i] oneratis cum stangno piscibus &c ac de portubus de Devynshyre. Somersetshyre applicant cum eorum navibus ad le bake cum fluxium maris. ad exonerandum & discarcandum earum naves de eorum mercandisis,

(252)

SUPER LE BAK

<u>Capella</u> decens longitudinis ... [j] virgarum

[k]super le bak Bristollie prope Mersh yate est edificatum per venerabilem Mercatorem cognominatum Knapp pro duobus capellanis sustinendis in terris et tenementis jta quod semper omni die hora .v.[ta] in mane. illi vel vnius dictorum suorum capellanorum. dicent Missam pro mercatoribus marinarijs & artificis ac seruientibus possunt adire & audiendas Missas tempore matutinali;

(253)

<u>Le Crane officium</u> jnstrumenti super le bake est scitum prope portam vocatam le Mersh yate. bene fundatum & fortiter in terra fixum;

(254)

Domus & hospicium pro communi vtilitate ville vocatum a cloth halle est super le bak ordinatum[l] quondam Roberti Sturmyn venerabilis mercatoris ville Bristollie manentis & hospicium amplum custodientis tam pro externeis mercatoribus quam alijs generosis

---

a   *sic,* error for *cachys* (properly *cachæ,* skiffs)
b   From this point to the end of this item, Talbot has drawn a vertical line down the left-hand side of the text, and written *havyns by West* in the margin alongside
c   Worcestre deleted *Myllford.havyn.,* then wrote *stet* above; cf. note e
d   Worcestre wrote *Mylford havyn* again here, and deleted it
e   *havyn* repeated
f   *havyn* deleted

(251)
Ships, boats and skiffs, also boats called (in English) 'woodbushes, ketches and picards' are from the ports of the Welsh towns. They are from the towns and havens of Tenby, Milford haven, Haverfordwest, Laugharne haven, Llanstephen haven, Kidwelly haven, Swansea haven, Neath haven, Cardiff haven, Newport haven, Usk haven, Caerleon haven, Tintern abbey on the river Wye, Chepstow haven, 'Betysley-water'[1] on the river Wye, and other harbours or havens from the counties and ports of Cornwall, laden with tin, fish etc., and from the ports of Devonshire [and] Somersetshire. They moor their ships at The Back on the rising tide, to unload and discharge their ships of their goods.

(252)
UPON THE BACK
A fine chapel, of -- yards length.
It is built upon The Back of Bristol near Marsh Gate, by a respected merchant surnamed Knapp, for two chaplains, maintained by lands and property; so that at 5 o'clock in the morning every single day his said chaplains or one of them say mass for the merchants, seamen, craftsmen and servants able to go and hear mass in the early morning.

(253)
The crane, a public machine, is situated upon The Back, near the gate called The Marsh Gate, well founded and firmly fixed into the ground.

(254)
A house and lodging for the public benefit of the town, called a Cloth Hall, was some time since set up upon The Back, formerly Robert Sturmy's, a respected merchant of the town of Bristol, for lodging and keeping ample hospitality both for foreign merchants and for other gentry.

---

1 Possibly Beachley at the mouth of R.Wye, which would fit the north-south sequence of places listed on the river

---

g   *sic*
h   *Gloucestre Teukysbery* deleted
i   *De* (probably for *Devynshyre* as below) deleted
j   Blank in MS
k   *Jtem* deleted
l   Worcestre originally wrote *ordinatus* and amended it

p.137

(255)
Ecclesia parochialis sancti Audoeni cum capella fraternitatis in honore sancti Johannis baptiste scita directa linea inter Ecclesiam sancte Wereburge ex^a parte occidentali et vicum vocatum Bradstrete ex parte orientali et magna fenestra orientalis altaris dicte Ecclesie scita super stratum Bradstrete,

(256)
Ecclesia parochialis sancte trinitatis scita in directa linea Ecclesie Audoeni ex parte occidentali dicte Ecclesie ac buttat super orientali parte vici Bradstrete et meridionalis pars dicte Ecclesie est scita cum porta eiusdem apud crucem altam in quadriuio de Bradstrete. hyghstrete. Cornstrete & Wynchestrete, quondam Castelstret. et dicta Ecclesia habet turrim quadratum cum campanis ac speram alta cum lapidibus de Frestoone condecenter operatam;

(257)
Ecclesia parochialis omnium sanctorum scita super vicum Cornstrete in parte boriali. et prope Crucem altam de hyghstrete ex parte orientali. et habet Turrim quadratum pro campanis pulsantibus,^{b}

(258)
Ecclesia parochialis beate marie de Radclyff in altera parte pontis Bristollie super altum montem scituata & edificata velut Ecclesia Cathedralis cum turri quadrata larga occupata cum ... ^{c} campanis large quantitatis & ponderis quarum

> prima Campana ponderat ... ^{d}
> Secunda Campana ponderat ...
> Tercia Campana ponderat ...
> Quarta campana ponderat ...
> Quinta Campana ponderat ...
> Sexta Campana ponderat ...

e

---

a   *ex* badly written, and then rewritten more clearly above
b   In the space between **(257)** and **(258)** is written *Ecclesia parochialis*, but nothing more. The space might have been intended for St Werburgh, fourth of this central group of churches
c   Blank in MS, but with *q'* (for *questio* or *query*?) deleted, as though Worcestre intended to fill in the total number of bells, but then added the list below

p.137

(255)
The parish church of St Ewen, with the chapel of the Fraternity in honour of St John the Baptist,[1] is situated in a straight line between St Werburgh's church on the west side and the street called Broad Street on the east side; and the great window of the eastern altar of the said church overlooks the street of Broad Street.

(256)
The parish church of Holy Trinity is situated directly [opposite] the church of [St] Ewen, [which is] on the west side of the said church; and it abuts upon the east side of the street of Broad Street.   And the south side of the said church, together with its door, is situated at the High Cross on the crossroads of Broad Street, High Street, Corn Street and Wynch Street (formerly Castle Street).   And the said church has a square bell-tower, and a high spire finely worked with masonry of freestone.

(257)
The parish church of All Saints is situated upon the street of Corn Street on [its] north side, and next to the High Cross of High Street on [its] east side; and it has a square tower for bell-ringing.

(258)
The parish church of the Blessed Mary of Redcliffe is situated on the other side of Bristol Bridge upon a high hill, and [is] built like a cathedral church, with a square tower of considerable extent, with ... bells of considerable size and weight, of which
    the first bell weighs ...
    the second bell weighs ...
    the third bell weighs ...
    the fourth bell weighs ...
    the fifth bell weighs ...
    the sixth bell weighs ...

---

1 The Fraternity of Merchant Tailors

---

d No figures are given for the weights of the bells; cf. **(335)**
e An unrelated jotting appears beneath this item, in a flowing 16th century hand, possibly Aldrich

p. 138

(259)
Ecclesia parochialis de sancta cruce quondam ordinis Templariorum in Templo Jerusalem modo de sancto Johanne baptista[a] ordine jn Jerosolimitana Ciuitate primo orta & fundata. ac diebus modernis Ecclesia Religionum ordinis prefate sancti Johannis baptiste apud jnsulam de Rodes florente,

Et dicta Ecclesia parochialis Bristollie in diocesi Bathoniensi et Wellensi super aquam de Avyn scituata in altera parte de Avyn scita
jn longitudine continet ... [b]
jn latitudine vero ... [b]
Altitudo Turris Quadrate de nouo fabricate circa annum christi .1460. per parachianos ville pro Campanis magnificis pulsandis et sonandis;

(260)
Capella sancti Johannis Euangeliste super le Bakke[c] fundata per magnificum virum mercatorem & burgensem Bristollie scita super le ... [d]

(261)
Capella pulcherima. cum volta larga & alta archuata cum lapidibus subtus capellam beate marie Virginis super medium locum pontis Bristollie ac super pontem fortissimum archuatum cum magnis boteraces. cuius pons extendit ab occidentali pontis Bristollie contigue cum longo ponte Bristollie &[e] archus dicte pontis. breuis respectu alterius pontis. ad partem orientalem super aquam Avyn.

Turris quadratus pro campanis pulsandis super fundum Capelle predicte continet in altitudine .18.[f]

(262)
Capella hospitalis sancte trinitatis in veteri Mercato anglice old Market,

---

a   *lodo,* possibly for *London,* deleted
b   Blank in MS
c   *bakke* repeated
d   Blank in MS
e   & repeated
f   *brachia* omitted: cf. **(247)**

p.138

(259)

The parish church of Holy Cross, formerly of the Order of Templars in the Jerusalem Temple, now of the Order of St John the Baptist, first begun and founded in the city of Jerusalem, and nowadays the church of the religious Order of the aforesaid St John the Baptist, flourishing on the island of Rhodes.

And the said parish church of Bristol, in the diocese of Bath and Wells, is situated upon the river Avon, sited on the other side of the Avon.
In length it measures ...
But in width ...
The height of the square tower, newly built about the year of Christ 1460 by the parishioners of the town for ringing and sounding the splendid bells.

(260)

The chapel of St John the Evangelist, founded upon The Back by a great man, a merchant and burgess of Bristol,[1] is situated upon The ...

(261)

The very beautiful chapel of the Blessed Virgin Mary, with a wide and lofty crypt arched with stone beneath the chapel, [is] over the middle area of Bristol Bridge, and very strongly arched over the bridge, with huge buttresses; of which a pier extends from the west [side] of Bristol Bridge, abutting onto the length of Bristol Bridge; and the arch of the said pier [is] short in comparision with the other pier over the river Avon on the east side.[2]

The square tower for bell-ringing upon the foundation of the aforesaid chapel, measures 18 [fathoms][3] in height.

(262)

The chapel of Holy Trinity hospital in the old market (in English 'Old Market').

---

1   i.e. Thomas Knapp
2   This complicated description only makes sense if *pons* is taken as sometimes meaning the main bridge, and sometimes the piers (cf. **(109)**) supporting the bridge and chapel
3   cf. **(247)**

(263)

Capella sancti spiritus antiquissima iuxta Ecclesiam beate marie de Radclyff,

p.139

(264)

Porta prima de Frome yate ex parte vie versus Ecclesiam sancti Johannis continet longitudine .20. gressus siue ... [a] virgas
Spacium longitudinis vie a dicta prima porta edificata et cum archu siue longitudo[b] pontis de Frome inter dictas duas portas continet ... [c] gressus siue ... [c] virgas
Porta secunda edificata desuper versus & prope Ecclesiam canonicorum quondam sancti Bertholomei continet in longitudine .12. gressus siue ... [c] virgas

(265)

Ecclesia parochialis sancti Augustini nouiter isto anno 1480 constructa & erecta in longitudine cum duabis[d] alis[e] excepto choro continet in longitudine .24. virgas

latitudo dicte Ecclesie viz Navis Ecclesie sancti Augustini continet .6. virgas jdest .18. pedes. Et quelibet Ela continet in latitudine 4. virgas siue .12. pedes jn toto eius latitudo continet .42. pedes mihi relatas per parochianum
longitudo cancelle continebit[f] quando constructum fuerit .10. virgas[g]

pp.140–148   *[Blank]*

p.149

(266)[h]
NOTULE DE CRONICIS MARIANI SCOTI APUD LIBRARIAM OMNIUM SANCTORUM JNUENTE,[i]
Cronica a Mariano Scoto veraci stilo digestus[j] sic jncipit

---

a   Blank in MS
b   *dic* (for *dictas*?) deleted
c   Blank in MS
d   *sic*
e   *sin* (for *sine*?) deleted
f   Originally *continet*, with ending deleted and changed to future tense
g   The rest of the page is blank

(263)

The most ancient chapel of the Holy Spirit, next to the church of the Blessed Mary of Redcliffe.

p.139

(264)

The first gate of Fromegate, on the side of the road towards St John's church, measures in length 20 steps or ... yards.

The extent of the length of the road from the said first gateway building and including the arch, or the length of Frome bridge between the said two gates, measures ... steps or ... yards.

The second gateway built on top, towards and near the church of the canons, formerly St Bartholomew's, measures in length 12 steps or ... yards.

(265)

The parish church of St Augustine, newly built and erected in this year 1480, in length together with the two aisles, not counting the quire, measures 24 yards in length.

The width of the said church, to wit the nave of St Augustine's church, measures 6 yards, that is 18 feet. And each aisle measures 4 yards or 12 feet in width. In all, its width measures 42 feet, as told to me by a parishioner.

The length of the chancel, when it shall be built, will measure 10 yards.

pp.140–148   *[Blank]*

p.149

(266)

BRIEF NOTES FROM THE CHRONICLES OF MARIANUS SCOTUS FOUND AT THE LIBRARY OF ALL SAINTS

The chronicle of Marianus Scotus, compiled in a convincing style, begins thus:

---

h   Item **(266)** was included in Harvey, *Itineraries*, pp. 316-321, with some variations in transcription and translation. Amended dates are based on Harvey's notes, which give fuller details

i   *q'* (for *questio* or *query*?), and O by Talbot, in margin opposite

j   *sic*

(266) [continued]

Meum nomen vt dignum cum pre illis cronica cronicorum cum pre illis seruo Euangelistarum, nulla cum cronica conseruat diem mensis solaris resurexionis christi iuxta historiam Euangelij nisi ista sola;

ā

Romanorum primus Imperator Gayus Jullius Cesar regnauit annis .4. mensibus sex vsque kalendas Marcij adde menses quinque supra fit annus

Romanorum^a secundus Octouianus Cesar Augustus regnauit annis quinquaginta sex mensibus sex, aliquantisque diebus Josepho teste hoc est vsque kalendas Octobras in anno sextodecimo Incarnacionis

ā

Crassus falcidius tribunus plebis legem tulit nequis testamento legaret plus quam vt quarta pars superesset

Cursus salussus in jnsula Arado cum quatuor cohortibus viuus combustus est eo quod tributa grauius exigeret

Cicero in firmano^b suo ab herennio et popilio occiditur sexagesimo septimo etatis sue anno Olimpius centum octogesima prima; pauses et hirsulus consules fuerunt in isto anno

Ovidius naso nascitur in pligna

.776. Dorobernia igne consumpta est,^c

.774. Cuthredus Westsaxonum & Rex Merciorum Athelbaldus iuxta Beorhtforda^d satis durum^e commisere prelium

Asclepiadoco Rege Britannie Regnante; orta est persecucio Diocliciani imperatoris in qua erat deletura tota christianitas in hac jnsula, et durauit ista persecucio annis viginti, Et in hac persecucione passus est beatus albanus^f anno gracie .223.^g

---

a   *Imperator* deleted
b   Worcestre actually wrote *in frmano suo*; see note 5 opposite
c   § by Talbot in margin opposite
d   *Beorhtforda* underlined, probably by Talbot, with § in margin opposite
e   *bellum* deleted
f   *albanus* underlined, probably by Talbot
g   *.223. Christi* in margin

---

8   A conflation of different events, all at different dates

(266) [continued]
I hold my name as worthy since in comparison with other chronicles of chronicles and even in comparison with those of the Evangelists, no chronicle preserves the day of the solar month of Christ's Resurrection according to the story of the Gospel, except this alone.

The first Emperor of the Romans, Gaius Julius Caesar, reigned 4 years six months[1] until the kalends[2] of March; adding five months more would complete a[nother] year.

The second [Emperor] of the Romans, Octavianus Caesar Augustus, reigned for fifty-six years six months and some days;[3] according to Josephus this is until the kalends of October in the sixteenth year of the Incarnation.

Crassus Falcidius, tribune of the plebs, passed a law that no one should bequeath by testament more than would leave a quarter part remaining.

Cursus Salussus was burned alive with four cohorts on the island of Aradus, because he exacted an oppressive tribute.

Cicero was killed in his litter by Herennius and Popilius, in the sixty-seventh year of his age, the hundred and eighty-first Olympiad.[4] Pauses and Hirsulus were consuls in that year.

Ovidius Naso was born in Paelignia.[5]

776   Canterbury was destroyed by fire.[6]

774   Cuthred of the West Saxons and Æthelbald King of the Mercians fought a very hard battle near 'Beorhford'.[7]

When 'King' Asclepiodotus was ruling Britain, there began the persecution of the Emperor Diocletian, in which all Christianity in this island was suppressed, and this persecution lasted for twenty years.   And during this persecution the Blessed Alban was martyred, in the year of grace 223.[8]

---

1   From the autumn of 49 BC to 15th March 44 BC
2   Error for 'Ides'
3   In fact, 21st November 43 BC (the *triumvir*) to 19th August AD 14
4   Cicero was in fact killed in his 64th year, in 43 AD, the third year of the 184th Olympiad
5   Ovid was born at Sulmo, in the territory of the Paeligni, in 43 BC
6   The fire at Canterbury in fact occurred in AD 754
7   This battle was in fact in AD 752. 'Beorhford' is unidentified, but for linguistic reasons is not now thought to be Burford in Oxfordshire

(266) [continued]

Quare Dani gentes huius Regni gubernacula tenuerunt, fuit desidia et negligencia[a] Ethelredi Regis patris Edwardi Regis et perfidia principum suorum et precipue nequissimi proditoris Edrici quem Rex Ethelredus Comitatui Merciorum prefecerat. Danis enim omnes portus infestantibus et leuitate pirata vbique discurrentibus occidentalis provincia que Devenshyre vocatur pessundata[b] euersis monasterijs et Exonia vrbe incensa, Rex interea strenuus et pulcre ad dormiendum factus tot negocia postponens in tam tristi pallore[c]

p.150

tot calimitatiue[d] vitam consumpsit. et mirum cum Rex provt a[e] maioribus accepimus neque multum fatuus erat nec nimis ignauus,

.357. Antonius monachus obijt

.369. Gregorius Nazanzenus floruit Episcopus Constantino-politanus Doctor Grecorum egregius

Summa librorum quos Augustinus doctor composuit 350 floruit circa annum christi .400. sed obijt circa annum Domini .440 anno etatis .70. secundum quosdam .76.[f]

Jeronimus fatetur se legisse sex milia volumina Origenis[g]

Cerdicius vir veteris[h] milicie post hengistum anno .8⁰. Britanniam cum Kenrico filio suo adolescente[i] adueniens bello est exceptus quos in fugam compellit

In Berwicia cepit primus regnare Yda

---

a　*fuit desidia et negligencia* underlined, probably by Talbot; *Aluredi Regis* deleted by Worcestre
b　*provincia* deleted
c　*pallore* repeated at the beginning of p.150, as a catchword
d　*sic*
e　*a* repeated
f　A vertical line down the side of this item, probably by Talbot
g　A wavy line down the side of this item, probably by Talbot
h　*h* deleted
i　Worcestre actually wrote *adlescente*

6　Bernicia (Worcestre's 'Berwick') was the territory north of R.Tees. Ida became the first of the Anglian kings of Northumbria in 547.

(266) [continued]
The reason why the Danish people seized the government of this kingdom was the sloth and negligence of King Ethelred, father of King Edward, and the treachery of his nobles, and especially of the most villainous traitor Edric, whom King Ethelred had made ealdorman over the Mercians. For the Danes were attacking all the harbours and swooping about everywhere in the west on piratical raids, the province which is called Devonshire destroyed, the monasteries overthrown, and the city of Exeter burnt. The King meanwhile, splendidly energetic at keeping his eyes closed [to the situation], put off so many affairs in such wretched indecision

p.150

that [his] life was wasted in calamities. And this is a wonder, since the King, as we have learned from our forefathers, was neither very foolish nor particularly cowardly.

357   Anthony the monk died.[1]

369   Gregory Nazianzen lived, Bishop of Constantinople, [and] eminent Doctor of the Greeks.[2]

Total number of books which Augustine the Doctor wrote: 350. He lived about the year of Christ 400, but died about A.D. 440, in his 70th year [or], according to others, [his] 76th.[3]

Jerome claimed that he had read 6,000 volumes of Origen.

Cerdic, a man experienced in warfare, came to Britain the eighth year after Hengist,[4] with Cynric his young son. In combat, he was intercepted [by the enemy] whom he put to flight.

In Bernicia Ida first started to reign.[5]

---

1 St Anthony, hermit, c.251–c.356
2 St Gregory Nazianzen, 329–389, one of the four great Greek doctors of the church, and briefly Bishop of Constantinople in 380-1
3 St Augustine of Hippo was born 354 and died 430, so the second estimate of his age is correct
4 Cerdic and Cynric are supposed, according to the Anglo-Saxon Chronicle, to have arrived in 495, which would be the eighth year after the death of Hengist (487-8), not after his arrival in England in 449

p.151ᵃ

(267)

ā

LE BAKE

Australis pars marisci sexies .60. vsque oppositum Ecclesie
Radclyff,

ā

secunda pars borialis ex opposito Ecclesie de Radclyff vsque
Gybtayllour & 60 gressus vltra sepcies .60. gressus

ā

.3.   Tercia pars ab extremitate banci coram arbore vocate
Gybtayllor   sunt   sexies   60   gressus   ad   Portam   de
Baldwynestrete

(268)

ā

jncepcio .prime. partis de le key Bristollie
jncipiendo a porta Baldwynestrete vsque Cornerium capitale
jncepcionis de le Key sunt .90. gressus;

(269)

ā

Memorandum quodᵇ tota longitudo de le key id est a le graunt
Corner place prope jncepcionem de le key ex opposito introitus
Ecclesie parochialis sancti Augustini sunt .quinquies .60.
gressus & .46. gressus

(270)

Item a cornerio jncipiente transcire ad Smalstrete eundo per
Templum & Ecclesiam sancti Egidijᶜ & sancti laurencij ad
portam sancti Johannis sunt .110. gressus
latitudo porte continet ... ᵈ virgas

(271)

Jtem longitudo Ecclesie sancti Johannis cum crippa volte
continet .50. gressus;

(272)

Jtem a porta sancti Johannis per Cristmasstrete vsque
principium porte & pontis de Fromeyate sunt .124. gressus.
Et pons de Fromeyate continet .24. gressus

---

a Items (267)–(285) are written upside-down, with (267) and (268) having
   apparently been added afterwards, squeezed into the available space
b The interlined phrase *tota longitudo de le key id est* should, according to
   its caret mark, precede *quod*, but sense suggests that the caret mark has
   been misplaced and should be after *quod*

p.151

(267)
THE BACK
The south side of the Marsh [is] six times 60 [steps] as far as opposite Redcliffe church.
The second, northern[1] side from opposite Redcliffe church as far as Gib Tailor and 60 steps further [is] seven times 60 steps.
3   The third side from the very end of the bank in front of the timber post called Gib Tailor: there are six times 60 steps to the gate from Baldwin Street.[2]

(268)
The beginning of the first side of The Key of Bristol:
Starting from the Baldwin Street gate,[2] as far as the end corner at the beginning of The Key: there are 90 steps.

(269)
Memorandum, that the whole length of The Key, that is from the great corner place near the beginning of The Key opposite the entrance of the parish church of St Augustine: there are five times 60 steps plus 46 steps.

(270)
Also, beginning from the corner to go along to Small Street, going past the Synagogue and church of St Giles and [that] of St Lawrence to St John's Gate, there are 110 steps.
The width of the gate measures ... yards.

(271)
Also, the length of St John's church, with the vaulted crypt, measures 50 steps.

(272)
Also, from St John's Gate along Christmas Street as far as the beginning of the gate and bridge of Fromegate, there are 124 steps. And the bridge of Fromegate measures 24 steps.

---

1   Error for 'western'; the third side, opposite the first, is the northern side
2   i.e. Marsh Street Gate

---

c   *vsque* deleted
d   Blank in MS

(273)

[a]Jtem a porta Fromeyate[b] per lewenysmede vsque murum cimiterij sancti Jacobi qui est finis eiusdem vici continet occies .60. gressus;

(274)

Jtem vicus vocatus le bake jncipit a fine predicti lewenysmede eundo de fromewater ad[c] dictam portam jntroitus cimiterium sancti Jacobi vbi scita est curta porta[d] vsque portam de Pyttey yate, continet .290. gressus;   Et pons ad ppyttey[e] yate continet .9. virgas

(275)

Jtem a porta vocata pyttey vsque le pylory ascendendo vocatus vicus pyttey vbi profundus fons scituatur, continet ... [f] gressus

(276)

Jtem vicus vocatus Wynchstret a porta newgate vsque Ecclesiam sancte trinitatis[g] continet ... [h] gressus;

(277)

Jtem via de le hygh crosse vsque portam sancti leonardi continet ... [h] gressus

(278)

Jtem via de le hyghcrosse ad portam sancti Johannis continet .290. gressus

(279)

Jtem via de le hygh cros ad portam sancti[i] Nicholai continet .200.[j] gressus

(280)

Memorandum latitudo vici vocati Brodemede continet .30. gressus
longitudo de le Brodemede continet vsque Kyngystrete ad murum fratrum predicatorum .300. gressus;

---

a   *ex* in margin, at worn edge of page, possibly for *extra*
b   *vsque* deleted
c   *ad* (to) inserted with a caret mark which appears to be written over
     original *a* (from), which in fact makes better sense
d   *continet* deleted
e   *sic*
f   Blank in MS
g   *le hygh crosse* is written above *sancte trinitatis*, with no caret mark,
     presumably as an alternative end-point for this measurement
h   Blank in MS

(273)

Also, from the gate of Fromegate along Lewinsmead as far as the wall of St James's churchyard, which is the end of that street, measures eight times 60 steps.

(274)

Also, the street called The Back, beginning from the end of Lewinsmead aforesaid, going along by the river Frome [from?][1] the said entry-gate to St James's churchyard, where the [church]yard gate is situated, [and] as far as the gate of Pithay Gate, measures 290 steps. And the bridge at Pithay Gate measures 9 yards.

(275)

Also, from the gate called Pithay climbing as far as the pillory, the street called Pithay, where the deep well is situated, measures ... steps.

(276)

Also, the street called Wynch Street, from the gate [of] Newgate as far as Holy Trinity church, measures ... steps.

(277)

Also, the road from the High Cross as far as St Leonard's Gate measures ... steps.

(278)

Also, the road from the High Cross to St John's Gate measures 290 steps.

(279)

Also, the road from the High Cross to St Nicholas's Gate measures 200 steps.

(280)

Memorandum, the width of the street called Broadmead measures 30 steps.
The length of the Broadmead measures 300 steps as far as King Street, to the wall of the Friars Preachers.

---

1   See note c, opposite

---

i   *leonardi continet* deleted
j   Worcestre originally wrote *.164.*, deleted it, wrote *.200.* above the line, then (without deleting *.200.*) *.164.* again, deleted that, and rewrote *200.* There are thus two *.164.*, both deleted, and two *.200.*, which figure is presumably his final version

(281)

longitudo Chori Ecclesie fratrum predicatorum continet .26. virgas[a] vel .44. gressus.

latitudo chori continet .8. virgas. vel .14. gressus

longitudo navis Ecclesie continet .31.[b] virgas vel .58. gressus

latitudo eiusdem continet .21. virgas vel .34. gressus.

(282)

ā[c]

Mauricius[d] Berkley chevalier dominus Castri de Beverstone obijt .5. die Maij post annum christi .1456.

(283)

longitudo Ecclesie navis fratrum[e] augustini continet .30. virgas[f] vel .54. gressus

.b.[g]

longitudo Chori Ecclesie Fratrum augustini idem viz chorus continet .30.[h] virgas; & eius.[i]

latitudo eius continet .9. virgas vel .16. gressus

longitudo[j] Chapiterhous .24. virge vel ... [k]

latitudo eius .8. virge,

longitudo Claustri continet .30 virgas latitudo eius continet .3. virgas,

latitudo Campanile .5. virge

(284)

1320.[l]

pridie jdus Jullij consecratus est locus fratrum heremitarum ordinis sancti Augustini

.a.[m]

longitudo navis Ecclesie fratrum heremitarum sancti Augustini. continet .30. virgas vel .60. gressus.

latitudo eius continet[n] .15. virgas

Est in Ecclesia vna navis & vna tantum ala. que ala continet ...[o]

---

a   *1* (possibly beginning *latitudo*?) deleted

b   *.31.* repeated above

c   Perhaps indicating a cross-reference to **(286)**

d   *Mauricius* underlined, probably by Talbot

e   *predicatorum* deleted

f   *.30.* repeated and *1* (possibly beginning *latitudo*?) deleted

g   A cross-reference to the measurements noted under .a. in **(284)**

h   *.30.* written again more clearly above

i   *sic*

j   *Claustri* deleted

(281)
The length of the quire of the church of the Friars Preachers measures 26 yards or 44 steps.
The width of the quire measures 8 yards or 14 steps.
The length of the nave of the church measures 31 yards or 58 steps.
Its width measures 21 yards or 34 steps.

(282)
Sir Maurice Berkeley, lord of Beverstone Castle, died 5th day of May in the year after Christ 1456.[1]

(283)
The length of the nave of the church of the Augustinian Friars measures 30 yards or 54 steps.
(b)
The length of the quire of the same church of the Augustinian Friars: to wit the quire measures 30 yards, and its[2]
Its width measures 9 yards or 16 steps.
The length of the chapter house: 24 yards or ...
Its width: 8 yards.
The length of the cloister measures 30 yards; its width measures 3 yards.
The width of the bell-tower: 5 yards.

(284)
1320.
On the day before the Ides of July,[3] the site of the Hermit Friars of the Order of St Augustine was consecrated.
(a)
The length of the nave of the church of the Hermit Friars of St Augustine measures 30 yards or 60 steps.
Its width measures 15 yards.

There is in the church one nave, and one aisle of the same size, which aisle measures ...

---

1   cf. **(286)**
2   *sic*, note breaks off
3   14th July 1320

---

k   Blank in MS
l   Written in margin, smudged and repeated
m   A cross-reference to .b. in **(283)**
n   Number, possibly *.60.*, deleted
o   Blank in MS

(285)[a]

Contra tussim.

j. handfull   di. handful   j. qrt. handfull

R[ecipe] yosopam. hoorhound. & origanum commune et coque in aqua fontena & cola extra pergaminum & tunc pone magnam quantitatem liquiricie munde puluerizate proiice &[b] & reserua & bibe mane et sero;

p.152

(286)[c]

Jn martilagio kalendarij fratrum predicatorum Bristollie,[d]

Johannes Vielle armiger primus vicicomes Bristollie obijt 29 die Marcij

Walterus Frampton obijt die .2.[do] Januarij

Willelmus Curteys qui fecit fieri magnam crucem in cimiterio die .2.[do] Aprilis

Ricardus Spicer mercator obijt primo die Junij

Henricus Rex tercius obijt .4. die Junij

Edwardus primogenitus Edwardi tercij obijt .7. die Junij

Edwardus Rex tercius obijt .23. die Junij

Edwardus Rex .2.[us] de Kaernarvan obijt die .2.[do] Augusti

Matheus de Gurnay obijt 28. die Augusti vnius[e] fundatorum fratris predicatorum

domina Matilda denys qui obijt die … [f] octobris anno christi .1422.

dominus Mauricius de Berkle & domina Johanna vxor eius qui iacet in choro in sinistra altaris die primo octobris

dominus Willelmus dawbeney miles qui iacet in choro

Cor domini Roberti de Gornay iacet in ista Ecclesia qui obijt die .20.º nouembris

dominus Ancelmus de Gurnay qui iacet in choro. die .15. nouembris

dominus Mauricius Berkley Miles obijt .26. die nouembris

---

a   Item **(285)** was included in Harvey, *Itineraries,* pp. 368-9, with some variations in transcription and translation.

b   A false start to *reserua,* deleted

c   Item **(286)** was included in Harvey, *Itineraries,* pp. 320-1, with some variations in transcription and translation

d   Added by Worcestre in different ink, at the same time as *Explicit* below, and the heading *DE PONTE BRISTOLLIE* of item **(287)**

e   *sic*

f   Blank in MS; the date of the next entry suggests that this one must be 1st October, as the martyrology should be in date order

(285)
Against a cough.
Recipe: hyssop (1 handful), horehound (½ handful), and common marjoram (¼ handful), and cook in spring water and strain through parchment, and then put in a large quantity of finely powdered liquorice; stir up, and store, and drink morning and evening.

p.152

(286)
In the obit book of the calendar of the Friars Preachers of Bristol.

John Vyell esquire, first Sheriff of Bristol, died 29th day of March.[1]
Walter Frampton died 2nd day of January.[2]
William Curteys, who had the great cross in the churchyard made: the 2nd day of April.
Richard Spicer, merchant, died the first day of June.
King Henry III died 4th day of June.[3]
Edward the firstborn son of Edward III died 7th day of June.[4]
King Edward III died 23rd day of June.[5]
King Edward II of Caernarvon died 2nd day of August.[6]
Matthew de Gurney, one of the founders of the Friars Preachers, died 28th day of August
Dame Matilda Denys, who died [1st?] day of October in the year of Christ 1422.
Sir Maurice de Berkeley and Dame Joan his wife, who lie in the quire on the left of the altar: first day of October.
Sir William Daubeny, knight, who lies in the quire.
The heart of Sir Robert de Gurney, who died 20th day of November, lies in this church.
Sir Anselm de Gurney, who lies in the quire: 15th day of November.
Sir Maurice Berkeley, knight, died 26th day of November.

---

1 John Vyell was Sheriff 1372-3 and 1373-4. Bristol was made a county on 8th August 1373. He died in 1399 (Wadley, *Bristol Wills*, p. 57)
2 Walter Frampton senior died 2nd January 1388/9 (Wadley, *Bristol Wills*, pp. 19-21)
3 In fact 16th November 1272. Harvey, *Itineraries*, p. 321, observed that no reason can be given for all the errors in the dates of death as listed. The incorrect dates are in sequence, but the correct dates are not, so the faults were in the obit book, not in Worcestre's copying of it
4 In fact 8th July 1376
5 In fact 21st June 1377
6 In fact, officially, 21st September 1327

(286) [continued]
.1429.
Frater Willelmus Bothoner obijt die .15. decembris a[nno]
Edwardus primus Rex Anglie obijt die .17. decembris
Explicit,

(287)
.1361.
DE PONTE BRISTOLLIE
Dedicacio capelle pontis Bristollie. die .4.to Februaris
longitudo capelle .25. virge
latitudo capelle .7. virgea
altitudo capelle .50. gradus computatur super quatuor Stages
Et est voltab jn jnferiori loco pro aldermannis ville continet
tantam longitudinem sicut Ecclesie cum navi
Et .4. fenestre magne quolibet latere & quelibet fenestra habet
.3. luces;
Et alta fenestra in orientali parte altaris continet ... c
Et aliud parum altare cum parua capella in orientaliori
principalis altaris, circa longitudinem .3. virgarum
Etd capella continet 1 voltam. 2 Capellam. ac 3 aulam. cum
officijs.e .4. altam cameram. ac .5. altiorem cameram, de
lapidibus,

(288)
Via Seynt Nicholasstrete de porta sancti Nicholai vsque ad
principium porte sancti Nicholaif continetg sexies .60.ta & 30
gressus;

(289)
LONGITUDO ECCLESIE SANCTI STEPHANI
Ecclesia sancti Stephani continet in longitudine .30.h virgas
latitudo eius continet .19. virgas,
altitudo eius continet .44. pedes.   Et continet .7. archus in
qualibet latere
Et continet .7. fenestras. et in qualibet latere & qualibet
fenestra continet .4. dayesi

---

a   .7. *virge* repeated
b   *des* (perhaps for *desuper*?) deleted
c   Blank in MS
d   Insertion, possibly *s...*, deleted and illegible
e   *1, 2, 3, .4., .5.* are written over the words which follow them
f   *sic*, error for St Leonard's Gate
g   *quinquies* deleted and *sexies* written twice above
h   *vir* (for *virgas*) smudged and deleted
i   Between the two parts of **(289)** is jotted: *philosophia / philosophia
    secundum platone est tedium & cura & studium et solicitudo mortis*
    (Philosophy: philosophy according to Plato is painstaking labour,
    [continued opposite]

(286) [continued]
1429.
Brother William Botoner died 15th day of December [that] year.
Edward I, King of England, died 17th day of December.[1]
The End.

(287)
1361/2
OF BRISTOL BRIDGE
Dedication of Bristol Bridge chapel: 4th day of February.
Length of the chapel: 25 yards.
Width of the chapel: 7 yards.
Height of the chapel: 50 stairs,[2] counted up four floors.
And there is a crypt on the lowest level, for the aldermen of the town; it measures the same length as the nave of the church.
And 4 great windows each side, and each window has 3 lights.
And the high window on the east side of the altar measures ...
And another small altar with a small chapel, further east of the main altar, about 3 yards long.
And the chapel comprises: (1) crypt; (2) chapel and (3) hall with offices; (4) upper room; and (5) topmost room, [all] of stone.

(288)
The road of St Nicholas Street, from St Nicholas's Gate as far as to the beginning of St Nicholas's Gate,[3] measures six times 60 plus 30 steps.

(289)
THE LENGTH OF ST STEPHEN'S CHURCH
St Stephen's church measures 30 yards in length.
Its width measures 19 yards.
Its height measures 44 feet; and it has 7 arches on each side.
And it contains 7 windows on each side, and each window contains 4 lights.

---

1 In fact 7th July 1307
2 vertical measurement in *gradus* (step of a stair), presumably reckoned up the actual staircase to the top of the building
3 Error for St Leonard's Gate

---

i [continued] attention to detail, application, and awareness of death); *secundum platone* is repeated above the line. This is probably derived from Plato, *Phædo* 67D,E; 80E and 81A. I am indebted to the Revd. Peter H. Thorburn for help in this identification

(289) [continued]
TURRIS SANCTI STEPHANI
longitudo partis occidentalis turris sancti Stephani exterius cum
lez boterasses triangularis. continet .9. virgas

p.153

(290)
ā
Memorandum   quod   kyngystrete   a   Monkynbrygge.   et
Erlesmede[a]
[b]in ista pagena .tres .3. articulos scripturorum[c] scrib[untur?]
legitando[d]
      In meridionali parte Ecclesie cimiterij sancti Jacobi
Kyngystrete qui continet .1000. gressus;[e] ad Erlesmede

KYNGYS STRETE,
longitudo vie a Monkynbrygge ex parte occidentali. eundo
versus orientem meridionalis cimiterij sancti Jacobi[f] dimitendo
per kyngystrete de cruce pontis cimiterij sancti Jacobi inter
angulum domus pandoxatorij. Pownam &[f] continuando ad
valuam[g] orientalem versus lez barres,[h] ad angulum tenementi
patris mee vbi mulieres meretrices manebant vocatum lez
barres, continet[i] 200. gressus
latitudo dicte vie, continet ... [j]
Et sic continuando viam de Kyngystrete ad pratum vocatum
Erles medew. ad vnam altam petram de Frestone scitam apud
fontem   clausum   de   Frestone   quadrate   vocatum
Beggerwell . . . . [k]

---

a   Worcestre originally wrote *Erlesmedew*, adding *mede* above
b   *cont* (probably for *continet*) deleted
c   The three items in order, with linking symbols, are
            (i)   the rest of **(290)**, ending with . . . .
            (ii) **(300)**, beginning with . . . . and ending with ∵
            (iii) **(295)**, beginning with ∵
d   *in ista pagena* ... *legitando* has been interpolated as an afterthought, and
    is cramped and confused with the line below
e   The 1000 steps are presumably made up of **(290)**: 200 steps, **(300)**:120
    steps, and **(295)**: 666 steps, totalling 986 steps

(289) [continued]
THE TOWER OF ST STEPHEN'S
The length of the west side of the tower of St Stephen's, outside, together with the triangular buttresses, measures 9 yards.

p.153

(290)
Memorandum, that King Street from Monkenbridge, and Earlsmead.
On this page: three (3) items of writing are noted down for checking.
On the south side of the burial ground of St James's church:
King Street, which measures 1000 steps to Earlsmead.

KING STREET
The length of the road from Monkenbridge on the west side, going eastwards, south of St James's churchyard, going along King Street from the cross of the bridge of St James's churchyard [set] into the corner of the house of Pownam the brewer; and going along to the east door towards the Bars, to the corner of my father's house where the wanton women live, called The Bars, measures 200 steps.
The width of the said road measures ...
And so going on along the road of King Street to the meadow called Earlsmead, to a tall stone of freestone standing at the well-head of square freestone called Beggarwell . . . . [1]

---

1 Worcestre's dots link to **(300)**; cf. notes c opposite and k below

f *ad* deleted
g *boria* deleted
h *200 gressus.* deleted, but then *stet* written above. This total is repeated at the end of the sentence, as shown
i *continet* repeated
j Blank in MS
k A row of 4 dots above *Beggerwell* link it to the beginning of **(300)**; cf. note c opposite

(291)
PARUA BAKK
Via coram aquam frome. vbi domus elemosiarij[a] scita est,[b] de
fundatione Margarete de Chedder tenementi Sopemaker.[c]
returnando de angulo Brodemede ad principium vie returnando
ad principium de le Slepe ex opposito hostij de le sopemaker.
continet 50. gressus

(292)
Via returnacionis ad le Pyttey yate alias alderych yate[d] per
pontem. continet .50. gressus

(293)
PYTTEY
TOURYATE[e]
Via de Pyttey yate per le welle vsque ad antiquam portam
Tourstrete walle[f] altiorem partem de montis de pyttey continet
.130. gressus intrando viam de Tourestrete versus cimiterium
sancti Johannis baptiste, coram portam antiquissimam.[g]

---

(294)
SEYNT THOMAS STRETE
Via vocata Seynt Thomas strete vsque murum de le tounewalle
versus portam de templestrete seu Radclyffstrete continet .424.
gressus a domo sororis mee sed a ponte [totidem?][h]

---

(295)
∴ ERLESMEDE[i]
latitudo de Erlesmede de Beggherswelle vsque aquam de Frome
& eundo versus castrum Bristollie & le wateryngplace vocat le
weere. continet .224. gressus,
longitudo vie de Erlysmede eundo per Fromewater ad angulum
muri Castri vocati le were[j] ad ponte. continet .666. gressus[k] in
parte meridionali

---

a   *sic*
b   *Vis* deleted
c   *de fundatione Margarete de Chedder tenementi Sopemaker* written mostly
    in the margin. The whole item contains many amendments and additions
d   *alias alderych yate* has been added subsequently in different ink
e   The heading *TOURYATE* has been added likewise
f   Originally read *... vsque altiorem partem ...*, but *ad antiquam portam
    Tourstrete walle* has been inserted likewise above the line
g   *coram portam antiquissimam* has been added likewise
h   Uncertain reading of an illegible word

(291)
LITTLE BACK
The road alongside the river Frome, where the almshouse is situated, of the foundation of Margaret de Cheddre, at the soapmaker's house: turning off from the corner of Broadmead to the beginning of the road turning off at the beginning of the slip, opposite the soapmaker's door, measures 50 steps.

(292)
The road turning to the Pithay Gate otherwise Aldrich Gate over the bridge measures 50 steps.

(293)
PITHAY
TOWER GATE
The road from Pithay Gate, past the well, as far as to the old gate of Tower Street wall at the upper end of Pithay Hill, going into the road of Tower Street, towards St John Baptist's churchyard, in front of the most ancient gateway, measures 130 steps.

---

(294)
ST THOMAS STREET
The road called St Thomas Street, as far as the wall of the town wall, in the direction of the gate[s] of Temple Street or Redcliffe Street, measures 424 steps from my sister's house, [and as much again?][1] from the bridge.

---

(295)
∴ EARLSMEAD[2]
The width of Earlsmead from Beggarswell as far as the river Frome, and going towards Bristol Castle and the watering-place called The Weir, measures 224 steps.
The length of the road from Earlsmead going by the river Frome to the corner of the castle wall called The Weir, and the bridge, measures 666 steps on the south side.

---

1   Uncertain reading
2   Worcestre's link symbol ∴ : see note i below

---

i   Worcestre's symbol ∴ links this item to the end of **(300)**: cf. **(290)** note c. Item **(295)** has been fitted afterwards into the space between **(294)** and **(296)**; hence the need to note scattered but related items
j   *weere* repeated
k   *666. gressus* repeated

(296)

Jn Castelstrete alias seynt petyrstrete[a]

.b.[b]

[c]Via defensiua deffendstrete[d] videlicet a Castellstrete veniente de Newyate vsque secundam venellam directe intrante in dictam viam a vico vocato seynt petyrstrete coram fonte nouo de Frestone nouiter erecto & fundato de bonis Willelmi Canyngys[e] ex transverso dictam viam intrantem & deffendentem magnum murum[f] inter Castell[g] ville Bristollie quem quidem murum adherebat[h] prope Murum deffensorum ville predicte,

(297)

a[i]

Venella prima proxima scituata post jntroitum de Newgate per viam de Castelstrete alias dictam[j] seynt peter strete ex parte boriali opposita Ecclesie parochialis sancti petri. vbi … [k] Olyuer[l] jurus peritus Reccordator Bristollie manebat, continet .circa .60. gressus

(298)

.c.[m]

SHAMELYS

Via vocata Worshypstrete aliter vocata[n] le Shamells alias dicta le Bochery ab antiquo vocabatur Worshypstrete. eo quod fuit vicus honoris. propter mercandisas lanarum veniencium et ad portum navium oneratarum,[o]

(299)

Via vocata defenciffestrete .continet in longitudine; …
latitudine …

---

a Heading added in different ink
b cf. *a* in **(297)** and *.c.* in **(298)**; this is the second of the three lanes leading off St Peter's Street
c *De Wynch strete eundo* deleted
d Worcestre first wrote *Defenstrete*, deleted it, then wrote *deffendstrete* above in the same ink as the heading
e *Willelmi Canyngys* underlined, probably by Talbot
f *tocius* deleted
g Worcestre originally wrote *tocius ville Bristollie*, then, realising the distinction between town and castle defences, deleted *tocius* and inserted *inter Castell*, but failed to add the *et* which is needed to make sense
h Poorly written, deleted and rewritten above
i cf. *.b.* in **(296)** and *.c.* in **(298)**

(296)
In Castle Street, otherwise St Peter Street.
(b)
The defensive road (Defence Street), to wit from Castle Street, coming from Newgate as far as the second lane running straight into the said road, to the street called St Peter Street, in front of the new well of freestone, newly set up and built out of the estate of William Canynges, at the crossing of the said road entering and defending the great wall between the Castle [and] the town of Bristol, which same wall clung closely to the defensive wall of the aforesaid town.

(297)
(a)
The first lane situated close after the entry from Newgate along the road of Castle Street, otherwise called St Peter Street, on the north side, opposite the parish church of St Peter, where ... Oliver, the jurist, Recorder of Bristol, dwelt,[1] measures about 60 steps.

(298)
(c)
THE SHAMBLES
The road called Worship Street, otherwise called The Shambles, otherwise termed The Butchery, from ancient times called Worship Street because it was a street of distinction on account of woollen goods arriving, and the lading of ships at the harbour.

(299)
The road called Defence Street measures in length ...
Width ...

---

1   Simon Oliver of the parish of St Peter, Queen's Seneschal, died May 1419 (Wadley, *Bristol Wills*, p. 104).   His house on the corner of St Peter Street and Church or Chequer Lane was mentioned in the will of Walter Seymour in 1410 (ibid. p. 85); see Leech, *Topography*, p. 111

---

j   *Wynchestr* (for *Wynchestrete*) deleted and *seynt peter strete* written above
k   Blank in MS
l   *Recor* (for *Recordator*) deleted
m   cf. *a* in **(297)** and *.b.* in **(296)**
n   *Worshypstrete aliter vocata* has been inserted subsequently above the line in different ink, which accounts for the repetitive phrasing
o   The last part of this item has been marked by Talbot, with § and a vertical wavy line, in the margin

(300)

. . . . [a]

Et sic continuando dictam viam de Kyngstrete a monkynbrygge per cimiterium sancti Jacobi ad angulum Carfox[b] per tenementa anguli patris mei, eundo continue ad pratum vocatum Erlesmedew ad vsque principium dicti prati ad vnam altam petram vnius virge altam ad Beggherswelle scituatam que est vltima libertas Franchesie ville Bristollie ex parte orientali continet in longitudine a dicta via anguli de Barrys .120. gressus. sic via Kyngystret[c] continet a monkerbrygge[d] vsque principium Erlesmedew 1000. gressus.[e] mille; ∴ [f]

p.154

(301)

ECCLESIA FRATRUM YN LEWELYNYSMEDE;

ā

Ecclesia & conuentus fratrum sancti Francisci Bristollie in parochia sancti Jacobi in vico lewenysmede. videlicet

Chorus Ecclesie continet in longitudine .28. virgas siue .50. gressus

latitudo Chori continet .9. virgas siue .18. gressus

longitudo Navis dicte Ecclesie. cum duabus magnis alis. continet .28. virgas siue .50. gressus[g]

latitudo dicte navis cum duobus alis continet .27. virgas siue .52. gressus

latitudo Campanilis turris quadrate continet .4. virgas siue gressus .7. gressus[h]

altitudo dicte turris continet; ... [i]

archus .4. sunt in boriali navis Ecclesie & tot in meridionali

---

(302)

Fromeyate. longitudo duarum portarum apud Fromeyate continet cum distancia duarum pontium ibi arched vt flumen de Frome. cum nauiculis pro bosco oneratis ad manentes super seynt Jamys bake. ac[j] ac lewnysmede[k] Brodemede. & apud Marchallstret[l] ad fratres predicatores per aquam de Frome

---

a　A row of 4 dots link this item with the end of **(290)**
b　Underlined, probably by Talbot
c　*continet* smudged and deleted
d　*sic*
e　Total of 1000 steps: cf. **(290)**
f　Worcestre's ∴ symbol indicates this item should precede **(295)**
g　Blotted *.50 g* above, and *50. gressus* repeated in margin opposite
h　*sic*

(300)

. . . .[1]

And thus going along the said road of King Street from Monkenbridge past St James's churchyard to the corner of the crossroads by the corner house of my father; going on along to the meadow called Earlsmead, as far as the beginning of the said meadow, to a tall stone, one yard high, situated at Beggarswell, which is the furthest liberty of the franchise of the town of Bristol on the east side; it measures in length from the said road at the corner of The Bars, 120 steps. Thus the road of King Street measures from Monkenbridge as far as the beginning of Earlsmead, 1000 (one thousand) steps. ∵ [2]

p.154

(301)

THE CHURCH OF THE FRIARS IN LEWINSMEAD

The church and community of the Franciscan Friars of Bristol, in St James's parish, in the street of Lewinsmead, to wit:

The quire of the church measures 28 yards or 50 steps in length.

The width of the quire measures 9 yards or 18 steps.

The length of the nave of the said church, with two great aisles, measures 28 yards or 50 steps.

The width of the said nave with the two aisles measures 27 yards or 52 steps.

The width of the square bell-tower measures 4 yards or 7 steps.

The height of the said tower measures ...

There are 4 arches on the north of the nave of the church, and as many on the south.

---

(302)

Fromegate: the length of the two gates at Fromegate measures, including the distance of the two arched piers there so that the river Frome [can be navigated] with boats laden with wood to storage areas upon St James Back and Lewinsmead, Broadmead and to the Friars Preachers at Marshal Street; they can carry

---

1 Worcestre's dots link to **(290)**
2 Worcestre's ∵ symbol links to **(295)**

---

i Blank in MS
j *Brodemede* deleted, then *ac* repeated
k *sic*
l *ac* deleted

(302) [continued]
possunt cariare boscum mearemium & alia necessaria. continet
via de Fromeyate .33. gressus
latitudo vie de Fromeyate inter dictas duas portas. continet
...ᵃ

(303)
Venella breuis & parua prope extra portas de dicta Fromeyate
in parte meridionali de horestrete alis dicte horstrete ex
opposito Ecclesie Religionum sancti Bertholomei. ad aquam de
Frome continet .20. gressus

(304)
LE BAKKE AD PEDEM STIPESTRET
locus vacuusᵇ ad proiciendum siue custodiendum boscum pro
igne domiciliorum & alia necessaria vocatus anglice a Bakkeᵇ
coram aquam de Frome continet in longitudine .33. gressus
latitudo dicti vacui spacijᵇ continet circa .20. gressus.

(305)
PORTA SANCTI JOHANNIS BAPTISTE
latitudoᶜ porte sancti Johannis baptiste continet .3. virgas cum
duobus pedibus;
Domus de Frestone in meridionali Ecclesie pro conducto aque
per canales plumbi; continet in longitudine ... ᵈ
latitudo eius continet ... ᵈ

p.155

(306)
Jn vico sancti Nicholai
VENELLE DUE IN BORIALI PARTE VIE SANCTI NICHOLAI
.2. Venelle jn vicoᵉ sancti Nicholai sunt due venelle quarum vna
transetᶠ ad partem orientalem Ecclesie sancte Werburge prope
le graun steyre & continet .120. gressus

Venella alia in eodem vico sancti Nicholai prope ibidem in dicta
parte alterius venelle, & transcit ex opposito directe hostij
Meridionalis Ecclesie sancte Werburge .135. gressus

---

a Blank in MS
b *locus vacuus, anglice a Bakke* and *vacui spacij* have been underlined by
   Talbot, with a line drawn through the whole note to link them, and *a
   back quid* (a back - what?) in the margin
c *Ecclesia de* deleted
d Blank in MS
e Worcestre originally started this sentence *jn vicus sancti Nicholai*,
   deleted *vicus* and wrote *vico* above, then added *.2. Venelle* in front

(302) |continued|
wood, timber and other goods along the river Frome.[1]   The
roadway of Fromegate measures 33 steps.
The width of the road at Fromegate between the said two gates
measures ...

(303)
A short and small lane close outside the gates of the said
Fromegate, on the south side of Horestreet, otherwise called
Horse Street, opposite the church of the community of St
Bartholomew, measures 20 steps to the river Frome.

(304)
THE BACK AT THE FOOT OF STEEP STREET
An open area for piling or storing wood for household fires,
and other goods (called in English 'a Back') alongside the river
Frome, measures 33 steps in length.
The width of the said open space measures about 20 steps.

(305)
ST JOHN THE BAPTIST'S GATE
The width of St John the Baptist's Gate measures 3 yards plus
two feet.

A freestone [conduit] house on the south of the church, for
drawing water through pipes of lead, measures in length ...
Its width measures ...

p.155

(306)
In St Nicholas's Street
TWO LANES ON THE NORTH SIDE OF ST NICHOLAS'S
ROAD
2 lanes: in St Nicholas's Street are two lanes, one of which
(near the great stairs) crosses to the east side of St
Werburgh's church and measures 120 steps.

Another lane in the same St Nicholas's Street [is] nearby, on
the same side as the other lane, and crosses to right opposite
the south door of St Werburgh's church: 135 steps.

---

1   Worcestre lost his way with this note to the extent that the translation
    tries to embody his idea rather than his words

---

f   Worcestre actually wrote *transct*

(307)
ECCLESIA SANCTI LAURENCIJ
Ecclesia sancti laurencij continet in longitudine .28. virgas.
latitudo eius continet .9. virgas;

(308)
GYLHALDA BRISTOLLIE
ā
latitudo Gylhalde[a] Bristollie in vico Bradstrete, continet cum
capella sancti Georgij & cellarijs continet .23. virgas,
longitudo eius continet ... [b]
Capella sancti Georgij continet in longitudine ... [b] virgas
latitudo eius continet ... [b]

(309)
ECCLESIA TEMPLI
Cimiterij amplitudo[c] ex omni parte continet .570. gressus
longitudo templi Ecclesie[d] continet .53. virgas bis[e] per me
numeratas,

(310)
venella jncipiente prope conductum aque de seynt Thomas
strete ad templestrete continet .160. gressus
latitudo venelle continet .3. virgas,

(311)
Ecclesia sancti Thome continet in longitudine .43. virgas
latitudo eius ... [f]

(312)
venella secunda de parte boriali templestrete eundo ad seynt
Thomasstrete continet .160. gressus
latitudo[g] venelle continet .3. virgas

(313)
VICUS SANCTI THOME
vicus sancti Thome intersecans venella[h] predictam[h] continet in
latitudine .14. gressus

(314)
venella alia de seynt Thomasstrete aducens ad Ratclyff strete.
continet longitudo .120. gressus.

---

a   *london* deleted
b   Blank in MS. The space beside and below this item is filled with later
    jottings and pen trials, including some Greek, probably by Aldrich
c   *amplitudo* smudged, deleted and rewritten more clearly
d   *Ecclesie* repeated
e   *comp* (for *computatas?*) deleted

(307)
ST LAWRENCE'S CHURCH
St Lawrence's church measures 28 yards in length.
Its width measures 9 yards.

(308)
THE GUILDHALL OF BRISTOL
The width of the Guildhall of Bristol, in the street of Broad
Street, measures, including the chapel of St George and the
cellars: it measures 23 yards.
Its width measures ...
The chapel of St George measures in length ... yards.
Its width measures ...

(309)
TEMPLE CHURCH
The circumference of the churchyard on all sides measures 570
steps.
The length of Temple church measures 53 yards, twice counted
by me.

(310)
The lane beginning near the water-conduit, from St Thomas
Street to Temple Street, measures 160 steps.
The width of the lane measures 3 yards.

(311)
St Thomas's church measures 43 yards in length.
Its width ...

(312)
The second lane on the north side of Temple Street, going to
St Thomas Street, measures 160 steps.
The width of the lane measures 3 yards.

(313)
ST THOMAS'S STREET
St Thomas's Street, cutting across the aforesaid lane, measures
14 steps in width.

(314)
Another lane leading from St Thomas Street to Redcliffe Street,
measures 120 steps in length.

---

f   Blank in MS
g   *Vie* deleted
h   *sic*

(315)

Vicus Radclyfstrete continet in latitudine contra dictam venellam .14. gressus.

(316)

Venella directe trium venellarum predicte deuencium de Radclyfstrete ex[a] parte boriali ad aquam de Avyn cum le Slepe continet[b] .100. gressus.

p.156

(317)

Jn parochia sancti Nicholai

Venella de vico sancti Nicholai ad Smalstrete[c] eundo .132. gressus

(318)

∵ [d] Pontis longitudine .184. gressus[e] a principio ad finem anguli vie de le bake

(319)

FROMEYATE

Longitudo vie inter duas portas pontium de Fromeyate continet .34. gressus. spacium vie sub qua edificantur duo pontes ... [f]

(320)

MURUS APUD LE KEY

Muri ville longitudo a fine key jncipiendo apud lez couerynges[g] vie de le key vbi murus altus jncepit edificij tenementorum abbatis de Bathe transceundo ad portam Smalstrete continet 40. gressus.   Et a dicta porta Smalstrete vsque portam sancti Johannis. per altum murum templi & Ecclesie sancti Egidij. continet .110. gressus;

(321)

longitudo venelle vie vocate Myghell hille de horsstrete jncipiendo ad ymaginem sancte marie ducendo ad Ecclesiam sancti Michelis in occidentali parte de[h] Stepestrete,[i] eundo per

---

a   *500* (deleted) in margin opposite, with another illegible deletion below.
    The linear total of **(312)–(316)**, however, is only **408** steps.
b   Worcestre first wrote *.106.*, then, without deleting it, *.100.*
c   *Smalstrete* rewritten above more clearly, in different ink
d   Worcestre's ∵ link symbol, although to what is not immediately clear; *q'*
    (for *questio* or *query?*) in margin opposite the beginning of this item
e   *gressus* repeated
f   Blank in MS
g   The last letters *...ges* of *couerynges* smudged and rewritten
h   *lymestrete* deleted

(315)
The street of Redcliffe Street measures in width over against the said lane 14 steps.

(316)
The aforesaid through lane (of the three lanes[1]), continuing from the north side of Redcliffe Street to the river Avon with the Slip, measures 100 steps.

p.156

(317)
In the parish of St Nicholas
The lane going from St Nicholas's Street to Small Street: 132 steps.

(318)
∵ [2] The length of the bridge: 184 steps from the beginning to the end at the corner of the road of The Back.

(319)
FROMEGATE
The length of the road between the two gates of the bridges of Fromegate measures 34 steps.   The area of roadway beneath which the two bridges are built ...

(320)
THE WALL AT THE KEY
The length of the town wall from the end of the Key, beginning at the covered way of the road from The Key, where the high wall of the Abbot of Bath's tenement-buildings begins, going along to the Small Street gate, measures 40 steps.   And from the said Small Street gate as far as St John's Gate, past the high wall of the synagogue and St Giles's church, measures 110 steps.

(321)
The length of the alleyway called Michael Hill, from Horestrete, beginning at the statue of St Mary [and] leading to St Michael's church, on the west side of Steep Street, going past the east

---

1   i.e. **(316)** is the short lane to the slip at Redcliffe Back, a continuation in a straight line of **(312)** and **(314)**, Michel Lane and Ivie Lane.   The first of the 'three lanes' is **(310)**, probably Long Row, which does not continue through to Redcliffe Back
2   Worcestre's ∵ link symbol; see note d opposite

---

i   *Pyle* deleted and *Stepe* inserted above

(321) [continued]
orientalem ortum fratrum Carmelitarum sic continuando ad crucem lapideam cum Fonte[a] lapidis de Frestone continet .170. gressus versus Ecclesiam sancti Michelis non multum a Cimiterio sancti Michelis

(322)
FROGSTRETE
longitudo venelle vocate Frogstrete prope finem venelle vocate Myghellhille jncipiendo ad crucem & fontem jn alciori parte de Stepstrete & eundo versus & a retro Ecclesiam abbathie sancti Augustini & le Gauntes continuando ad finem sanctuarij sancti Augustini eundo ad locum vocatum lymotes continet 840. gressus. ad principium Montis sancti Brendani

(323)
Mons[b] sancti Brandani[c] Ecclesie eiusdem altitudo jncipiendo a principio finis de Froglane.[d] prope quadam Murum in parte dextra sic eundo per dictum Murum & prope ibidem ascendendo semper vsque Capellam sancti Brandani in summitate montis predicte continet in altitudine & longitudine vie continet circa .840. gressus.   Et dicitur ab heremita custode dicte capelle quod altitudo supprema dicte montis[e]

(324)
Capelle longitudo sancti Brandane continet .8. virgas cum dimidio
latitudo eius .5. virgas, continet,[f]
Circuitus muri[g] capelle sancti Brandani continet .180 gressus.

(325)
Altitudo montis[h] Capelle sancti Brandani[i] dicitur vt heremita ibidem michi retulit quod naute & discreti homines dicunt esse alciorem alicuius pinaculi siue Ecclesie de Radclyff quam aliarum Ecclesiarum per spacium altitudinis .18. brachiorum anglice a vathym.[j] et quodlibet brachium continet .6. pedes,

---

a *Fonte* smudged and rewritten more clearly above
b Worcestre originally wrote *montis*, then altered it to *Mons*
c Talbot has written in the margin:
   est alius visus nominis in hibernia. ante fo. 14
   (there is another observation of the name in Ireland, earlier: fo.14).
   This probably refers to **(241)**, also annotated by Talbot, although the page is now numbered 132
d *Froglane* repeated above
e The item breaks off at the end of a line; it continues in **(325)**
f *sic*
g *muri* rewritten more clearly above

(321) [continued]
garden of the Carmelite Friars [and] thus going on to the stone cross, with the well of freestone, measures 170 steps in the direction of St Michael's church, not far from St Michael's churchyard.

(322)
FROG STREET
The length of the lane called Frog Street near the end of the lane called Michael Hill, beginning at the cross and well at the upper end of Steep Street, and going towards and behind the church of St Augustine's abbey and The Gaunts, going on to the boundary of St Augustine's precinct, going to the place called the Bounds, measures 840 steps to the beginning of St Brandon's Hill.

(323)
St Brandon's Hill; the height of its church: beginning first at the end of Frog Lane, next to a certain wall on the right-hand side, and so going along by the said wall and climbing always close by it as far as the chapel of St Brandon on the summit of the aforesaid hill, measures in height and in the length of the road: it measures about 840 steps. And it is said by the hermit, guardian of the said chapel, that the topmost height of the said hill.[1]

(324)
The length of St Brendan's chapel measures 8 yards and a half.
Its width measures 5 yards.
The circumference of the wall of St Brendan's chapel measures 180 steps.

(325)
The height of the hill of St Brendan's chapel is said, as the hermit there told me that sailors and knowledgeable men say, to be higher than any pinnacle, whether of Redcliffe Church or of other churches, by the space of 18 fathoms (in English 'a vathym') in height, and each fathom measures 6 feet. And

---

1   Continued in **(325)**.   See note e opposite

---

h   *montis* inserted above the line with a caret mark first placed after
      Capelle, but deleted and another put after *Altitudo*: i.e. Worcestre is
      describing the height of the hill, not of the chapel building
i   *siue montis sancti* deleted, presumably as a result of the amendments
      above, note h
j   *a vathym* is underlined, probably by Talbot

(325) [continued]
Et nota quod Turris & spera siue pinaculum. cum turri quadrato Ecclesie[a] beate Marie de Radclyffe continet in[b] altitudine videlicet Turris ... [c] pedes et spera pinaculi integri continebat ... [c] pedes. sic summa tocius altitudinis tam Turris quam spere continet in toto ... [c] pedes,

(326)
Venella tercia super Myghell hylle citra Ecclesiam sancti Michelis. crucem lapideam. & Fontem de Stepestrete viz occidentaliorem fontem duarum Fontium de petra circumgirata qui[d]

p.157

(327)
            Ecclesia canonicorum sancti Augustini
dominus Ricardus Newton Craddok[e] Miles justiciarius de communi banco & Miles obijt anno christi .1444. die sancte lucie, .13. die decembris[f]

CHORUS SANCTI AUGUSTINI BRISTOLLIE
Capella sancte marie jn longitudine continet .13.[g] virgas
latitudo eius continet .9. virgas & dimidium
Spacium siue via[h] processionum a retro altaris principalis coram capellam sancte marie continet .5. virgas,[i]
Chori longitudo de le Reredos principalis altaris vsque ad finem chori continet .29. virgas jncipiendo a fine predicti spacij.
latitudo. tam navis chori quam duarum Elarum chori continet .24. virgas
Capella decens edificata. in boriali parte Ele chori continet in longitudine ... [j] virgas
latitudo eiusdem capelle continet, ... [j]

---

a   *templi* deleted
b   *alti* (for *altitudine*) at end of line with insufficient space, and rewritten without deletion
c   Blank in MS
d   Note breaks off
e   *just* (for *justiciarius*) deleted
f   These opening lines of **(327)** were included in Harvey, *Itineraries*, pp. 320-321, with some variations in transcription and translation. They, with the heading, appear to have been added after the rest was written
g   *gr* (for *gressus?*) deleted

(325) [continued]
note that the tower and spire or pinnacle, with the square tower of the church of St Mary Redcliffe, measure in height, to wit the tower ... feet, and the spire [and] pinnacle together measured ... feet, so the sum total of the height of both tower and spire measures in all ... feet.

(326)
A third lane[1] above Michael Hill this side of St Michael's church, the stone cross and the well of Steep Street, to wit the more western well of the two wells surrounded by stone, which[2]

p.157

(327)
The church of the Canons of St Augustine.
Sir Richard Newton Craddock,[3] knight, Justice of the Common Bench, and knight, died in the year of Christ 1444, on St Lucy's day, 13th day of December.

THE QUIRE OF ST AUGUSTINE'S, BRISTOL
The Lady chapel measures 13 yards in length.
Its width measures 9½ yards.
The space or processional way behind the high altar, in front of the Lady chapel, measures 5 yards.
The length of the quire, from the reredos of the high altar as far as the end of the quire, beginning at the end of the aforesaid space, measures 29 yards.
The width of the central quire together with the two quire aisles measures 24 yards.
A fine chapel built on the north side of the quire aisle measures ... yards in length.
The width of that chapel measures ...

---

1 The first two lanes being **(321)** and **(322)**
2 Note breaks off
3 Harvey notes (p.321) that Sir Richard Newton became Justice of Common Pleas in 1439 and Chief Justice in 1440/41; he died in fact in 1448 and has an effigy in Yatton church; father of Sir John Newton: see **(157)**, **(339)**

---

h *via* rewritten more clearly above
i *.5. virge* rewritten more clearly in margin alongside
j Blank in MS

(328)

FROGLANE [?VERE VT PERFECITUR EXAMINATA?][a]

Via vocata <u>Froglane</u> cuius principium est in parte boriali
Ecclesie[b] Religionum de Gauntes ad finem de le seyntuarye[b] in
parte[c] occidentali & boriali[d] dicti sanctuarij sancti Augustini
ordinis. et sic continuando dictam viam per posteriorem viam
gardinorum de Gauntes. & per Murum occidentalis Ecclesie
fratrum Carmelitarum[e] sic continuando vsque ad crucem &
fontem de superiori vico vocato pylestrete ex opposito Ecclesie
sancti Michelis super montem vbi tres vie concurrunt & obuiant
videlicet via Stepstrete.[f] eundo ad horsstrete, alia via in parte
occidentali eundo ad Gistonclyff Tercia via eundo ad Ecclesiam
Collegij de Westberye Et alia via versus orientem ad venellam
longam sancti Jacobi
continet in[g] longitudine .720. gressus

(329)

Via vocata <u>Stanley</u> jncipiente ex opposito crucis & fonte alcioris
Monticule[h] de Stipestrete. transceundo vsque ad Gyston clyff.
per villam de Clyffton. continet in longitudine. eundo per
montem altissimum Capelle de Brandonhille[i] dimittendo
capellam in dextra manu continet ... [j] gressus[k]

(330)

Via vocata seynt Myghelle hylle versus[l] Ecclesiam Religii
Religionum[m] nouitarum de sancta maria Magdalena aceciam ad
Ecclesiam & turrim sancti Michelis & similiter ad petram de
Frestone prope locum justitie vocate anglice lez Fourches siue
Galowes & sic transceundo Cathedralem[n] Ecclesiam de
Westbery.[o] continet in longitudine ad montem Ecclesie Michelis
& Ecclesiam Religiósarum mulierum sancti Magdalene ... [p]
gressus

(331)

Venella siue via de <u>le stipestrete</u> ad crucem & Fontem
Stypestrete[q] retornando ad horstrete ad ymaginem beate marie
continet .120. gressus,

---

a Very uncertain reading of an illegible marginal heading
b *de* deleted
c *occita* (mis-spelling *occidentali*) deleted
d *dt* (mis-spelling *dicti*) deleted
e *sci* (mis-spelling *sic*) deleted
f *vis se* (perhaps for *secunda*) deleted
g *loni* (mis-spelling *longitudine*) deleted
h *Monticule* lit. of the molehill
i *de Brandonhille* underlined, probably by Talbot
j Blank in MS
k *Gressus* repeated
l *Myghelle hylle versus* underlined, probably by Talbot

(328)

FROG LANE [?AS FULLY EXAMINED AS CAN BE MANAGED?][1]

The road called Frog Lane, the beginning of which is on the north side of the Church of the community of The Gaunts at the edge of the precinct, on the northwest side of the said precinct of the order of St Augustine; and thus going along the said road past the back road of The Gaunts' gardens, and past the west wall of the church of the Carmelite Friars; thus going along as far as the cross and well of the upper street called Pyle Street, opposite St Michael's church upon the hill, where three roads meet and come together: to wit, the Steep Street road going to Horestreet; another road on the west side going to Ghyston Cliff; a third road going to the church of the College of Westbury. And another road to the east, to the long lane of St James's.

It measures 720 steps in length.

(329)

The road called Stanley, beginning opposite the cross and well of the upper hillock of Steep Street, going along as far as Ghyston Cliff through the village of Clifton, measures in length going past the very high hill of Brandon Hill chapel, leaving the chapel on the right hand: it measures ... steps.

(330)

The road called St Michael's Hill, in the direction of the church of the nuns of the community of novitiates of St Mary Magdalene, and also to the church and tower of St Michael's, and likewise to the stone of freestone near the place of execution (called in English the gibbet or 'gallows') and thus going on to the cathedral[2] church of Westbury, measures in length to the hill of [St] Michael's church and the church of the nuns of St Magdalene ... steps.

(331)

The lane or road of Steep Street, to the Steep Street cross and well, turning off to Horestreet, at the statue of the blessed Mary, measures 120 steps.

---

1 Very uncertain reading: see note a opposite
2 Error for 'Collegiate'

---

m   *M* (for *Maria*?) deleted
n   *sic*, error for *Collegium*
o   *Cathedralem Ecclesiam de Westbery* underlined, probably by Talbot
p   Blank in MS
q   *ad* deleted

p.158

(332)
Crux magnifica apud hyghstrete, vel vocata le hyghcrosse
in ... [a] continet .2. virgas vel .6. gressus

(333)
GYLDHALLE
latitudo domus officij justitie vocate Gylhalda Bristollie
continet. per viam de Bradstrete, 33. gressus siue .23.
virgas.

(334)[b]
Vicus latitudo de Radclyffstrete jncipiente ad pontem Bristollie
continet in principio dicte vie 4. virgas siue .7.[c] gressus; Sed
ampliat versus Ecclesiam de Radclyff ita quod ante venellam
proximam in boriali parte Ecclesie sancti Thome latitudo dicte
vie continet .12. gressus

latitudo de[d] venelle predicte ex parte boriali Ecclesie sancti
Thome. continet .2. virgas

(335)
Turris quadratus Ecclesie de Radclyff continet in altitudine
.108. pedes altitudinis Et spera ... [e]

maxima Campana de Radclyff continet in pondere de lyggeyng
wyght .7000. 70024. septem milia 24[ll]
Secunda campana fere .v. milia[ll] vel iiij milia & ... [e]
Tercia campana continet xxxiij[C] [ll] lvij[li]
Quarta campana continet ponderat[f] M[l]M[l].ij[C] [ll]
Quinta Campana minor. continet. xv[C]. [li] .lxx.[li]
Sexta minima campana continet .M[l] iij[C]. [ll].[g]

(336)
Turris sancti Stephani continet in altitudine .120. pedes
Et habet 163. gradus idest anglice stappys, et quilibet gradus
continet .8. pedes[h]

---

a   Blank in MS
b   Marginal heading GYLDHALL, presumably misplaced from **(333)**, deleted
c   The figure 7 has been written over 8, with q' (for *questio* or *query*?) in
    the margin opposite, presumably before the figures were noted
d   Worcestre in fact wrote only *d*, above the line, presumably for *de*
e   Blank in MS
f   *sic*
g   Talbot has drawn a vertical line beside this item, with a note: *whatt
    was the weyght off owr cloccher belles then*, i.e. at Norwich

p.158

(332)

    The splendid cross at High Street, otherwise called
the High Cross in ... measures 2 yards or 6 steps.[1]

(333)
THE GUILDHALL
The width of the public courthouse called the Guildhall of
Bristol, measures 33 steps or 23 yards along the road of
Broad Street.

(334)
The width of the street of Redcliffe Street, starting at Bristol
Bridge, measures 4 yards or 7 steps at the beginning of the
said road; but it widens out towards Redcliffe church, so that
in front of the lane next to the north side of St Thomas's
church the said road measures 12 steps.

The width of the aforesaid lane on the north side of St
Thomas's church measures 2 yards.

(335)
The square tower of Redcliffe church measures 108 feet in
height; and the spire ...

The biggest bell of Redcliffe weighs, in hanging weight,[2]
    7024 lbs.
The second bell: about 5,000 lbs., or 4000 and ...
The third bell weighs 3357 lbs.
The fourth bell weighs 2200 lbs.
The fifth, smaller bell weighs 1570 lbs.
The sixth, smallest bell weighs 1300 lbs.

(336)
The tower of St Stephen's measures 120 feet in height.
And it has 163 stairs (that is, in English, 'steps'), and each
stair measures 8 feet.[3]

---

1   Either *gressus* is an error for *pedes* (a 12 inch foot), or Worcestre's
     measurement is wrong
2   This curious term, presumably gleaned from the bell-master or John
     Norton the master mason, cf. **(337)** and **(228)**, perhaps means that the
     bells were, unusually, weighed with their headstocks in place
3   Error for 'inches': cf. **(207)**

---

h   *sic*, error for *pollices*; cf. **(207)**

(337)

ā

Turris altitudo Ecclesie de Radclyff continet ... [a]

ā

Spere altitudo. vt isto die stat quamuis defalcatur ex fortuna procelle & fulminis .200. pedes ∵[b] per relacionem .n. norton magistri Ecclesie de Radclyff,
Memorandum de le[c] Severee duorum fenestrarum vnius ex opposito alterius. inter duos[d] columpna. continet et apud Ecclesiam Radclyff continet .22. pedes et in longitudine .16. pedes,

(338)

Turris & spera. siue le broche. Ecclesie Carmelitarum de fratribus Carmelitarum Bristollie continet altitudine 200. pedes latitudo dicte turris continebat nisi .9. pedes ex omni parte densitudo Murorum turris continet nisi duas pedes

p.159

(339)[e]

Istas notulas scripsi Bristollie mense Septembris in anno christi .1480. de libro papiri magne voluminis cronicorum cuiusdem presbiteri Johannis Burton de Ecclesia sancti Thome Bristollie,

Secundum diuersitatem celi & facies hominum & colores, corporis qualitates & animarum diuersitates existunt et hinc Romanos graues. Gayos.[f] leues. Affros versipelles
Gallos natura feroces & acriores ingenio;

Videmus[g] quod natura Climatum facit non necessitate sed quadam inclinacione vel disposicione &c

Item Jeronimus super[h] ysaiam dicit quod[i] omnes historie referunt Romanorum & Judeorum gentes nil fuisse auarius

---

a   Blank in MS
b   This note continues in the margin, linked by Worcestre's ∵ symbol
c   *Severyng* deleted
d   Worcestre originally wrote *duos*, and appears to have deleted the *s*
e   Item **(339)** was included in Harvey, *Itineraries*, pp. 322-5, with variations in transcription and translation. The heading appears to have been added afterwards
f   *Gayos* underlined, with *pro Grecos* added in the margin, by Talbot

(337)
The height of the tower of Redcliffe church measures ...

The height of the spire, as it stands today, as it was thrown down by chance of a storm and lightning: 200 feet, according to – Norton,[1] Master [mason] of Redcliffe church.
Note, that the bay between two windows at Redcliffe church, one opposite the other, [and] between two pillars, measures 22 feet, and in length 16 feet.

(338)
The tower and spire or steeple of the Carmelites' church, of the Carmelite friars of Bristol, measures 200 feet in height.
The width of the said tower measures scarcely 9 feet on each side.
The thickness of the tower wall measures scarcely two feet.

p.159

(339)
These notes I wrote at Bristol in the month of September, in the year of Christ 1480, from a paper book, a great volume of chronicles of a certain priest, John Burton, of the church of St Thomas at Bristol.[2]

According to the variation of climate, there arise variations in both the features of men and the colour and characteristics of their bodies and spirits; and hence we see the Romans serious, the Greeks inconstant, the Africans crafty, the Gauls fierce by nature and sharper in disposition.

We see that the nature of the climate acts not by compulsion but by a certain inclination or disposition, etc.

Also Jerome upon Isaiah says that all histories relate of the Roman and Jewish peoples [that] none have been more greedy.

---

1   John Norton, freemason: cf. **(228)**
2   Worcestre makes another brief reference to Burton's 'book of ancient chronicles' in **(416)**

---

g   *Videmus* on it own on the line above, appears to be a false start
h   *ysaam* deleted
i   *quod* repeated

(339) [continued]
Item nota quod eleccio anime multum jnclinatur ex complexione corporis vnde medici indicant aliquem esse jucundum tristem vel lassiuum vel aliud huiusmodi

Judicia autem hec frequentanda vera sunt eo quod in pluribus racio passionibus succumbit et ab eis deducitur quamuis non de necessitate eo quod racio jmperium super passionibus habet

ā
Anglici a Saxonibus animorum jnconditam ferocitatem a Flandricis corporum eneruem moliciem, a Danis potacionem nimiam, dedicerunt tempore Regis Edgari

Pirati in mare. predones in bello spoliatores in seculari dominio raptores in meatu publico latrones in locis absconditis latitantes. fures in tenebris noctium bona aliorum clandestine captantes[a]

C .xx. dragme idest .xxv. s. monete nostre[a]

Nota pro J.Fastolf:[b]
Rarus jmperator aut nullus filium reliquit successione sed heredes habuerunt aut hostes aut ignotos

Contra racionem nemo sobrius. contra scripturam nemo christianus. contra Ecclesiam nemo pacificus sentit hoc Augustinus de trinitate capitulo 4[to] [c]

ā
Jn excidio Jerusalem vndecies centena milia Judeorum gladio & fame perierunt. Centum milia Captiuorum sunt vendita semper xxx. pro vno denario et nongenta Milia sunt dispersa
Hoc Egesippus de excidio vrbis, quem transtulit Ambrosius. Josephus historiographus .libro .7⁰. non est miranda de tanta multitudine Judeorum mortua capta aut occisa. nam Nerone inquirente de numero Judaico Judaice plebis quam omnino vilipendebat rescripsit Cestius preses quemadmodum Dedicerat a pontificibus reperta fuisse in die Festo Jerosolimis vicesies Centena et septingenta Milia absque polutis et viciatis personis quibus hostias conferre non licuit

---

a A wavy line has been drawn by Talbot down the side of these two
   paragraphs
b Added in the margin
c Talbot has bracketed this paragraph, with § in margin opposite

(339) [continued]
Also note that the inclination of the spirit is much influenced by the complexion of the body, whence the doctors diagnose someone as happy, sad or languid, or something else of this kind.

These judgements, however, are often true because in many the reason gives way to the passions, and by them is led astray, though not of necessity, because reason has rule over the passions.

The English, in the time of King Edgar, learnt from the Saxons an uncouth ferocity of spirit; from the Flemings, effeminate weakness of the body; from the Danes, excessive drinking.

Pirates at sea, plunderers in war, extortioners in civil government, robbers in public gatherings, brigands lurking in hidden places, thieves stealing other men's goods secretly in the darkness of night.

120 drachmæ, that is, 25s. of our money.

Note for J.Fastolf:[1]
Rarely or never has an Emperor left a son in succession, but has had either enemies or unknown [people] for heirs.

No prudent man [is] against reason, no Christian against Scripture, no peaceable man against the Church. This [from] Augustine on the Trinity, 4th chapter.

At the fall of Jerusalem, 1,100,000 Jews perished by the sword and of starvation; 100,000 captives were sold at 30 for a penny; and 900,000 were scattered.
This from Hegesippus on the fall of the city, which Ambrosius translated. Josephus the historian in the 7th book:[2] it is not surprising that such a multitude of Jews died, were captured or slain, for when Nero inquired about the number of the Jews (of the Jewish people, which he utterly despised) Cestius the governor wrote back as to how it was given out by the priests that there had been found at Jerusalem on the day of the Feast 2,700,000, not including polluted and corrupt persons to whom it was not permitted to join in the sacrifices.

---

1 A quotation seen by Worcestre as relevant to the circumstances of Sir John Fastolf, who had died in 1459, and the disputes over his will
2 Noted by Harvey, *Itineraries*, p. 323 n.3 as Josephus, *De Bello Iudaico* Lib. VI. 420–427 (cap. ix. 3)

(339) [continued]
newton chivaler:[a]
Manus Jullij Cesaris non minus apta stilo quam gladio fuerat

p.160

Nota J.Paston:[a]
Ingens Dedecus et miserabile vt nouus aduena veteres colonos
arare compellat

Nobilis animus semel jncitatus in ampliora conatur

<u>Oracius</u> et verba pondus habeant. nec fides verbis deficiat

Facilius toleratur opes non habuisse. quam habitas, amisisse

(340)
longitudo   duarum   portarum   de   Fromeyate   cum   spacio
longitudinis[b] pontis duarum archuum subtus[c] aquam de Frome
fluencium continet cum spacio[d] intercepto dictarum duarum
portarum continet .22. virgas
longitudo Muri prime porte desuper edificate continet .8.[e]
virgas cum volta lapidis desuper edificate
latitudo secunde porte desuper edificate continet ... [f] virgas
siue ... [f] gressus siue .6. virgas cum domo desuper edificato
Spacium interceptum. inter duas portas continet .8. virgas

---

(341)
Memorandum[g]
quod in cimiterio sancti Jacobi. quasi versus fratres sancti
francisci Capella pulcra quadrangula totum de Frestone fundata
tam in coopertura tecti quam fenestris et continet ex qualibet
latere capelle .10. pedes quadrales cum .8. boterasses

---

a   Added in margin
b   *duo* deleted
c   Worcestre originally wrote *super* then altered it to *...btus*
d   *intercep* deleted for lack of space at end of line, and rewritten
e   *8* rewritten more clearly above
f   Blank in MS
g   *stet* in margin opposite *Memorandum*, probably because *Memorandum* was
    accidentally crossed through by the horizontal line above

---

3   Literally, to plough

(339) [continued]
Newton, knight:[1]
The hand of Julius Caesar was no less fitted for the pen than
for the sword.

p.160

Note: J.Paston:[2]
A monstrous and wretched disgrace that the newcomer should
force the old inhabitants to labour.[3]

A noble mind once roused ventures still further.

Horace: and let the words have weight, nor faith in words be
lacking.

Not to have had wealth is easier to bear than to have had [it
and] to have lost [it].

(340)
The length of the two gates of Fromegate, together with the
space of the length of the two-arched bridge beneath [which]
the river Frome flows, measures with the intervening space
between the said two gates: it measures 22 yards.
The length of the wall of the first gate built on top, with the
stone arch built above, measures 8 yards.
The width of the second gate built on top, with the house built
above, measures ... yards or ... steps or 6 yards.
The intervening space between the two gates measures 8
yards.

---

(341)
Memorandum:
That in St James's churchyard, somewhat towards the
Franciscan Friars, [is] a beautiful square chapel, entirely built
of freestone, as well in the roof tiles as in the windows; and it
measures on each side of the chapel 10 feet square, with 8
buttresses.

---

1   A quotation seen by Worcestre as relevant either to Sir John Newton (cf.
    (157)), or to his father Sir Richard Newton as suggested by Harvey. Sir
    Richard Newton had died over thirty years previously, but was still
    well remembered: cf. **(327)**, **(345)**
2   Similarly, a quotation seen by Worcestre as a tart comment on John
    Paston and the wrangling over Sir John Fastolf's estate

(342)
LE BAKE
Capella vocata Knap per ipsum fundata pro ij presbiteris super
bak. continet in longitudine .13. virgas[a] & in latitudine sex.
virgas

(343)
latitudo Porte sancti Nicholai continet .7. virgas
[b]

(344)
LONGITUDO VILLE A BORIA IN MERIDIEM
Via longitudo. jncipiendo[c] ad pedem pontis[d] sancti Johannis[e]
infra bradstrete et continuando per altam crucem de
hyghstrete; eundo directe ad portam sancti Nicholai per
hyghstrete. continet dicta integra longitudo ad interius partis
dicte porte sancti Nicholai. vndecies .60. que faciunt .660.
gressus que fuit[f] integra medietas. tocius ville videlicet ... [g] a
boreali parte in meridionale

(345)
Via longitudo ab oriente in occidens videlicet a loco longitudinis
antique porte ville. citra portam nouam vocatam ... [h] ex
opposito venelle in Wynchstrete alias Castellstrete. directe qua
itur ad portam siue hostium Ecclesie[i] sancti Petri per domum
vbi Ricardus Newton justiciarius Regis manebat quando fuit
Recordator ville Bristollie. et est proxima venella citra
Newyate; continet ... [j] gressus citra newyate que via est[k] altera
medietas tocius integre vie ab oriente in occidens

p.161

(346)
Ecclesia parochialis sancti Jacobi prope Ecclesiam prioratas in
parte orientali ville Bristollie continet. ... [l]
Cimiterium & circuitus dicte Ecclesie parochialis continet ... [l]

---

a   *virgas* repeated
b   *longitudo* deleted, probably a false start to **(344)**
c   Worcestre actually wrote *jnpiendo*
d   *sic*, error for *porte*
e   *ex* deleted
f   *jnte* (for *jntegra*) smudged and deleted
g   Blank in MS, with smudged underlining
h   Blank in MS
i   *de p* deleted

(342)
THE BACK
The chapel called Knapp's, upon the Back, founded by him for 2 priests, measures 13 yards in length and six yards in width.

(343)
The width of St Nicholas's Gate measures 7 yards.

(344)
THE LENGTH OF THE TOWN FROM NORTH TO SOUTH
The length [of] the road starting at the foot of St John's bridge[1] within Broad Street, and going on past the High Cross of High Street, going straight along High Street to St Nicholas's Gate: the said entire length measures, to the inner side of the said St Nicholas's Gate, eleven times 60, which makes 660 steps, which was the complete mid-line of the whole town to wit from the north side to the south.

(345)
The length [of] the road from east to west, to wit from the place alongside the ancient gate of the town, this side of the new gate called ... , opposite the lane into Wynch Street otherwise Castle Street, which goes straight to the gate or door of St Peter's church, past the house where Richard Newton, the King's justice, dwelt when he was recorder of the town of Bristol. And it is the nearest lane this side of Newgate. It measures ... steps this side of Newgate; which road is the other mid-line of the whole complete road from east to west.

p.161

(346)
The parish church of St James, next to the priory church on the east side of the town of Bristol, measures ...
The churchyard and circumference of the said parish church measure ...

---

1   Error for 'Gate'

---

j   Blank in MS
k   *proxima* deleted
l   Blank in MS

(347)

Ecclesia parochialis prope Abbathiam Canonicorum regularium sancti Augustini in honore sancti Augustini dedicata,

(348)

Ecclesia parochialis in sanctuario sancti Augustini ex parte boriali ville Bristollie. vocata. le Gauntes vbi Ecclesia Religiosa in honore sancti Marci dedicata

(349)

Ecclesia parochialis sancti philippi in meridionali parte ville Bristollie in loco quondam prioratus Religionum ordinis sancti Benedicti

(350)

Ecclesia parochialis sancti petri iuxta turrim Bristollie scita in loco vbi quondam prioratus Religionum ordinis sancti Benedicti

(351)

Ecclesia parochialis sancti Stephani. prope le Key Bristollie in loco scituata vbi quondam ab antiquo tempore vt audiui fuit Ecclesia prioratus Religiosorum monachorum ordinis sancti Benedicti et fuit Cella pertinens Monasterio de Glastynbery

(352)

Ecclesia parochialis Sancti Egidij[a] sciatuata.[b] in alto loco ad finem vici de Smalstrete[c] super portam ad finem vie dicte Smalstrete[d] ad introitum principij de le Kay pro nauibus applicandis cum mercandisis. sed diu dicta Ecclesia est vnita ad Ecclesiam sancti laurencij parochialem vel ad Ecclesiam parochialem sancti leonardi. circa tempus regni regis Edwardi tercij;

(353)

Templum[e] judeorum quondam scituatam sub antiquas voltas directe subtus Ecclesiam quondam parochialem sancti Egidij super principium de la Kay scituatam[f] nomine certe dee appollinis vel huic simile honorificatum. vt quam plures gentes michi retulerunt et modo sunt Cellarij pro mercandisis custodiendis in dicto templo prophanato,

---

a   *super solarium veluti* (upon the upper floor, as it were) deleted
b   *sic*
c   *prope jntroitum porte* (near the entry of the gate) deleted
d   *prope* deleted
e   Preceded by capital *T* above the opening words: probably a false start
f   *in* deleted

(347)

The parish church near the abbey of the Regular Canons of St Augustine [is] dedicated in honour of St Augustine.

(348)

A parish church in the precinct of St Augustine's, on the north side of the town of Bristol, [is] called The Gaunts, where the church of the community [is] dedicated in honour of St Mark.

(349)

The parish church of St Philip [is] on the south[1] side of the town of Bristol, on the site formerly a priory of monks of the order of St Benedict.

(350)

The parish church of St Peter next to the keep of Bristol [is] situated on the site where [there was] formerly a priory of monks of the order of St Benedict.

(351)

The parish church of St Stephen [is] situated near The Key of Bristol, on the site where there was formerly, in ancient times as I have heard, a priory church of a monastic community of the order of St Benedict, and it was a cell belonging to the monastery of Glastonbury.

(352)

The parish church of St Giles [is] situated in a high place at the end of the street of Small Street, above the gate at the end of the said road of Small Street, at the entry to the head of The Key, for mooring ships with cargoes; but the said church was long since united to the parish church of St Lawrence or to the parish church of St Leonard, about the time of the reign of King Edward III.

(353)

The Jewish Synagogue [was] formerly situated down in the ancient vaults, directly beneath the former parish church of St Giles situated at the head of The Key, dedicated in the name of a certain god Apollo[2] or some such, according to what many people have told me; and now there are cellars for storing merchandise in the said profane synagogue.

---

1   Error for 'east'
2   *sic*: Worcestre has perhaps confused Apollo and Apollyon in his derogatory reference to the 'profane' place of worship

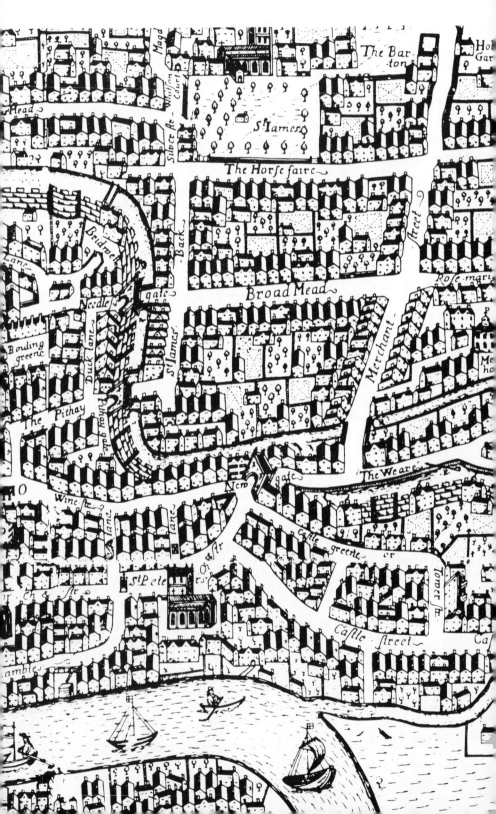

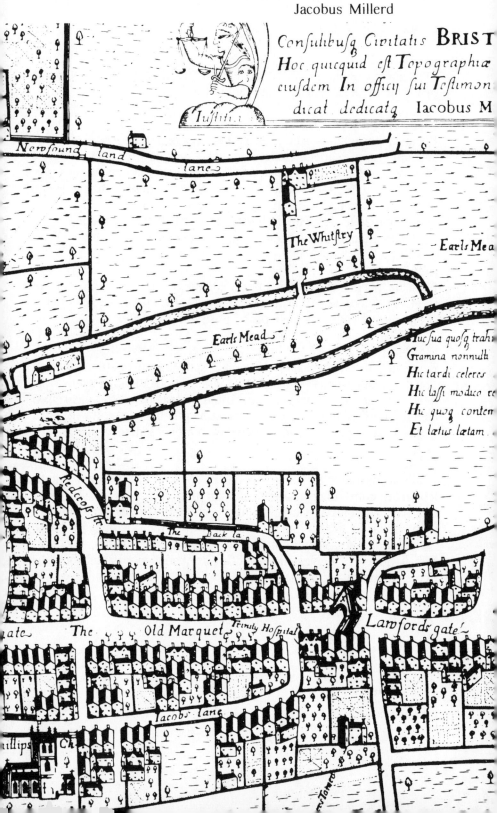

EASTERN SUBURBS

BRISTOL IN 1673

Jacobus Millerd

Confulibufq Civitatis **BRIST**
Hoc quicquid eft Topographiæ
eiufdem In officij fui Teftimon
dicat dedicatq Iacobus M

Iuftitia

Newfound land lane

The Whitftry

Earls Mea

Earls Mead

Huc fua quofq trahi
Gramina nonnulli
Hic tardi celeres
Hic laffi modico re
Hic quoq conten
Et lætus lætam

Redcrofs ftr

The Back la

gate   The   Old Marquet   Trinity Hospital   Lawfords gate

Iacobs lane

Phillips Ch

p.162

(354)
Ecclesia parochialis sancti laurencij scita directa linea ex parte orientali Ecclesie parochialis sancti Egidij

(355)
Ecclesia parochialis sancti Johannis baptiste cum volta[a] jnferius archuata cum capella sancte crucis, in qua Ecclesia famosus Mercator. burgensis ville predicte in tumulo iacet desuper sepultus[b] et fecit de nouo fundare & construere tam Ecclesiam quam portam pulcram cum turre cum alta Spera de Frestone cum campanis desuper pulsantibus. Et dicta porta est scita contigue[c] Ecclesie laurencij ex parte[d] occidentali;

(356)
Ecclesia parochialis beate marie vocata Seynt marye a port, et iacet in vico seynt Marye at port directa linea ex parte occidentali Ecclesie sancti petri a[e] turris Bristollie

(357)
Ecclesia parochialis sancti Nicholai. scita supra portam pulcram vocatam, seyntcolas yate idest porta[f] sancti Nicholai cum turri quadrata et de magnum pinaculum siue spera de mearemio eleuato cum plumbo cooperto Et cum pulcherima volta de arcu lapidum ac fenestris cum capella in honore sancte crucis;

(358)
Ecclesia parochialis sancti leonardi scita supra portam sancti leonardi. cum turri desuper portam pro campanis pulsantibus. sed parua Ecclesia. sic scita inter vicum Baldwynestrete in quo vico. aqua de Frome currebat ab antiquis temporibus. ex parte meridionali ac viam eundo ad keyam. & vicum vocatum Merstrete[g] & Ecclesiam sancti Stephani ex parte boriali. Ecclesie sancti leonardi

---

a   *de* deleted
b   *sic*
c   *tam* deleted
d   *orie* (for *orientali*) deleted
e   *sic*, probably an error for &
f   Worcestre actually wrote *prta*
g   *sic*

p.162

(354)
The parish church of St Lawrence [is] sited in a straight line on the east side of the parish church of St Giles.

(355)
The parish church of St John Baptist with the vaulted crypt, together with the chapel of Holy Cross, below: in which church a famous merchant, burgess of the aforesaid town, lies in a tomb [with] an effigy upon it;[1] and he caused to be newly built and constructed both the church and the fine gateway, together with the tower and the high spire of freestone, with the ring of bells, on top. And the said gate is sited right next to [St] Lawrence's church on its western side.

(356)
The parish church of the blessed Mary [is] called St Mary le Port, and it lies in St Mary le Port Street, in a straight line from the west side of St Peter's church and the keep of Bristol.

(357)
The parish church of St Nicholas [is] sited on top of a fair gateway called St Colas Gate, that is, the gate of Saint Nicholas, with a square tower and a great pinnacle or spire built up in timber covered with lead; and with a most beautiful stone-arched crypt, and windows, and with a chapel in honour of the Holy Cross.

(358)
The parish church of St Leonard [is] sited on top of St Leonard's Gate, with the tower for bell-ringing on top of the gate; but [it is] a small church. It stands thus, between the street of Baldwin Street, in which street the river Frome flowed in ancient times, on the south side; and the road going to The Key, and the street called Marsh Street, and St Stephen's church, on the north side of the church of St Leonard.

---

1 Walter Frampton, d.1388/9: see **(176)**. His tomb chest with effigy, now in a recess in the chancel, was originally freestanding

(359)
Ecclesia parochialis sancte Wereburge cum turre condecenti operate artificiose pro campanis pulsantibus; scituata in vico principali vocato Cornstrete, inter Ecclesiam sancti leonardi directa linea[a] ex parte orientali.[b] et[c] Ecclesiam sancti Audoeni ex parte orientali directe,

p.163

(360)
Templestrete latitudo eius est 30 gressus in principis et[d] per totum vicum .22. gressus .144. gressus.

(361)
Venella[e] Via ex opposito Ecclesie sancti Thome
latitudo dicte vie continet .10. pedes eundo ad templestrete

(362)
Et a fine dicte venelle. continuando ad templestrete. et retornando versus Stallagecrosse vsque a cornerium vici vocati Tokerstrete retornando ad pontem. ex opposito Stallagecrosse in boriali parte de Stallage crosse versus Toukerstret continet illa pars vie de templestret. continet .100. gressus in longitudine

(363)
Via dextre partis de Tokerstrete vltra Stallage crosse versus magnam fontem ad le Slepp in angulo finis de Toukerstrete continet .140. gressus[f] a Stalage crosse,

g
(364)
SEYNT THOMAS STRETE
Via vocata. Seynt Thomasstrete jncipiendo ad pontem vsque mansionem sororis mee in longitudine continet continuando versus Muros Bristollie per le condyt in Seynt Thomas strete. retornando versus Redclyff chyrch sic[h] de dicta ponte vsque mansionem predictam sororis mee continet .160.[i] gressus & ab inde continuando ad le toune walles continet ... [j]

---

a *et Ecclesiam* deleted
b *sic*, error for *occidentali*
c *Et* repeated
d *et* is written over, and obscures, another word, probably *sunt*
e *Venella* has been added afterwards, in front of *Via*
f *ad* deleted
g *Via* written above marginal heading, perhaps a false start to **(364)**

(359)
The parish church of St Werburgh, with a fine tower for bell-ringing, skilfully worked, [is] situated in the main street called Corn Street, in a straight line between St Leonard's church on the east[1] side and St Ewen's church straight on the east side.

p.163

(360)
Temple Street: its width is 30 steps at the beginning, and 22 steps throughout the street: 144 steps.

(361)
The alleyway opposite St Thomas's church:
The width of the said road, going to Temple Street, measures 10 feet.

(362)
And from the end of the said lane, going to Temple Street, and turning towards Stallage Cross, as far as the corner of the street called Tucker Street, turning to the bridge, opposite Stallage Cross, on the north side of Stallage Cross towards Tucker Street: that part of the road of Temple Street measures 100 steps in length.

(363)
The road on the right side of Tucker Street beyond Stallage Cross, towards the great well at the slip, on the corner at the end of Tucker Street, measures 140 steps from Stallage Cross.

(364)
SAINT THOMAS STREET
The road called St Thomas Street, beginning at the bridge, measures in length as far as the dwelling house of my sister, going along towards the walls of Bristol, past the conduit in St Thomas Street, turning towards Redcliffe church: thus from the said bridge as far as the aforesaid dwelling house of my sister measures 160 steps; and going on from there to the town walls measures ...

---

1   Error for 'west'

---

h   *vsque* deleted
i   *.160.* has been written afterwards, in a space left for the figures
j   Blank in MS

(364) [continued]
longitudo dicte vie vsque le toune wallys .305. gressus
latitudo vie seynt Thomasstret continet .22. gressus.

(365)
latitudo pontis Bristollie continet .9. gressus vel ... [a]

(366)
Via de hyghstrete longitudo eius est ad altam crucem per
cokery de seynt Nicholas yate sunt[b] 176. gressus
latitudo dicte vie sunt ... [c]

(367)
Via vocata Cornerstrete ab alta cruce ad portam sancti
Nicholai[d] continet .300. gressus.
latitudo dicte vie ad finem porte sancti leonardi continet .22.
gressus. vel: ... ;[e]

(368)
Via de mershstrete ad portam de Mershyate continet 396.
gressus. versus le mersyate
latitudo eius continet .9. gressus ad portam de mershyate

(369)
Via quod jncipit a porta de mershyate ad principium de le key
a[f] turri rotunda vbi Burton shyp fuit edificatam, vsque ad
mansionem Cornerij de lapidibus magnis vocatam vielle place
continet 220. gressus;   Et[g] sic continuando a dicti cornerio
domo henrici vielle[h] per[i] longitudinem de le key vsque finem
eius erga domum Johannis Pavye prope templum Ecclesie sancti
Egidij prope vicum vocatum Smalstrete, continet .480. gressus
Et sic continet longitudo tocius key[j] coram aquam de Frome
.700. gressus
latitudo dicte key continet, ... [k]

---

a   Blank in MS
b   *180* deleted
c   Blank in MS
d   *sic*
e   Blank in MS
f   *por* (perhaps for *porta*?) deleted
g   *Et* smudged and rewritten
h   *vsque l* deleted and *per* written above

(364) [continued]
The length of the said road as far as the town walls: 305 steps.
The width of the road [of] St Thomas Street measures 22 steps.

(365)
The width of Bristol Bridge measures 9 steps or ...

(366)
The road of High Street: its length is from St Nicholas Gate past cooks' row to the High Cross: there are 176 steps.
The width of the said road is ...

(367)
The road called Corn Street, from the High Cross to St Nicholas's Gate,[1] measures 300 steps.
The width of the said road to the end at St Leonard's Gate measures 22 steps, or ...

(368)
The road of Marsh Street, to the gate of Marsh Gate, measures 396 steps in the direction of the Marsh Gate.
Its width measures 9 steps at the gate of Marsh Gate.

(369)
The road which starts from the gate of Marsh Gate to the head of The Key, from the round tower where Burton's ship was built, as far as the dwelling house [with] the corner of huge stones, called Vyell's Place, measures 200 steps.   And thus going on from the said corner house of Henry Vyell, along the length of The Key as far as its end opposite the house of John Pavye, near the synagogue of St Giles's church [and] near the street called Small Street, measures 480 steps.   And thus the length of the whole Key alongside the river Frome measures 700 steps.
The width of the said Key measures ...

---

1   Error for St Leonard's Gate

---

i   *per* repeated
j   *key* repeated
k   Blank in MS

p.164

(370)
HORSTRETE
Via de exteriore parte de Fromeyate. vocata Horstrete vsque
vlteriorem domum prope jntroitum sanctuarij abbathie sancti
Augustini. videlicet vsque Fratres Carmelitas ad cornerium in
manu sinistra. edificatam coram aquam de Frome; continet
.360. gressus   Et continuando a dicto cornerio prope fratres
Carmelitas ad jntroitum sanctuarij sancti Augustini. continet
alias .360. gressus in toto .720. gressus

(371)
PYTTEY
Via de Pyttey a pyttey yate porta vocata nether pyttey vsque ∵
antiquam portam pyttey[a] vsque viam ducentem ad Wynchstrete
continet .140. gressus
Pons longitudo apud Frome de Pytteyyate continet .10. virgas
Porta pyttey continet .4. virgas;

(372)
VENELLA PER[b] CIMITERIUM SANCTI JOHANNIS
Via. a fine pyttey vsque Wynshstrete. jncipiendo ab angulo de
Wynchstrete[c] ex opposito de le Pyllorye continuando ab illo
loco ad Cimiterium sancti Johannis ad locum vocatum le Blynde
yate continet 240 gressus et a dicta porta vocata le Blyndyate
vsque vicum de Bradstrete per Ecclesiam sancti Johannis
baptiste continet ... [d] gressus
Et[e] dicta via continet in longitudine .140. gressus,
latitudo dicte vie venelle continet .6. pedes

(373)
Via a[f] Porta vocata le Blyndyate veniente de Pyttey yate per
vicum vocatum le Gropelane, & de Gaole vocatum le
Monkenbrygge continet, .180.[g] gressus,

(374)
Porta blynde yate continet in longitudine & latitudine quadrate
.4. virgas

---

a   *antiquam portam pyttey* has been added in the margin, with Worcestre's
    ∵ link symbol
b   *cimit*, a false start for *cimiterium*, abandoned for lack of space
c   illegible word with *ex* written over it and then deleted
d   Blank in MS
e   *dicta* deleted

p.164

(370)
HORESTREET
The road called Horestreet, from the outer side of Fromegate, as far as the furthest house by the entry of the precinct of St Augustine's abbey, to wit as far as the Carmelite Friars, to the corner on the left hand, [is] built up alongside the river Frome; it measures 360 steps. And going on from the said corner by the Carmelite Friars, to the entry of St Augustine's precinct, measures another 360 steps; in all, 720 steps.

(371)
PITHAY
The road of Pithay, from Pithay Gate (the gate called Nether Pithay) as far as the old gate of Pithay, to the road leading to Wynch Street, measures 140 steps.
The length [of] the bridge from Pithay Gate over the Frome measures 10 yards.
Pithay Gate measures 4 yards.

(372)
THE LANE PAST ST JOHN'S CHURCHYARD
The road from the end [of] Pithay as far as Wynch Street, starting from the corner of Wynch Street opposite the pillory, continuing along from that spot to St John's churchyard, to the place called the Blind Gate, measures 240 steps. And from the said gate called the Blind Gate as far as the street of Broad Street, past St John the Baptist's church, measures ... steps.
And the said road measures 140 steps in length.
The width of the said alleyway measures 6 feet.

(373)
The road from the gate called the Blind Gate, coming from Pithay Gate along the street called the Grope Lane, and from the gaol called the Monkenbridge, measures 180 steps.

(374)
The Blind Gate gate measures in length and width, 4 yards square.

---

f   *Via a* added by Worcestre afterwards, in front of the original opening
   words *Porta vocata*
g   *virgas* deleted

(375)
GROPELANE
Via a porta pyttey vsque per Gropelane vsque ad portam vocatam le blyndeyate supra nominata cum vno returno continet vt supra .180 gressus. vsque murum in anglice vocate le tounewalle.

Via de pyttey yate vocata Gropelane ad viam jncidentem[a] vsque Blynde yate continet .120. gressus
latitudo vie predicte continet .10. pedes

(376)
PONS SUPER[b] AQUAM FROME
Via a monkenbrygge vsque cimiterium sancti Jacobi continet .60. gressus ad crucem super pontem coram cimiterium portus[c] sancti Jacobi.
latitudo vie predicte ⋯ [d]

(377)
latitudo vie de Bradstrete prope portam sancti Johannis continet .20 gressus

(378)
latitudo vie de[e] smalstrete ad finem porte sancti Egidij continet .15. gressus

(379)
porta latitudo noua prope ibidem continet .10. pedes
longitudo porte continet. de edificacione prioris de Bathe continet … [f]

(380)
latitudo vie vocate Cornstrete ad Portam sancti leonardi continet .31. gressus. vel … [f] virgas

(381)
latitudo vie cimiterij sancti leonardi. est .10. pedes
longitudo dicte vie a porta sancti Nicholai vsque seynt Leonardes yate continet. … [f]

---

a   *eu* (for *eundo?*) deleted
b   PONS SUPER is repeated in the margin
c   Uncertain reading of an illegible word

(375)
GROPE LANE
The road from Pithay gate along Grope Lane as far as the above-named gate called the Blind Gate, with one bend, measures as above 180 steps as far as the wall, in English called 'the town wall'.

The road from Pithay Gate called Grope Lane measures 120 steps to the side road to Blind Gate.
The width of the aforesaid road measures 10 feet.

(376)
THE BRIDGE OVER THE RIVER FROME
The road from Monkenbridge as far as St James's churchyard measures 60 steps to the cross on the bridge in front of the parish churchyard of St James.
The width of the aforesaid road ...

(377)
The width of the road of Broad Street by St John's Gate measures 20 steps.

(378)
The width of the road of Small Street at [its] end at St Giles's Gate measures 15 steps.

(379)
The width [of] the new gate near there measures 10 feet.
The length of the gate from the prior of Bath's building measures ...

(380)
The width of the road called Corn Street at St Leonard's Gate measures 31 steps, or ... yards.

(381)
The width of the St Leonard's churchyard road is 10 feet.
The length of the said road from St Nicholas's Gate as far as St Leonard's Gate measures ...

---

d   Blank in MS
e   *Bra* (for *Bradstrete*?) deleted   ,
f   Blank in MS

p.165

(382)
Hospitalis domus pro pauperibus jn Ecclesia quondam[a]
Canonicorum regularium ordinis sancti Augustini[b] et modo
domus hospitalis pro pauperibus sustinendis in Ecclesia sancti
Bertholomei

(383)
Capella[c] decens ab antiquo fundata. per se scita. in Meridionali
parte Ecclesie de Radclyff in honore sancti spiritus dedicata

(384)
Capella ampla in honore sancti Georgij fundata par Ricardum
Spicer famosum mercatorem & burgensem dicte ville circa
tempus Regis Edwardi tercij seu Ricardi Regis secundi. et est
Fraternitas dignissima Mercatorum et marinariorum Bristollie
dicte capelle pertinencia;

(385)
Capella in parte Meridionali Ecclesie parochialis sancti Audoeni.
que capella est in honore sancti Johannis baptiste et Fraternitas
magnifica pertinet dicte capelle

(386)
Capella pulcra scita in amplo cimiterio[d] Ecclesie parochialis
sancti Jacobi. totum de Frestone fundata. et continet[e] .10.
pedes longitudinis & 10 pedes latitudinis

(387)
Ecclesia prioratus de kalenders Collegij siue Fraternitatis
vocate[f] et fundate in honore festi Corporis christi. et ab
antiquissis[g] temporibus Fundata. ante tempus Willelmi
Conquestoris Anglie circa annum christi .700[mo] vt per litteras
certificatorias tempore sancti Wolstani Episcopi Wigorniensis
sub antiqua manu vidi & legi que Ecclesia scita est in
meridionali parte Ecclesie parochialis omnium sanctorum et
ante tempus Edwardi Regis tercij fuit scita in Ecclesia parochiali
sancte trinitatis. vt per relacionem ... [h] prioris dicti prioratus
certificatum fuit,

---

a   Illegible deletion, possibly *sancti A* (for *Augustini*)
b   Illegible deletion, possibly *in b*
c   *p* deleted
d   *sancti* deleted
e   *q'* (for *questio* or *query*?) deleted; the *.10.* may have been added later
f   *p* deleted

p.165

(382)
The hospital for the poor in the church, formerly of the Regular Canons of the Order of St Augustine and now a hospital for the care of the poor, in the church of St Bartholomew.

(383)
A handsome chapel, founded long ago, sited on its own on the south side of Redcliffe church, dedicated in honour of the Holy Spirit.

(384)
A spacious chapel in honour of St George, founded by Richard Spicer, famous merchant and burgess of the said town, about the time of King Edward III or King Richard II; and there is a most worthy fraternity of merchants and seafarers of Bristol attached to the said chapel.

(385)
A chapel on the south side of the parish church of St Ewen, which chapel is in honour of St John the Baptist, and a wealthy fraternity is attached to the said chapel.

(386)
A fair chapel, entirely built of freestone, sited in the large churchyard of the parish church of St James: and it measures 10 feet in length and 10 feet in width.

(387)
The priory church of the College or Fraternity of Kalendars, called and founded in honour of the Feast of Corpus Christi, and founded in most ancient times, before the time of William the Conqueror of England, about the year of Christ 700, as I have seen and read in confirmatory documents in an ancient hand, of the time of St Wulstan, bishop of Worcester. Which church is sited on the south side of the parish church of All Saints; and before the time of King Edward III it was sited in the parish church of Holy Trinity, as was confirmed by the account of ... prior of the said priory.[1]

---

1 cf. **(82)** and see N.Orme, 'The Guild of Kalendars, Bristol', *T.B.G.A.S.* xcvi (1978), 33

---

g   *sic*
h   Blank in MS

p.166

(388)
Volte & Cellarij .10. jn numero idest .5. volte in orientali parte vie de Bristow brygge et .5. alie volte in occidentali parte de Bristow brygge cum fortissimis archibus petri clausis et fundatis,

Volte due in parte orientali vie eundo ad Bristow brygge vnde vna pulcra volta^a prope Portam sancti Nicholai, vnde vna est ... ^b

Volta principalyssima & amplissima. sub capella beate marie fundata;

p.167

(389)
Turris rotundus .24. gressus tunc sunt 100 gressus &^c
Turris quadratus .12. gressus. tunc murus infra duas turres murus spacium continet 120. gressus
Turris 3.us quadratus continet .9. virgas,
murus vacuus proxime sequens continet 110. gressus
Turris^d .4.^{tus} Quadratus continet 10 virgas
Murus vacuus sequiter^e continet .94. gressus
Turris .5.^{tus} rotundus continet .8. virgas,
Murus vacuus sequitur^e vsque portam Templeyate continet 100 gressus
Porta cum turre quadrata. vocata Templeyate,
Turris alius^e citra portas temple^f gate latitudinis^g sex virgarum
Turris alia^h ex opposito Seynt Thomas strete latitudinis sex virgarum
Turris alius^h inter finem Seynt Thomas Strete & portas duas vocatas Radclyff yates. & continet .6. virgas latitudinis
Porte due vocate Radclyff yates super edificate continet in longitudine ... ⁱ

---

a   *sub* deleted
b   Blank in MS
c   *tunc sunt 100 gressus &* appears to have been added in a different ink
d   *4* smudged and deleted
e   *sic*
f   *ge* (mis-spelling *gate*?) deleted

p.166

(388)

Vaults and cellars, 10 in number: that is, 5 vaults on the east side of the road of Bristol Bridge, and 5 other vaults on the west side of Bristol Bridge covered over and constructed with very strong arches of stone.

Two vaults on the east side of the road going to Bristol Bridge, of which one fair vault near St Nicholas's Gate, of which [the other?] one is ...

The most important and most spacious vault constructed below the chapel of St Mary.

p.167

(389)

A round tower (24 steps), then there are 100 steps, and
A square tower (12 steps), then the wall between the two towers.
The extent of wall measures 120 steps.
A 3rd tower, square, measures 9 yards.
The blank wall next following measures 110 steps.
A 4th tower, square, measures 10 yards.
The blank wall following measures 94 steps.
A 5th tower, round, measures 8 yards.
The blank wall following as far as the gate of Temple Gate measures 100 steps.
The gate with a square tower called Temple Gate.
Another tower beside the gates of Temple Gate, of six yards width.
Another tower, opposite St Thomas Street, of six yards width.
Another tower, between the end of St Thomas Street and the two gates called Redcliffe Gates; and it measures 6 yards in width.
The two gates called Redcliffe Gates, built upon, measure in length ...

---

g   *.6.* deleted
h   *sic*
i   Blank in MS

(390)
Memorandum in mansione pulcherima de le bake ex posteriori parte de Radclyf strete super aquam de Avyn. est pulcher. Turris. per Willelmum Canynges edificatum continet 4 fenestras vocatas Bay wyndowes ornatissimo modo cum cameris continet circa .20. virgas. in longitudine 16. virgas

(391)
Vna porta apud primam portam Mershyate per le bakk continet in latitudine muri portarum in qualibet latere porte non desuper edificate .2. virgas
Turri due sunt apud le Mersh walle. & quelibet turris continet .16. virgas in rotunditate exterius
Porta alia in altera parte Mershyate. que continet .16. virgas in rotunditate non edificata desuper
Turris alia jncipiente vbi navis Johannis Burton edificata fuit. in circumferentia .16. virgarum
Turris alia in Muro jncipiente le graunt key continet vt supra
Turris prenobilis per Johannem Vyelle armigerum edificata continet in circuitu vltra .30. virgas super primum angulum de le key
Turris alius super Murum de le key
Porta sancti Johannis baptiste
Turris alius magnus quadratus non multum a Cimiterio sancti Johannis ... [a]. mercator manet
Porta prima in alciori loco de pyttey yate prope Wynchstrete non super edificata cum domibus,

p.168

(392)
Turris quadratus cum mansionibus desuper pro honesto viro ad murum ville per 60 gressus vltra pytteyyate vocatus aldrych yate super pontem de frome
Porta vocata pyttey yate supra pontem aque de frome
Turris rotundus ex opposito Brodemede
Turris rotundus ex opposito le seynt Jamys bake

---

a   Blank in MS

(390)

Memorandum, in the very fair dwelling house on The Back, on the side behind Redcliffe Street upon the river Avon, there is a fair tower built by William Canynges. It contains 4 windows called bay windows, highly decorated, like the rooms. It measures about 20 yards, in length 16 yards.[1]

(391)

A gate at the first Marsh Gate gateway by The Back measures 2 yards, in the width of the gate-walls, on each side of the gate (not built above).

There are two towers along the Marsh wall, and each tower measures 16 yards around the outside.

Another gate on the other side of Marsh Gate, which measures 16 yards around (not built above).

Another tower, 16 yards around, beginning where John Burton's ship was built.

Another tower in the wall at the beginning of The Broad Key measures as above.

A most splendid tower built by John Vyelle Esquire upon the first corner of The Key measures more than 30 yards in circumference.

Another tower upon the wall of The Key.

St John Baptist's Gate.

Another great square tower not far from St John's churchyard [where] ... , merchant, lives.

The first gate in the upper area of Pithay Gate near Wynch Street, not built upon with houses.

p.168

(392)

A square tower, with dwellings on top for a worthy man, at the town wall 60 steps beyond the Pithay Gate called Aldrych Gate, upon the Frome bridge.

The gate called Pithay Gate upon the bridge of the river Frome.

A round tower opposite Broadmead.

A round tower opposite St James's Back.

1　It is unclear, from Worcestre's phrasing, whether 20 yards is the depth of the house front to back, and 16 yards its length along the river frontage, or the other way round; but *in longitudine* tends usually to precede the measurement to which it refers, and studies of the site, such as R.H.Jones, *Excavations in Redcliffe 1983-5* (1986), suggest a long, narrow property with its shorter side towards the river frontage

(392) [continued]
Turris alius principalissimus Quadratus cum multis mansionibus. ad pontem vocatem Monkenbrygge^a vbi quondam fuit locus fortissimus pro prisonarijs custodiendis.
Turris Rotundus.
Turris Rotundus
Turris alius quadratus citra Fromeyates. edificatus in fine de Cristmassestrete prope cimiterium sancti laurencij vbi in quo turri^b honestus vir manet

(393)
Porte due apud Fromeyate fundate & ambo desuper bene edificate,
Turris quadratus. prope portas Fromeyates directe in angulo finis Cristmas strete super paruum pontem siue archus coopertus subtus viam anglice vocatam. vnum Slepe siue gradus. circa .30. numero ad aquam de Frome. et vna crux de Frestone desuper edificata super archum. anglice vnum vowt,
Turrus longus & largus quadratus versus turrim de Monkenbryge^c opposito Ecclesie conuentus Fratrum sancti Francisci. in quo turri. Bagot manet
Turrus Rotundus. non amplus. proximus de Turri de le Monkenbrygge. ex opposito Chori

pp. 169–172
[Notes written 1480 about the Battle of 'Wenlyngg', Great Yarmouth, memorandum re Henry Calbras, accounts at Yarmouth, Bury St Edmunds,^d various saints and dates, Thrigby (Norfolk), Hereford and Aristotle] ^e

p. 173
[Accounts, written 1480, which commence in Oxford but move to Castle Combe and then to Bristol]

---

a *Monkenbrygge* underlined by Talbot, with a diagonal line linking it to the next reference to Monkenbridge in **(393)**: note c, below
b *in quo turri* has been inserted above the line as if to replace *vbi*, but *vbi* has not been deleted
c *Monkenbryge* underlined by Talbot and linked to previous reference in **(392)**, note a, above; *expp* (error for *ex opposito*) deleted
d Dated 1479 by Harvey, *Itineraries*, pp. 160–1, together with Worcestre's other dated notes on Bury St Edmunds, although all the other notes on these pages are ascribed to 1480

(392) [continued]
Another very important square tower with many dwellings, at the bridge called Monkenbridge, where there was formerly a very strong place for keeping prisoners.
A round tower.
A round tower.
Another square tower, built at the end of Christmas Street, this side [of] Fromegate, near the churchyard of St Lawrence; in which tower lives a worthy man.

(393)
Two gates constructed at Fromegate, and both well built above.
A square tower near the gates [of] Fromegates, right on the corner of the end of Christmas Street, above a small bridge or covered arch below the road (called in English a 'slip' or stairway) numbering about 30 [stairs] to the river Frome; and a cross of freestone built on top, upon the arch (in English, a 'vault').
A long and large square tower, in the direction of the Monkenbridge tower, opposite the church of the house of the Franciscan friars; in which tower Bagot lives.
A round tower, not big, near the tower of Monkenbridge, opposite the quire.[1]

pp.169–172
>   [Notes written 1480 about the Battle of 'Wenlyngg', Great Yarmouth, memorandum re Henry Calbras, accounts at Yarmouth, Bury St Edmunds, various saints and dates, Thrigby (Norfolk), Hereford and Aristotle]

p.173
>   [Accounts, written 1480, which commence in Oxford but move to Castle Combe and then to Bristol]

---

1   i.e. of the Franciscan Friars' church

---

e   The notes on these pages do not relate to Bristol, and were included in Harvey, *Itineraries*, pp. 344-5, 266-7, 262-3, 160-1, 266-9, 328-9 and 330-1, according to his reconstruction of the original order

(394)[a]

In primis debeo hospiti meo ad signum tauri Oxonie	.4.d
Item hospiti meo Benet de Castelcombe	12.d
Item mutuaui de Thoma Bole de lewenysmede	.13.s .4d
Item de Roberto Assh consanguineo meo	3s 4d
[b]sorore mea Mutuaui	.4d.de[c]
[d]Johanne Grene mutuaui	.4.d
Item de ... [e] & Alicia Nele pro relaxacione dampnorum Thome Neel	6.s .8.d

Soluciones Bristollie a die sancti Bartholomei	
In primis in expensis meis minutis vsque ... [e] diem Septembris per estimacionem vinis panibus et potacionibus per estimacionem	10.s
Item pro .2. cucurbitis	.5.d
pro 12 punctis	.2.d
pro[f] ferrura equorum meorum	.12.d.
pro dimidia lagena vini presentata Magistro Mundford chivaler	.8.d.[g]
Memorandum datum fuit michi per ipsum .3. pastella venyson	
Item prestiti sorori meo	12.d
... [h] die exaltacionis sancte crucis in vino	12d

Memorandum ad deliberandum Cobbald de Mylkstrete
Mercer summam xiij.s. iiij.d. ad mittendum sorori mee
pro tot denarijs michi prestitis per manus magistri
Willelmi prowte nomine piers Whyte de seynt Thomas
strete wefer

Eciam ad Mittendum Thome Bole de lewenysmede alias
xiij.s iiijd michi prestitis. per dictum Thomam
Item solutum pro dimidio groos de poyntes .9.d et pro[i]
Et pro .4.[bus] duodenis punctuum, 8.d

---

a　Item **(394)** was included in Harvey, *Itineraries*, pp. 264-5, with some variations in transcription and translation. It gives background information relating to Worcestre's 1480 visit to Bristol

b　*Item de* deleted

c　*de* presumably anticipates the next entry

d　*Item de* deleted

e　Blank in MS

f　*pro* repeated

g　*Magistro Mundford* and *.8.d.* underlined, probably by Talbot

h　Blank in MS; *die exaltacionis ... 12d* underlined by Talbot, who has written *M[emorandum] quod egij* [*sic*] *is of the church* in the margin

(394)[1]

First I owe to my host at the sign of the Bull,[2] Oxford   4d.
Also to my host Benet at Castle Combe   12d.
Also I borrowed from Thomas Bole of Lewinsmead   13s. 4d.
Also from Robert Assh my kinsman   3s. 4d.
Of my sister I borrowed   4d.
Of John Grene I borrowed   4d.
Also from ... and Alice Nele, for release of the
damages of Thomas Nele   6s. 8d.

Payments at Bristol from St Bartholomew's day[3]
First in my petty expenses up to ... September, by
estimation, in wine, bread and drinks, by estimation   10s.
Also for 2 cucumbers   5d.
for 12 points   2d.
for shoeing of my horses   12d.
for half a gallon of wine presented to Master
Mundford,[4] knight   8d.
Memorandum, 3 venison pasties were given to me by him.
Also I have lent to my sister   12d.
... on the day of the Exaltation of the Holy Cross,[5]
on wine   12d.

Memorandum, to deliver to Cobbald of Milk Street,
mercer,[6] the sum of 13s 4d. to send to my sister,
for the same amount of money lent to me by the
hand of Master William Prowte in the name of Piers
Whyte of St Thomas Street, weaver.

Also to send to Thomas Bole of Lewinsmead another
13s 4d. lent to me by the said Thomas.
Also paid for half a gross of points, 9d.; and for[7]
And for 4 dozen points, 8d.

---

1   The accounts **(394)/(438)** partner Worcestre's diary **(395)/(437)**
2   The Bull, off Cornmarket Street in Oxford, was later partly incorporated
    into the Golden Cross Inn, part of which still survives
3   24th August
4   Master Mundford cf. **(423)**
5   14th September
6   Milk Street, London. Robert Cobolt/Cobold was a member of the
    Mercers' Company, a warden in 1468 and 1474-5, and still actively
    involved in the Company's proceedings in 1478-9
7   See note i below

---

i   *sic*, presumably anticipating the next line

(394) |continued|
Item cuidam Thome davy de Brode[a] manente cum
Thoma prowte poyntmaker pro reparacione sepelturarum
parentum meorum & fratrum ac sororum meorum   5.d
Item pro .2. Cepis de Spayn .j.d pro bysquey cakys jd

[These accounts are continued as item **(438)***]* [b]

p.174

*[Diary of Worcestre's journeys in late summer
1480, arriving in Bristol on 24th August, to
partner the accounts, item* **(394)***]*

(395)[c]
Sabato die 22. jullij. die Magdalene. equitaui post meridiem
vsque Norwych de london

Lune vltimo die jullij reequitaui de Norwico vsque london

Veneris xj .11. die augusti equitaui de london vsque Oxonford
et continuaui

Sabbato .19. die augusti equitaui de Oxonia per Malmesbery &
Castelcumbe vsque Bristollie.

Dominica 20 die augusti applicui Castelcombe

Jovis .24. augusti de Castelcombe applicui Bristollie

lune .28. Augusti decollacionis sancti Thome[d] fui apud
Bedmynster[e] loquendo cum Johanne Choke justiciario pro
remedio .ij. acrarum terre in knollefeld raptarum de sorore
mea

Item locutus fuit sibi pro iiij. li redditus in henton blewet
Templecloude & henton. pertinentes michi ex dono Johannis
Torynton & Johannis Vyell modo in possessione Johannis

---

a   *sic,* for *Brodemede?*
b   Harvey suggests that other accounts written by Worcestre on pages 202
    and 225 of his notes and printed in Harvey, *Itineraries,* pp. 264-7 are
    also dated 1480 and could be continuations of these accounts. There
    are, however, no obvious links or Bristol references, whereas **(438)** is
    clearly a continuation of **(394)**
c   Item **(395)**, which provides background to Worcestre's Bristol visit, was
    included in Harvey, *Itineraries,* pp. 260-1, with some variations in
    transcription and translation

(394) [continued]
Also to a certain Thomas Davy of Broad[mead?] dwelling
with Thomas Prowte, pointmaker, for the repair of the
graves of my parents and brothers and sisters   5d.
Also for 2 Spanish onions, 1d.; for biscuit cakes,[1] 1d.

*[These accounts are continued as item **(438)**]*

p.174
>*[Diary of Worcestre's journeys in late summer*
>*1480, arriving in Bristol on 24th August, to*
>*partner the accounts, item **(394)**]*

(395)[2]
Saturday 22nd day of July, St Mary Magdalene's day, I rode in
the afternoon from London as far as Norwich.

Monday the last day of July I rode back from Norwich as far
as London.

Friday 11th day of August I rode from London as far as
Oxford, and stayed.

Saturday 19th day of August I rode from Oxford through
Malmesbury and Castle Combe as far as Bristol.

Sunday 20th day of August I reached Castle Combe.

Thursday 24 August from Castle Combe I reached Bristol.

Monday 28 August, the Decollation of St Thomas, I was at
Bedminster speaking with John Choke, the justice, about a
remedy for the 2 acres of land in Knoll Field seized from my
sister.

There was also talk with him about the £4 of rent in Hinton
Blewett, Temple Cloud, and Hinton belonging to me by gift of
John Torynton and John Vyell, now in the possession of John

---

1   Harvey, *Itineraries*, p. 265 n.2 suggested that these could be small cakes
    (cf. Spanish *bizcocho*) or hard ship's biscuit to carry on a journey
2   The diary **(395)**/**(437)** partners Worcestre's accounts **(394)**/**(438)** for the
    same period

---

d   *apud* deleted
e   *apud Bedmynster* underlined, probably by Talbot

(395) [continued]
Choke militis ex dono ... [a] vxoris relicte Johannis Viel filij Johannis Vielle & desiderauit videre cartas meas reseruandi sunt londonijs

> *[The rest of page 174 covers Worcestre's journeys to Wells and Glastonbury on 28th–30th August. He returned to Bristol on 31st August: item (437)]* [b]

p.175

(396)[c]
The quantite of The Dongeon of the Castell of Bristow aftyr the jnformacion of ... [d] porter of the Castell[e]

ā
The Tour[f] called the dongeon ys in thyknesse at fote. ys 25. pedes. and at the ledyngplace vnder the leede cuveryng .9. feete & dimidium
and in lenght Este & west[g] .60. pedes
and[h] north and south .45. pedes wyth .iiij. Toures standyng vppon the fowre corners
and the hyest Toure called the Mayn idest myghtyest Toure abofe all the .iiij. Towres. ys .v. Fethym in hyght abofe all the iiij. Toures. and the wallys be yn thyknesse there .vj. fote,
Item the lenght of the Castelle wythynne the wallys. Est & west ys .180. virge
and the breede of the Castell from the north to[i] the south wyth the grete gardyn[j] that ys from the Wateryate to the mayng rounde of the Castell walle to the walle[k] northward toward blake Frerys, 100. yerdes,
Item a bastyle. lyeth[l] southward. beyond the water gate conteynyth yn lenght .60. virge
Item the lenght from the bulworke at the vtteyate by seynt Phelippes chyrch yerde conteynyth .60. yerdes large
Item the yerdys called Sparres[m] of the halle ryalle. conteynyth yn lenght about .45. fete of hole pece
Item the brede of euery Sparre at fote conteynyth[n] .12. onch. and .viij. onch

---

a   Blank in MS
b   The rest of page 174 was printed in Harvey, *Itineraries,* pp. 260-1
c   This item was included in Harvey, *Itineraries,* Appendix I, p.400: transcription only, with some minor variations
d   Blank in MS
e   *Castell* rewritten more clearly above.   This heading is in different ink
f   *Tour* rewritten more clearly above

(395) [continued]
Choke, knight, by gift of ... the widow of John Vyell son of John Vyell; and he desired to see my deeds; they are to be kept in London.

> *[The rest of page 174 covers Worcestre's journeys to Wells and Glastonbury on 28th–30th August. He returned to Bristol on 31st August: item* **(437)***]*

p.175

(396)[1]
The size of the Keep of Bristol Castle, according to the information of ... , porter of the Castle.

The tower called the Keep is 25 feet thick at the base, and 9½ feet at the eaves under the lead roofing, and 60 feet in length east to west, and 45 feet north to south, with 4 towers standing at the four corners.
The highest tower, called the main [tower], that is, the most massive of all the 4 towers, is 5 fathoms higher than the other 4 towers,[2] and the walls at that point are 6 feet thick.
Also, the length of the Castle within the walls, east to west, is 180 yards, and the width of the Castle from north to south, including the great garden (that is, from the Watergate to the main circuit of the castle wall, northwards to the wall in the direction of Blackfriars): 100 yards.
Also a barbican stands to the south, beyond the Watergate; it measures 60 yards in length.
Also, the length from the bulwark at the outer gate by St Philip's churchyard measures 60 yards in extent.
Also the 'yards', called 'spars',[3] of the Royal Hall measure about 45 feet in length, all in one piece. Also, the width of every 'spar' at its base measures 12 plus 8 inches.

---

1   For a Latin description of the Castle see **(422)**; also diary **(437)**
2   *sic*, error for *3*
3   Perhaps the porter was a retired sailor, using a seaman's terms to convey the size of the roof beams

---

g   *y* deleted
h   *yn* deleted
i   *to* deleted
j   *ys* deleted
k   *toward* deleted
l   Worcestre started to write *l[yeth?]* again above
m   *f* (error for *of*?) deleted
n   *x* (for *xij*?) deleted

p.176

(397)
Hospitalis domus in

Hospitalis domus in

Hospitalis domus

Ecclesia hospitalis domus sancte trinitatis apud laffordysyate in mercato

(398)
Ecclesia hospitalis domus[a] sancte marie Magdalene leprosorum in Occidentali parte de Radclyffhylle in boriali parte[b] vie ad pontem Bryghtbow

(399)
Hospitale domus. jn Ecclesia Religionum prioris et Conuentus. sancti Johannis baptiste scitum super aquam. Avyn in altera parte Ecclesie de Radclyffe

(400)
Hospitalis domus in Ecclesia sancte katerine vbi magister Henricus Abyndon musicus de Capella Regis est Magister

(401)
Hospitalis domus. in vico vocato lewelynsys mede ex opposito Ecclesie fratrum & Conuentus. sancti Francisci fundata per ... [c] Spencer mercatorem & burgensem ville de bonis. domini Willelmi Canyngys decani[d] .Collegij Westbery. et circa annum christi[e] .1478.

(402)
Hospitalis domus cum pulcra Ecclesia. in honore sancti laurencij. in occidentali[f] parte ville[g] per dimidium miliare de laffordysyate sicut itur londonijs pertinenti modo vt dicitur Collegio[h] Canonicorum Ecclesie de Westbery;

---

a *apud* deleted
b *de* deleted
c Blank in MS
d *C* deleted
e *Anno* deleted

p.176

(397)

The hospital in

The hospital in

The hospital

The church of the hospital of Holy Trinity at Lawford's Gate in the market.

(398)

The church of the lepers' hospital of St Mary Magdalene, on the west side of Redcliffe Hill, on the north side of the road to Brightbow Bridge.

(399)

The hospital in the church of the order of the prior and community of St John Baptist, sited upon the river Avon on the other side of Redcliffe church.

(400)

The hospital in the church of St Katherine, where Master Henry Abingdon, musician of the Chapel Royal, is master.

(401)

The hospital in the street called Lewinsmead, opposite the church of the friars and community of St Francis, founded by ... Spencer, merchant and burgess of the town, out of the estate of Sir William Canynges, Dean of the College of Westbury, and about the year of Christ 1478.

(402)

The hospital, with a fair church in honour of St Lawrence, on the west[1] side of the town half a mile from Lawford's Gate as one goes to London, now belongs, so it is said, to the College of canons of the church at Westbury.

---

1   Error for 'east'

---

f   *sic*, error for *orientali*
g   *Br* (for *(Bristollie)* deleted
h   *Ecclesie* deleted

(403)

Ecclesia heremitagij[a] super montem altissimum sancti Brendani.
pertinenti prioratus Religionum sancti Jacobi & vt dicitur.
dictus mons est similis monti Caluarie prope Jerusalem[b]

(404)

Ecclesia pulcherima domus Templi in honore sancte crucis
fundate. in dominio & vico vocato Templestrete. et est de
magnis libertatibus & franchesijs[c]

(405)

[d]Heremitagium cum Ecclesia in rupe periculosissima scita.
vocata Ghyston Clyffe[e] in profundo loco Rupis.[f] viginti
brachiorum profunditatis in dicta[g] Rupe super aquam de Avyn.
in honore sancti Vincencij;

pp.177–180　　　　　　　*[Blank]*

pp.181–183

　　[Notes, probably written 1480, of proverbs,
　　and of events at the abbey of St Benet Hulme
　　(Norfolk) and Yarmouth] [h]

p.184　　　　　　　*[Blank]*

p.185

　　[Notes on Madeira and the Canary Islands] [i]

p.186

　　[Blank, but with jottings in Latin and Hebrew
　　in a later hand] [i]

p.187

(406)[j]

Blake Stonys, scita[k] in aqua de Severn apud holowbakkes
distans a Bristollia vltra[l] hungrode per .4. Miliaria vbi naves

---

a　*domus* deleted
b　*montem altissimum sancti Brendani* and *similis monti Caluarie prope*
　　Jerusalem underlined by Talbot, with § in margin alongside
c　*& libertatibus* repeated
d　*Ecc* (for *Ecclesia*) deleted
e　*Ghyston Clyff* underlined by Talbot, with Θ in margin opposite
f　*super* deleted
g　Vertical wavy line by Talbot alongside the last part of this item
h　Included in Harvey, *Itineraries*, pp. 364-7, 346-7

(403)

The church of the hermitage upon the very high hill of St Brandon belongs to the priory of the community of St James, and, so it is said, the said hill is similar to the hill of Calvary near Jerusalem.

(404)

The most fair church of the Temple [was] founded in honour of the Holy Cross, in the lordship and street called Temple Street, and there are extensive liberties and privileges.

(405)

The hermitage with a church, in honour of St Vincent, sited on a most dangerous rock called Ghyston Cliff, in a deep place of the rock, at a depth of twenty fathoms down the said rock,[1] above the river Avon.

pp.177–180   *[Blank]*

pp.181–183

[Notes, probably written 1480, of proverbs, and of events at the abbey of St Benet Hulme (Norfolk) and Yarmouth]

p.184   *[Blank]*

p.185

[Notes on Madeira and the Canary Islands]

p.186

[Blank, but with jottings in Latin and Hebrew in a later hand]

p.187

(406)

Blackstones sited in the river Severn at Hollowbacks, 4 miles distant from Bristol beyond Hungroad, where ships and boats

---

1   i.e. 20 fathoms down from the cliff top: cf. **(63)**, **(66)**

---

i   Included in Harvey, *Itineraries*, pp. 372–5, 394, 396.   The jottings are
     probably by Henry Aldrich
j   Item **(406)** was included in Harvey, *Itineraries*, pp. 302–3, with some
     variations in transcription and translation
k   *apud* deleted
l   *kyngrode per .4.* deleted

(406) [continued]
& nauicule morantur pro nouo refluxu maris. et dicti rupes parue. quando mare de Severne jncipit refluere versus Bristolliam per kyngrode hungrode & per Ghyston Clyff ac ...ᵃ cooperiuntur cum mare & quam scito sic per refluxum jncepcionis maris. omnes Naves apud le Holow bakkys de hispania portugalia Burdegalia Bayona Vasconia. Aquietania Britannia Islandia Irlandia. Wallia. & ceteris patrijs trahunt eorum anchora. et disponunt ea velare versus Bristolliam,

Kyngrode

Hungrode in parte altera Ghystonclyff sed non multo jnferius versus kyngrode inᵇ dominio ville de lye. in Comitatu Somersetie

p.188   *[Blank]*

p.189

> *[Notes, written 1480, on mileages between Bristol and Chester, and on bridges along the route]* ᶜ

p.190

(407)
Ecclesia hospitalis sancti Bertholomei longitudo eius continet .18. virgas vel .32. gressus

(408)
longitudo a pede vie ducens ad Ecclesiam Religionum [trium]ᵈ Marie magdalene usque ad separationem vie vocate lez barres versus Westberye prope Ecclesiam sancti Michelis continet .420 gressus ascendendo ad Ecclesiam sancti Michelis
latitudo vie predicte continet ... ᵉ

(409)
ECCLESIA MARIE MAGDALENE
longitudo Ecclesie Religionum continet .27. gressus. cum cancella.
latitudo constat ex navi et tribus alis. ac .4. arches

---

a   Blank in MS
b   *parte* deleted
c   Except that the mileages start from Bristol Bridge, this page does not
    relate to Bristol, and was included in Harvey, *Itineraries*, pp. 330–331

(406) [continued]
wait for the next incoming tide. And when the tide begins to rise from the Severn towards Bristol past Kingroad, Hungroad and past Ghyston Cliff and ... , the said small rocks are covered by the sea; and, as I learned, thus on the turn of the tide, all the ships at the Hollowbacks (from Spain, Portugal, Bordeaux, Bayonne, Gascony, Aquitaine, Brittany, Iceland, Ireland, Wales and other countries) weigh their anchors and set sail towards Bristol.

Kingroad

Hungroad [is] on the other side [from] Ghyston Cliff, but not much lower, towards Kingroad, in the lordship of the village of Leigh in the county of Somerset.

p.188   *[Blank]*

p.189

  [Notes, written 1480, on mileages between Bristol and Chester, and on bridges along the route]

p.190

(407)
The church of St Bartholomew's Hospital: its length measures 18 yards or 32 steps.

(408)
The length on foot of the road leading to the church of the community of [three] of Mary Magdalene, as far as the fork of the road called The Bars, in the direction of Westbury, near St Michael's church, measures 420 steps, climbing to St Michael's church.
The width of the aforesaid road measures ...

(409)
THE CHURCH OF MARY MAGDALENE
The length of the church of the community measures 27 steps, including the chancel.
The width consists of nave and three aisles, with 4 arches.

---

d   Illegible word, probably *trium*: cf. *trium monacharum* in **(139)**
e   Blank in MS

(410)
ECCLESIA SANCTI MICHELIS
longitudo Ecclesie sancti Michelis continet 46. gressus vel .26. virgas
latitudo eius continet .10. virgas .20. gressus.
Turris quadratus Campanile noue continet quadrate. ex quatuor partibus. quelibet costera continet extra murum .5. virgas
altitudo[a] turris per estimacionem continet; ... [b]
Porta borialis Ecclesie continet .xj. pedes. & latitudo .10. pedes

(411)
GROPELANE
Via vocata Gropelane jncipiente ad portam sancti Johannis baptiste ducens per voltam sancti Johannis ad prisonam de Monken brygge ad angulum finis dicte vie continet .300. gressus
latitudo vie continet .8.[to] gressus

(412)
Via parua ab[c] predicti ad Monkenbrygge ad venellam. veniente & obuiantem viam Gropelane ducente ad[d] blyndeyate. continet 100 gressus

(413)
PORTA SANCTI JOHANNIS
Porta[e] sancti Johannis continet in[f] longitudine versus brodestrete .7. virgas
latitudo eius continet ... [g]

(414)
VIA SANCTI LAURENCIJ
latitudo vie sancti laurencij ad finem de Bradstrete continet
... [g] virgas

(415)
HYGHSTRETE
longitudo alte vie de hyghstrete[h] de alta cruce usque portam sancti Nicholai continet .152. gressus

---

a   *pro* or *per* smudged and deleted
b   Blank in MS
c   *anguli* deleted, although *predicti* is not
d   *usque* deleted as superfluous after *ducente ad* inserted above the line
e   *long* (for *longitudo?*) deleted

(410)
ST MICHAEL'S CHURCH
The length of St Michael's church measures 46 steps or 26 yards.
Its width measures 10 yards [or] 20 steps.
The new square bell-tower measures a square on the four sides; each side measures, on the outside, 5 yards.
The height of the tower, by estimation, measures ...
The north door of the church measures 11 feet, and [its] width 10 feet.

(411)
GROPE LANE
The road called Grope Lane, beginning at St John Baptist's Gate, leading past St John's crypt to the prison of Monkenbridge, to the corner at the end of the said road, measures 300 steps.
The width of the road measures 8 steps.

(412)
The small road from the [corner][1] aforesaid at Monkenbridge, to the lane meeting and crossing the road of Grope Lane, leading to Blind Gate, measures 100 steps.

(413)
ST JOHN'S GATE
St John's Gate measures 7 yards in length towards Broad Street.
Its width measures ...

(414)
ST LAWRENCE ROAD
The width of the St Lawrence road at the end of Broad Street measures ... yards.

(415)
HIGH STREET
The length of the highway of High Street, from the High Cross as far as St Nicholas's Gate, measures 152 steps.

---

1   'corner' has been deleted, but 'aforesaid' has not: see note c opposite

---

f   *latitudine* deleted
g   Blank in MS
h   *usque* deleted

p.191

　　*[Henry I's invasion of Normandy, 1105-6;
　　proverb]* [a]

(416)[b]

ANGLIA

Anglia jnsularum maxima habet in longitudine .800. Miliaria
hoc est a Totenesio in Cornubia usque ad Catenesiam in Scocia
Et in [c]
Et in latitudine .300. Miliaria hoc est a Sancto Dauid in Wallia
ad Doroberniam in Cancia
Et in Circuit[d] tria Milia Miliaria 340. sed oblongata. hec jnueni
quodam libro antiquorum cronicorum domini ... [e] capellani
Ecclesie sancti Thome Bristollie notarij vulgariter vocatus
Burtonpreeste;

　　　*[There follow annals relating to St Patrick, St
　　　Augustine and the Saxon kingdoms, which may
　　　or may not have been taken from the same
　　　chronicle]* [f]

p.192

　　[Annals continued] [f]

p.193

　　*[The works and sayings of Robert Grosseteste,
　　Bishop of Lincoln 1235-1253; the place-name
　　Shrewsbury; proverb; note on Bucephalus;
　　Saxon rulers]* [f]

p.194

　　*[Quotations from Ovid, note on Boethius, list
　　of different names for the sun]* [g]

---

a　The notes on this page, with the exception of **(416)**, do not relate to
　　Bristol, and were included in Harvey, *Itineraries*, pp. 324-5.　Harvey
　　observed that the notes on Henry I's Normandy campaigns derive
　　ultimately from Florence of Worcester, but William Worcestre does not
　　give his immediate source
b　Item **(416)** is included in Harvey, *Itineraries*, pp. 324-7, with some
　　variations in transcription and translation.　Harvey (p. 326 n.1) noted
　　the similarity to measurements given in *A Cronicle of Yeres* (1550-1)
c　Probably a false start to the next line
d　*sic*
e　Blank in MS

p.191

    [Henry I's invasion of Normandy, 1105-6; proverb]

(416)

ENGLAND

England, largest of the islands, is 800 miles in length, that is from Totnes in Cornwall[1] as far as to Caithness in Scotland. And in

And in width 300 miles, that is from St David's in Wales to Canterbury in Kent.

In circumference it is 3,340 miles, but [of] oblong [shape]. I found these things in a certain book of ancient chronicles of Sir ... , chaplain of St Thomas's church in Bristol, notary, commonly called Burton priest.[2]

    [There follow annals relating to St Patrick, St Augustine and the Saxon kingdoms, which may or may not have been taken from the same chronicle]

p.192

    [Annals continued]

p.193

    [The works and sayings of Robert Grosseteste, Bishop of Lincoln 1235-1253; the place-name Shrewsbury; proverb; note on Bucephalus; Saxon rulers]

p.194

    [Quotations from Ovid, note on Boethius, list of different names for the sun]

---

1 *sic*, error for Devon

2 See **(339)** for other notes from what is probably the same 'great volume of chronicles of ... John Burton, of the church of St Thomas at Bristol'

---

f Included in Harvey, *Itineraries*, pp. 326-9

g Included in Harvey, *Itineraries*, p. 391

p.195

(417)[a]
Johannes Jay secundus maritus Johanne sororis mee obijt die
.15. Mensis Maij anno christi ... [b]

... [c] filius Roberti Assh[d] quasi etatis ... [e] annorum obijt .19.
die Septembris & sepelitur in Ecclesia sancti Thome

(418)[f]
1480 die .15. Jullij. Navis ... [g] et Johannis Jay junioris
ponderis .80. doliorum jnceperunt viagium apud portum
Bristollie de kyngrode usque ad jnsulam de Brasylle[h] in
occidentali parte hibernie. sulcando maria per ... [i]

et ... [j] Thloyde est magister navis. scientificus marinarius
tocius Anglie. et noua venerunt Bristollie die lune 18. die
Septembris quod dicta navis velauerunt[k] maria per circa .9.
menses[l] nec jnuenerunt jnsulam sed per tempestas maris
reuersi sunt vsque portum ... .[m] in hibernia pro reposicione
navis & marinariorum;

p.196

(419)[n]
ARBOR APUD ALTAM CRUCEM
Memorandum quod quidem Dynt artifici vnius plumpmaker
ville Bristollie dixit diuersis hominibus. ab auditu senium &
antiquorum gencium quod retulerunt sibi. videre vnum
arborem vocatum anglice a hawtree crescentem in loco
hyghstrete vbi Crux magnifica scita est,

---

a Item **(417)** was included in Harvey, *Itineraries*, pp. 308-9, with some
   variations in transcription and translation
b Blank in MS. ⊖ by Talbot in margin opposite this note
c Blank in MS. O by Talbot in margin opposite *filius Roberti Assh*
d cf. **(394)**: 'Robert Assh my kinsman'
e Blank in MS
f Item **(418)** was included in Harvey, *Itineraries*, pp. 308-9, with some
   variations in transcription and translation
g Blank in MS
h *jnsulam de Brasylle* underlined by Talbot, with § in the margin
i Note breaks off
j Blank in MS
k Talbot has drawn a wavy vertical line alongside the note from this point
   to the end, with § in the margin alongside
l *sic*: see note 3 opposite
m Blank in MS
n Item **(419)** is included in Harvey, *Itineraries*, pp. 330-1, with some
   variations in transcription and translation

p.195

(417)
John Jay, second husband of my sister Joan, died the 15th day of the month of May in the year of Christ [1480?].[1]

... the son of Robert Assh, almost ... years of age, died the 19th day of September and is buried in St Thomas's church.

(418)
1480. On the 15th day of July, the ship of ... and John Jay the younger, of the weight of 80 tons, began a voyage from Kingroad at the port of Bristol, to the island of Brazil to the west of Ireland, sailing over the sea by ... [2]

And ... Lloyd was the ship's master, the most knowledgeable mariner in all England. And news came to Bristol on Monday the 18th day of September that the said ship had sailed the sea for about 9 months,[3] not finding the island, but was driven back by storms at sea to the port of ... in Ireland, for refitting the ship and [reorganising] the crew.

p.196

(419)
A TREE AT THE HIGH CROSS
Memorandum, that one Dynt, a pumpmaker by trade, of the town of Bristol, said to several people that he had heard from elderly and aged people that told him they had seen a tree, called in English a hawthorn tree, growing on the spot [in] the High Street where the splendid Cross is sited.

---

1   There has been considerable confusion over John Jay, husband of Worcestre's sister Joan.   John Jay who died between April and July 1468 (Wadley, *Bristol Wills* pp. 142-3) had a wife Joan, a [?half-]brother John and a son John; he also had two daughters called Joan, either or both of whom might have been daughters-in-law. He was to be buried in the quire of St Mary Redcliffe. However, the brass in the quire of St Mary Redcliffe commemorating John and Joan Jay and their 14 children is very late 15th century in style, and bears the incomplete date 148... . Joan Worcestre, it is suggested, married not John Jay (d. 1468) but his [?half-]brother John who, if he was dead before Worcestre's visit in September 1480, presumably died 15th May 1480. He is therefore not the same as John Jay the younger who went in search of Brazil, who was still alive in September 1480 and who was presumably the son of John Jay (d. 1468)
2   The missing words might be 'Blasket island', or similar: cf. **(239)**
3   Harvey, *Itineraries*, p. 309 n.8 found this 'unintelligible', but '9 months' is probably an error for '9 weeks'. The dates of departure and of news

(420)[a]
<u>PYLLENEDE</u>

Item apud vicum vocatum le pylle ende[b] inter portam sancti leonardi & introitum cimiterij Ecclesie sancti Stephani fuerunt domus edificate & pro fundamento. fuit ita debile fundamentum quod foderunt .47. pedes ad bassum[c] terre secure fundamenti. & ibi jnuenerunt jn profundo fundamenti vnam cimbam cum vna toga de Raycloth. ac eciam jnuenerunt vnam magnum[d] arborem longitudinis .16. pedum squaratum et demiserunt in fundo nec coruptum sed integre sanum, &c,

(421)[e]

Radclyff chyrch

Dimencio siue proporcio artificiosissime. de Fremasonwork operata in Porta hostij. occidentalis Ecclesie Radclyff,[f]

The west Dore[g] fretted yn the hede wyth grete Genlese & smale, and fylled wyth entayle, ennyng[h] with[i] a double Moolde costley don & wrought

latitudo porte .7. pedes

altitudo porte .9. pedes.[j]

The square yn the dore[k]	.b.	a Casement
a champ		a Fylet
a bowtelle		a bowtelle
a Casement		a Fylet
a fylet		a Casement
a double ressant wyth a filet		
a Casement		a Fylet
a Fylet		a bowtelle
a bowtelle		a Fylet
a Fylet		a lowryng casement
a Casement		a Fylet
a Fylet		a Resaunt
a grete bowtelle		a fylet
a Fylet		a Ressant lorymer
a Casement		a Casement
a filet		[l]a cors wythoute[m]
.a. a grete bowtelle		<u>Explicit</u> proporcio[n] fenestre

---

a Item **(420)** was included in Harvey, *Itineraries*, pp. 330–3, with some variations in transcription and translation

b *prope* deleted

c The *a* in *bassum* has been rewritten more clearly above

d *sic*

e Item **(421)** was included in Harvey, *Itineraries*, pp. 332–3, with some variations in transcription and translation

f *q'* (for *questio* or *query*?) in margin opposite the beginning of this subheading. The details that follow appear to have been added later

g *ys* deleted

h *sic*, perhaps intended for *ending*?

i Repeated, spelt *wyth*

(420)
PYLLE END
Also, at the street called the Pylle End, between St Leonard's
Gate and the entrance of St Stephen's churchyard, houses were
built; and because the foundation was so weak at bottom, they
dug 47 feet downwards in the ground for a firm foundation.
And there they found at the bottom of the foundation[-trench]
a skiff with a gown of raycloth, and they also found a great
tree,[1] 16 feet in length, squared, not rotten but entirely
sound, etc., and they left [it] in the depths.

(421)

Redcliffe church

The measurement or layout most skilfully carved in
freemasonry work, in the porch of the west door[2] of Redcliffe
church.
The west door [is] carved at the top with great and small
cusps, and filled with carving, ending[3] with a double moulding
lavishly made and worked.
Width of the door 7 feet.
Height of the door 9 feet.
The square [frame] in the doorway:[4]
(a) a chamfer, a bowtel, a casement, a fillet, a double ogee with
a fillet, a casement, a fillet, a bowtel, a fillet, a casement, a
fillet, a large bowtel, a fillet, a casement, a fillet, a large
bowtel,
(b) a casement, a fillet, a bowtel, a fillet, a casement, a fillet, a
bowtel, a fillet, a lowering casement, a fillet, an ogee, a fillet,
an ogee drip, a casement, and a course outside [for the?]
frame.[5]
End of the layout.[6]

---

1   *sic*, but clearly not a natural treetrunk, as it is squared: a worked
    timber, a beam, ship's timber or perhaps even part of a mast
2   The architectural mouldings suggest this is the actual west door of
    Redcliffe church, and not the north porch which Worcestre sometimes,
    e.g. **(424)**, regarded as being at the west end
3   Harvey read this as *euuys*, and translated it as 'ivy leaves'
4   For terms, see glossary
5   Harvey translated this as 'a course without fillet', leaving *fenestre* as
    part of the next line; see note 6 below, and notes m,n below
6   Harvey translated this as 'End of the details of the frame', having left
    fenestre associated with the (deleted) *Explicit proporcio*; see note 5
    above, and notes m,n below

---

j   These two measurements have been jotted in the margin
k   *ys* deleted
l   Illegible deletion, possibly *et*
m   Illegible deletion, possibly *for the*? See note n, below
n   *Explicit proporcio* has been deleted, which Harvey failed to note. The
    line above may therefore be intended to read *Et a cors wythoute [for
    the?] fenestre*

(421) [continued]
Isti .4. proporciones in ambabus a champ asshler
a cors wyth an arch buttant
a boterasse
a body boterasse & a corner
boterasse

p.197

(422)[a]

De Castro & le dongeon de Bristowe;[b]

Memorandum
Porticus jntroitus aule[c] .10.[d] virge longitudinis cum volta archuata desuper ad jntroitum magne aule,

The jnner entre ad Porticum aule[e] .140. gressus. hoc est intelligere. spacium & longitudo inter portam muri de fortificacione murorum de area de le vtterward

longitudo aule[e] .36. virge jn gressibus .54. vel .52.[f] gressus longitudinis, per me computatis
latitudo aule .18. virge vel .26. gressus continet
altitudo murorum aule .14. pedes extra aulam mensuraui
aula quondam magnifica in longitudine latitudine & altitudine. est totum ad Ruinam
Fenestre in aula duplate altitudo de .ij. days continet .14. pedes[g] altitudinis
longitudo tignorum aule anglice raffters. continet .32. pedes

Camera principis[h] longitudo .17. virgarum in[i] sinistra parte aule Regis & per duas columpnas ∴[j] de magnis trabis operatas sed valde veteres.
latitudo eius Camere .9. virge continet
longitudo de le Front coram aula cum cameris 18[k] virge
longitudo tabule de marble stone .15. pedes. scita in alta parte aule pro mensa Regum ibi sedencium

---

a Item **(422)** was included in Harvey, *Itineraries*, pp. 399–400, in Latin only, with some variations in transcription
b *De Castro ... de Bristowe;* was written in first, as a heading
c *Porticus aule* was written in first, as a heading, and *jntroitus* added afterwards above the line
d *.10.* repeated above
e *The jnner entre ad Porticum aule* and *longitudo aule* were written in first, as headings
f *.52.* written above *.54.*, and *vel* added after
g *longitudinis* deleted
h *Camera principis* was written in first, as a heading
i *dextra* deleted

(421) [continued]
These four shapes on both sides:
a chamfered ashlar, a course with a flying buttress, a buttress, a wall buttress, and a corner buttress.[1]

p.197

(422)[2]
Of the Castle and The Keep of Bristol.
Memorandum:
The entrance porch of the hall: 10 yards in length, with an arched vault above the entrance of the great hall.

The inner entrance to the porch of the hall: 140 steps, that is taking the area and length between the gate of the wall from the defences of the walls of the yard of the outer ward.

The length of the hall: 36 yards; in steps: 52 or 54 steps in length, counted by me.
The width of the hall measures 18 yards or 26 steps.
The height of the walls of the hall I have measured: 14 feet outside the hall.
The hall, formerly splendid in length, width and height, is wholly ruinous.
The height of a double window in the hall, of 2 lights, measures 14 feet high.
The length of the beams of the hall (in English, 'rafters') measures 32 feet.

The length of the prince's[3] chamber: 17 yards, on the left-hand side of the King's hall, and past two pillars worked from great timbers, but extremely old.
The width of that chamber measures 9 yards.
The length of the facade in front of the hall with the chambers: 18 yards.
The length of the slab of marble set at the upper end of the hall, for the table of kings sitting there: 15 feet.

---

1   Harvey rendered course as 'string course', wall and corner buttresses as 'a solid buttress and an angle buttress'
2   For Worcestre's English version see **(396)**; see also his diary **(437)**
3   *sic*, unless Worcestre's *principis* is an error for his more usual *principalis* (the main chamber); either would suit the context

---

j   ∴ *de magnis trabis operatas sed valde veteres* is in the margin, linked by Worcestre's ∴ symbol. The whole paragraph is so full of amendments that his final intended order is uncertain
k   *18* repeated above

(422) [continued]
Turris longitudo.[a]   Jn orientali parte turris .36. virgas
continet
latitudo eius ex parte occidentali et meridionali .30. virgas[b]
continet

longitudo de le vtterward castri a media porta & muro separata
ab interiori warda Capelle principale, aule camera, continet
.160. gressus,

longitudo primi jntroitus ad castrum per portam .40. gressus.
hoc est intelligendum de vico Castelstrete jntrando ad primam
portam Castri siue vocatam le vtterewarde

Capella in le vtterward idest prima warda in honore sancti
Martini est dedicata tamen in deuocione sancti Johannis
baptiste. et monachus prioratus sancti Jacobi omni die deberet
in dicta capella tamen non celebrat nisi per dominicam
mercurium & venerem in septimana

Capella alia magnifica pro Rege & dominas[c] ac dominabus[c] scita
in[d] principalissima warda ex parte boriali aule vbi Camere
pulcherime sunt edificate sed discooperte nude & vacue de
planchers & coopertura

Domus Officiariorum coquine & hee[e] pertinentes sunt in
jnteriori warda iuxta aulam in parte sinistra idest in meridionali
parte aule,

Domus Officij Constabularij est scita in exteriori warda prima.
in parte meridionali turris magnifici, Sed totum ad terram
prostrate & dirute, vnde magna pietas surgit

p.198

(423)[f]
Illebrygge, lokbrygge, Serlesmyte vbi Mundford tendebatur

Memorandum
         [The rest of the page is blank]

---

a   *Turris longitudo* was written in first, as a heading
b   *30. virgas* repeated
c   *sic:* Worcestre first wrote *dominis*, before putting *a* over the *i*
d   *le* deleted
e   *sic:* probably Worcestre's spelling of *hæ*
f   Item **(423)** was included in Harvey, *Itineraries*, pp. 332-3, with some
    variations in transcription and translation

(422) [continued]
The length of the Keep: on the east side of the tower, it measures 36 yards.
Its width on the west and south side measures 30 yards.

The length from the outer ward of the Castle, from the middle gate and the wall separating [it] from the inner ward, to the chapel of the main hall chamber, measures 160 steps.

The length of the main entrance to the Castle through the gate: 40 steps; that is, taking [it] as from the street of Castle Street, entering at the main gate of the Castle, otherwise called the outer ward.

The Chapel in the outer ward, that is the first ward, is dedicated in honour of St Martin; [now,] however, in the service of St John the Baptist; and a monk of the priory of St James should [be] in the said chapel every day. However, he only celebrates on Sunday, Wednesday and Friday each week.

Another splendid chapel for the King and the lords and ladies [is] sited in the most important ward, on the north side of the hall, where very beautiful chambers were built, but [now] roofless, bare and stripped of floors and ceilings.

The kitchen quarters and their appurtenances are in the inner ward next to the hall, on the left hand side, that is on the south side of the hall.

The Constable's quarters are sited in the first, outer ward, on the south side of the splendid Keep; but the whole thing is thrown down to the ground and ruinous, whence arises great sadness.

p.198

(423)
[H?]illbridge, Lockbridge,[1] 'Serlesmyte',[2] where Mundford[3] was cared for.

Memorandum
[The rest of the page is blank]

---

1   cf. **(71)**
2   Harvey suggested that this might be a corruption of Earlsmead
3   cf. **(394)**: 'Master Mundford, knight' received a gift of wine

p.199

(424)

Radclyff

nota.[a] Cimiterium Ecclesie de Radclyff continet .500. gressus
Crux pulcherima artificiose operata est in medio dicti Cimiterij
hostium occidentalis Ecclesie continet .9. virgas[b] preter .6.[c]
pollices

latitudo capelle beate Marie de Radclyff in occidentali[d] parte
Ecclesie continet .10. virgas
longitudo dicte capelle ... [e]

altitudo volte frette archuate vsque cooperturam plumbi

altitudo volte archuate tocius Ecclesie tam navis Ecclesie quam
duarum   alarum   necnon   quatuor   alarum   voltarum   &
archuatarum[f] a parte boriali in meridiem continet computando
per numerum graduum. ad numerum .80. anglice steppys[g] de
terra ad superiorem partem cooperture tignorum & plumbi
cooperancium   totam   Ecclesiam   secundum[h]   relacionem
plumbatoris dicte Ecclesie michi dicte .7. die Septembris anno
1480 in dicta Ecclesia operante. 80 steppys superius recitatis
Et quilibet gradus siue Stepp. anglice dictus. continet .8.
pollices ad minus. sic in toto altitudo operis cooperture dicte
Ecclesie continet[i] .53. pedes & .4. pollices

CAPELLA
longitudo Ecclesie navis cum choro de Radclyff preter capellam
orientalem beate marie continet .113. gressus.
latitudo[j] brachiorum Ecclesie ante chorum a meridie in boriam
continet .67. gressus
longitudo Capelle beate Marie in orientalyssima parte Ecclesie
predicte continet .16. virgas

---

a This reconstructs the probable order in which Worcestre originally wrote
   this item. After the heading, he described (in matching ink) the interior
   of the church, beginning with *latitudo capelle* ... and then the outside
   (see pp. 244–5). The two lines beginning *nota. Cimiterium* ... and *Crux
   pulcherima* ... were fitted between the heading and the existing
   description in a different ink; the third line, *hostium occidentalis* ...,
   was added last, also in this different ink, above the heading Radclyff for
   lack of any other space
b *virgas* repeated
c *pollices* smudged and deleted
d *sic*

p.199

(424)

Redcliffe

Note: the churchyard of Redcliffe church measures 500 steps.
There is a very beautiful cross, skilfully worked, in the middle
of the said churchyard.
The door at the west [end] of the church measures 9 yards less
6 inches.

The width of the chapel of the Blessed Mary Redcliffe, at the
west end of the church,[1] measures 10 yards.
The length of the said chapel: ...

The height of the carved arched vault as far as the lead roof

The height of the arched vault of the whole church, both of the
nave of the church and of the two aisles, and also of the four
vaulted and arched aisles, from the north side to the south,
measures (counting up the number of stairs) to the number of
80 (in English) 'steps', from the ground to the upper side of
the roof of beams and lead covering the whole church,
according to the account of the plumber at the said church
(working in the said church) to me on the 7th day of
September in the year 1480: 80 steps [as] given above; and
each stair or 'step' (so-called in English) measures 8 inches at
least, so that in all the height of the roof construction of the
said church measures 53 feet and 4 inches.

THE CHAPEL

The length of the nave of Redcliffe church together with the
choir, excepting the eastern Lady chapel, measures 113 steps.
The width of the transepts of the church in front of the quire,
from south to north, measures 67 steps.
The length of the Lady chapel at the easternmost end of the
aforesaid church measures 16 yards.

---

1   i.e. the north porch, which lies towards the west end of the church

---

e   Blank in MS
f   *in* deleted
g   Worcestre originally wrote *.98. anglice steppys*, deleted *.98.* and wrote
    .80. steppys above
h   Illegible deletion, possibly *compu* (for *computantem*?)
i   *per* deleted
j   *E* deleted

(424) [continued]
ā
Et omnes boterasse in meridionali parte tocius Ecclesie cum boterasses Campanile continet, .25. in numero preter lez boterasses Campanilis, que continet in numero ... ᵃ boterasses

.a.ᵇ
latitudo trium alarum in meridionali parte Ecclesie continet .26. gressus. & .26. gressus in parte boriali Ecclesieᶜ

In boriali parteᵈ Ecclesie beate Marie de Radclyff sunt .16. boterasses. ab orientaliᵉ capella beate Marie usque ad principalem capellam. sunt .16. boterasses magne. quorum aliqui sunt in latitudine inferius apud le table. versus & prope terram .2. virgarum & alique boterasses minus

Quantitas rotunditatis principalis capelle sancte Marie cum ymaginibus Regum operatis subtiliter in opere de Frestone continet in circuitu cum hostio jntroitus subtiliter operatus .44. virgasᶠ

(425)ᵍ
VIA DE RADCLYFF STRETE
In via de Radclyfstert in parte ... ʰ sunt ... ʰ venelle et prima venella est prope murum de le tounewalle vocata ... ʰ

[**(424)** continued]
.b.ⁱ
latitudoʲ trium alarum in parte boriali Ecclesie de Radclyff continet 15. virgas & tot virge latitudoᵏ in parte boriali Ecclesie

---

a   Blank in MS
b   For .*b*., the other half of this set of measurements, see the section in the middle of **(425)**, and note c below
c   The sentence *latitudo trium alarum ... boriali Ecclesie* is very small and cramped, probably inserted afterwards; its partner .*b*. has been fitted into the next available space, part way through **(425)**, below.
d   *Ec* (for *Ecclesie*) smudged and deleted
e   *sic*
f   .*44. virge* repeated more clearly in the margin, linked by Worcestre's ∴ symbol
g   Part of **(425)** has been fitted in between sections of **(424)** as indicated, for lack of other space
h   Blank in MS
i   .*b*. is a continuation of .*a*. in **(424)**, added afterwards and fitted into the first available space
j   *sic*: Worcestre appears to have become muddled, perhaps when revising his notes. He originally wrote *longitudo*, then amended it to *latitudo* as [continued opposite]

(424) [continued]
And all the buttress[es] on the south side of the whole church, with the buttresses of the bell-tower, comprise 25 in number, except for the buttresses of the bell-tower which comprise ... buttresses in number.

(a)[1]
The width of the three aisles on the south side of the church measures 26 steps, and 26 steps on the north side of the church.

On the north side of the church of the Blessed Mary at Redcliffe there are 16 buttresses. From the eastern Lady chapel as far as the main chapel there are 16 great buttresses, some of which are 2 yards in width lower down at the plinth, towards and near the ground, and other buttresses [are] less.

The measurement around the main chapel of St Mary,[2] with statues of kings finely carved in freestone-work, with the exquisitely carved entrance door, measures 44 yards in circumference.

(425)
THE ROAD OF REDCLIFFE STREET
In the road of Redcliffe Street, on the [south][3] side, there are [five] lanes, and the first lane, called ... , is next to the wall of the town wall.

[**(424)** continued]
(b)
The width[4] of the three aisles on the north side of Redcliffe church measures 15 yards, and as many yards in width[4] on the north side of the church.

---

1 See **(425)** for .*b.*, which follows this sentence; see notes b,c opposite
2 i.e. the north porch chapel
3 Since **(426)** is the 'north' side of Redcliffe Street, Worcestre must have intended **(425)** to be the 'south' side; but he was perhaps uneasy about this from the start. Redcliffe Street, except at its north end near Bristol Bridge, runs almost due north-south, and Worcestre was well aware of the east ends of nearby churches. In fact, **(425)** is the east or south-east, and **(426)** the west or north-west side
4 *sic*, see note j opposite and below

---

j [continued] shown. He then rewrote *longitudo*, deleted it and wrote *latitudo* above it. His final preference would seem to be *latitudo*; but this makes the second half of his note (see k below) contradictory
k *sic*

(425) [continued]
Secunda venella sequens est howndonlane & continet ... [a]
gressus

Tercia venella est in meridionali parte Ecclesie sancti Thome &
continet ... [a] gressus

Quarta venella in[b] meridionali parte[c] Ecclesie sancti Thome
prope ibidem Ecclesiam & continet ... [d] gressus

Quinta venella est ex altera parte cimiterij sancti Thome vbi
tumba dauid Ruddoke est facta. in quodam muro
Et continet .180. gressus

---

(426)
VENELLE IN RADCLYFF STRE[e] IN PARTE BORIALI
In alia parte vie de Radclyfstrete proxima aque de Avyn. in
boriali parte vie de Radclyff. est prima venella a porta de
Radclyff yate. vsque aquam Avyn. et continet[f] .150. gressus
vbi domus Moysi lumbardi maneba[g]

Porte due in fine de Radclyffstrete cum spacio de le wateryng
place ac conducto paruo in le wateryngplace continet .32.
gressus, sed spacium inter duas portas continet .20. gressus

p.200

[h]venelle in parte boriali de Radclyf strete transciens
vsque avyn water

Venella secunda alia versus pontem Bristollie non multum distat
a prima venella quasi spacium .60. gressuum; & continet in
longitudine circa .110. gressus

---

a　Blank in MS
b　*boriali* deleted
c　Illegible deletion, possibly *Sancti*
d　Blank in MS
e　*sic*
f　*.150.* deleted
g　*sic*: the note breaks off

(425) [continued]
The second lane next along is Hounden Lane, and measures ...
steps.

The third lane is on the south side of St Thomas's church, and
measures ... steps.

The fourth lane [is] on the south side of St Thomas's church,
right next to that church, and it measures ... steps.

The fifth lane is on the other side of St Thomas's churchyard,
where the tomb of David Ruddock is set in a certain wall.
And it measures 180 steps.

---

(426)
LANES IN REDCLIFFE STREET ON THE NORTH SIDE
On the other side of the road of Redcliffe Street, next to the
river Avon, on the north side of the road of Redcliffe, is the
first lane from the gate of Redcliffe Gate to the river Avon,
where [there is] the house [where] Moses Lombard dwelt.[1]
And it measures 150 steps.

The two gates at the end of Redcliffe Street, including the area
of the watering-place, and the small conduit in the watering-
place, measure 32 steps; but the space between the two gates
measures 20 steps.

p.200

Lanes on the north side of Redcliffe Street, going along
to the river Avon

Another lane, the second towards Bristol Bridge, not far from
the first lane (a distance of about 60 steps); and it measures
about 110 steps in length.

---

1   Worcestre appears to have changed the subject midway through this
    incomplete phrase

---

h   *Md qd* (for *Memorandum quod*) has been added later in the margin in
    front of this heading.   Perhaps it, and the heading, were to indicate the
    continuation of **(426)** on the new page

(426) [continued]

<u>Venella</u> tercia in eadem forma coram aquam de Avyn. transciens.[a] cum vna via ad aquam de Avyn vocatum anglice a Slepe aliter ... [b]

et continet in longitudine ad aquam de Avyn; et est ex opposito venelle in altera parte venelle eundo ad Ecclesiam sancti Thome;

(427)

longitudo vie in parte[c] occidentali Ecclesie Religionum & hospitalitatis sancti Johannis baptiste ex altera parte turris Ecclesie de Radclyff continet .154.[d] gressus vsque aquam Auene,

latitudo dicte vie continet .3. virgas

<u>Heremitagium</u> est scitum in occidentali parte Ecclesie sancti Johannis super aquam Auene in Rubeo Cliuo, super aquam Abone anglice Avyn;

(428)

VIA AD MOLENDINA

longitudo vie in parte boriali super Radclyfhill vltra Ecclesiam de Radclyff in parte[e] dextra versus calcetum de Brisghtbow.[f] et citra domum hospitalis beate marie Magdalene conducentem ad Molendina super aquam Avyn scita; de lapidibus Murata continet[g] .400. gressus que vocatem ... [h] myllys

latitudo vie Molendinorum continet .3. virgas

(429)

HOSPITALE SANCTI JOHANNIS

Ecclesia hospitalis sancti Johannis baptiste.[i] ex opposito. Ecclesie beate marie de Radclyff

latitudo continet ... [j]

longitudo aule continet .21. gressus

latitudo aule continet .13. gressus

longitudo Claustri continet .32. gressus

latitudo Claustri continet .30. gressus

stagnum aque conductus quadratus est in medio Claustri

---

a   *et continet circa* deleted
b   Note breaks off
c   *orientali* deleted
d   *.150.* written above
e   *sini* (for *sinistra*) deleted
f   *sic*, suggesting Worcestre started to write *Bristollia*, before changing it to *Brightbow*
g   *in* deleted

(426) [continued]
A third lane going along to the water-front of the Avon in the same way, with a way called in English 'a slip', otherwise … ; and it measures in length to the river Avon, and it is opposite a lane on the other side: the lane going to St Thomas's church.

(427)
The length of the road on the west side of the church of the order and hospital of St John Baptist, on the other side of the tower of Redcliffe church, measures 154 steps as far as the river Avon.
The width of the said road measures 3 yards.

The hermitage is sited on the west side of the church of St John, above the river Avon on Redcliffe, above the river Abona, in English 'Avon'.

(428)
ROAD TO THE MILLS
The length of the road on the north side upon Redcliffe Hill, on the right side beyond Redcliffe church, towards the path from Brightbow and this side of the hospital of the Blessed Mary Magdalene, leading to the mills, walled in stone, sited upon the river Avon, which are called [Treen] Mills, measures 400 yards.
The width of the road of the mills measures 3 yards.

(429)
ST JOHN'S HOSPITAL
The church of St John the Baptist's hospital, opposite the church of the Blessed Mary of Redcliffe:
The width measures …
The length of the nave measures 21 steps.
The width of the nave measures 13 steps.
The length of the cloister measures 32 steps.
The width of the cloister measures 30 steps.
There is a pool of water, a square conduit,[1] in the middle of the cloister.

---

1   i.e. a square water tank

---

h   Blank in MS
i   *Jn* deleted
j   Blank in MS

(430)

Porta ad venellam siue viam in parte[a] occidentali de Ecclesie quam prope murum Ecclesie predicte usque ad aquam de Frome continet .150. gressus.　latitudo porte & vie 4. virge,

---

(431)

longitudo Ecclesie sancti Thome continet .73. gressus siue .48.[b] virgas

latitudo eius continet .21. virgas siue ... [c] gressus

altitudo turris ... [c]

latitudo turris ... [c]

(432)

latitudo porte sancti Nicholai .4. virge

longitudo porte .9. virge .14. gressus

(433)

latitudo porte sancti leonardi .4. virge

longitudo porte .9. virge in parte orientali

(434)

latitudo porte sancti Johannis .4. virge

longitudo porte .7. virgas

(435)

latitudo porte Newgate .4. virge

longitudo dicte porte, .9. virge

(436)

latitudo vie sancti Thome jncipiente apud pontem Bristollie .4. virge

latitudo vie principij prope pontem ad Radclyffstrete, ... [c]

latitudo vie Toukerstrete prope pontem, ... [c]

d

---

a　*orientali* deleted
b　*.48.* deleted
c　Blank in MS
d　In the bottom left-hand corner of the page is one of Worcestre's jotted
　　reckonings, deleted:

	Memorandum	*.14.*	*celers*
	A.	[?.2]*1.*	*celers*
	A.	*.16.*	*parte dextre* (on the right-hand side)
		.12.	

(430)
The gate at the lane or road on the west side of the church, which [goes] by the wall of the aforesaid church as far as to the river Frome,[1] measures 150 steps. The width of the gate and the road: 4 yards.

---

(431)
The length of St Thomas's church measures 73 steps or 48 yards.
Its width measures 21 yards or ... steps.
The height of the tower: ...
The width of the tower: ...

(432)
The width of St Nicholas's Gate: 4 yards;
the length of the gate: 9 yards [or] 14 steps.

(433)
The width of St Leonard's Gate: 4 yards;
the length of the gate: 9 yards on the east side.

(434)
The width of St John's Gate: 4 yards;
the length of the gate: 7 yards.

(435)
The width of the gate of Newgate 4 yards;
the length of the said gate: 9 yards.

(436)
The width of the St Thomas's road, beginning at Bristol Bridge: 4 yards.

The width of the main road near the Bridge at Redcliffe Street: ...

The width of the Tucker Street road near the Bridge: ...

---

1   error for Avon

p.201

[Worcestre's Bristol diary, August–September
1480, continued from item (395)]

(437)[a]
Jovis vltimo die Augusti. applicui Bristollie

Dominica .10. die Septembris, equitaui ad Collegium Westberi
& locutus fui cum Johannes Griffyth de Bristollie marchant ibi
morante

Item equitaui vsque Shyrehampton loquendo cum Thoma Yong
armigero pro ij. libris meis recuperandis vnum de libro magno
Ethicorum, alium de libro vocato le Myrrour de Dames
cooperto rubeo corio, & jantaui secum dedit michi letum
vultum pro amore patris sui. cum vxore eius sui favore

[b]Dominica predicta applicui Bristollie

Martis .12. .7.[bris] vidi Castellum Bristollie dirutum & valde
malum in reparacionibus

Dominica .27.[c] die .7.[bris] fuit[d] apud Ghyston Clyff &
mensuraui Rupem profundum vsque heremitagium ad
profunditatem .20. brachiorum. Et vnus juuenis officij fabri
dixit mensura residuum Rupis dicte die michi ad aquam[e] anglice
Ebbyng Water, et dixit mensurare a[f] Capella dicti heremitagij
.44. brachia sic in toto continet .64. brachia profunditatis

Martis .26. die .7.[bris] fui apud heremitagium vltra aquam de
Avyn quando mare exijt idest Ebbyngwater per villam Rownam.
in batilla conductus directe in monte opposita. seu contraria
Ghyston Clyff in dominio Asshton cuius dominus est Johannes
Chok chivaler,

... die .7.[bris] deo auxiliante propono ... [g]

---

a   Item **(437)** was included in Harvey, *Itineraries*, pp. 262–3, with some
    variations in transcription and translation
b   This entry originally began *Jovis predictus*, deleted
c   Worcestre clearly wrote 27, perhaps anticipating the reference to the
    7th month; the correct date should be Sunday 24th September
d   *sic*
e   *de* deleted
f   *di* (probably *dicti*, left unfinished)
g   The page is torn off at this point

p.201

> *[Worcestre's Bristol diary, August–September 1480, continued from item* **(395)***]*

(437)[1]
Thursday the last day of August I arrived at Bristol.

Sunday 10th day of September I rode to Westbury College and spoke with John Griffyth of Bristol, merchant, who lives there.

I also rode as far as Shirehampton, to speak with Thomas Yong esquire, to get back 2 of my books: one a large book of *Ethics*, the other a book called *The Ladies' Mirror*, bound in red leather; and I breakfasted with him. He, with his wife, kindly made me most welcome, for his father's sake.

Sunday aforesaid I arrived [back] at Bristol.

Tuesday 12 September I saw Bristol Castle, broken down and in an extremely bad state of repair.[2]

Sunday 2[4]th[3] day of September I was at Ghyston Cliff, and measured the cliff depth down to the hermitage, as 20 fathoms down. And a young man of the trade of a smith said to me that the measurement of the rest of the cliff, [down] to the water at, in English, 'low-water' on that day: and he said [it] measured 44 fathoms from the chapel of the said hermitage; so in all it measures 60 fathoms downwards.[4]

Tuesday 26th day of September I was at the hermitage above the river Avon; when the tide went out, that is at low-water, I was taken in a little boat[5] along by Rownham village, straight to the hill opposite or facing Ghyston Cliff, in the lordship of Ashton, of which John Choke, knight, is the lord.

... day of September, with God's help, I intend ... [6]

---

1 The diary **(395)**/**(437)** partners Worcestre's accounts **(394)**/**(438)** for the same period
2 Probably the visit described in **(396)** and/or **(422)**
3 See note c opposite; cf. **(66)**
4 For another version, see **(63)**
5 Probably the occasion of Worcestre's notes in **(52)**
6 The page is torn off at this point

p.202

[Accounts, continued from **(394)***]*

(438)[a]
Item dicto mense Septembris solui pro vno paruo pane. de zucrelofe. ponderis .2.li. .j. quarter. precij lb. .5.ob. xiijd. pro alio zucrelofe ponderis .iij.lb. .j. quarter. 17.d.ob. pro .5. bscakes[b] 2.d pro anulo .jd　pro .pare precularum .2.d. pro .3. cepis 2.d　pro filo pakthrede .jd　pro vno bosco ad custodiendum le pakthrede j.d.

c

p.203

(439)[d]
ā
Memorandum quod isto anno christi .1465. Bristollie relatum fuit mihi per Elizabet Nicholl quod die Epiphanie. Elizabet Nicholle commater mea obijt per .35. annos preteritos viz quando leycestre fuit maior londoniensis[e]

ā
Et dicto anno scilicet in anno christi .14... .[f] viz die Commemoracionis animarum. Willelmus Nicholl & ... [g] maritus Elizabet consortis sue uelauerunt in duobus nauibus. vnus in navi phish vocato le cog Anne[h] & alter viz maritus Elizabet in navi Thome Erle extra le kyngrode & ambo perierunt in vigilia sancte katerine proxima post cogita de die transitus eius[i] viz le cog Anne submersus & alius navis captus per hispanos

---

a　Item **(438)** was included in Harvey, *Itineraries*, pp. 264-5, with some variations in transcription and translation
b　*sic*, cf. *bysquey cakys* in **(394)**
c　The bottom quarter of the page has been torn off (cf. end of **(437)**). The space that remains has been filled with jottings in Latin, Hebrew, Greek and French by Henry Aldrich (for details, see Harvey, *Itineraries*, p. 266 note a). The page appears to have been torn before Aldrich scribbled on it
d　Item **(439)**, memoranda on Worcestre family history, was included in Harvey, *Itineraries*, pp. 308-313, with variations in transcription and translation
e　*sic*; O by Talbot in the margin opposite
f　*.14...* . inserted above the line, with a small space left for addition of the last two digits
g　Blank in MS
h　Θ by Talbot in the margin opposite

p.202

[Accounts, continued from (394)]

(438)[1]
Also in the said month of September I paid for one small sugarloaf weighing 2¼ lbs., at 5½d. per lb., 13d.
For another sugarloaf weighing 3¼ lbs., 17½d.
For 5 biscuit cakes,[2] 2d.; for a ring, 1d.; for a rosary, 2d.; for 3 onions, 2d.; for packthread twine, 1d.; for one box to keep the packthread, 1d.

3

p.203

(439)
Memorandum, that in this year of Christ 1465, at Bristol, it was told to me by Elizabeth Nicholl, that Elizabeth Nicholl my godmother died on the Feast of the Epiphany 35 years before,[4] to wit, when Leycestre was mayor of London.[5]

And in the said year, namely in the year of Christ 14[30], to wit on All Souls Day,[6] William Nicholl and ... the husband of Elizabeth his wife,[7] sailed out of the Kingroad in two ships, the one in a fishing boat called the *Cog Anne*, and the other, to wit Elizabeth's husband, in the ship of Thomas Erle; and they both perished on St Katherine's Eve[8] next following (work out the day of their death)[9] to wit, the *Cog Anne* sunk, and the other ship captured by Spaniards.

---

1   The accounts **(394)/(438)** partner Worcestre's diary **(395)/(437)** for the same period
2   cf. **(394)**
3   The bottom quarter of the page has been torn off at this point
4   6th January 1430/1
5   Error for Bristol. John Leycestre was Mayor of Bristol in 1430, which is 35 years before 1465
6   2nd November
7   It is unclear whether the nameless seaman was husband of Elizabeth Nicholl, Worcestre's godmother, or of Elizabeth Nicholl who told him about the disasters 30 years later; or whether 'Elizabeth his wife' is an error for 'Elizabeth his sister', using her maiden name. Either way, the implication is that the two men lost on the same day in separate disasters were related, perhaps brothers or brothers-in-law
8   24th November
9   The date was added afterwards: see note i below

---

i   *cogita de die transitus eius* is part of the original note, written before the exact date was inserted

(439) [continued]

ā

Memorandum quod die sancte trinitatis proxima[a] ante capcionem dictarum Nauium. Elizabet Nicholl filia Isabelle Nicholle erat sponsata; cuidam mercatori[b]

Memorandum quod die sancte Margarete anno christi .1402., Matilda Botoner[c] auia mea obijt. et executores eius fuerunt. Thomas Botoner filius eius & Willelmus Wyrcestre filiaster eius, & habuit exitus dictum Willelmum[d] Botoner Elizabet sponsata Willelmo Wyrcetyr & Aliciam sponsata Thome Benisham,[e]

Memorandum quod mense Jullij anno quinto regni Regis Henrici quinti. Willelmus Wyrcetyr primo jnhabitauit in tenemento Colyns in Brodemede,[f]

Anno .48. regni Regis Edwardi tercij. tenementum patris mei in Brodemede fuit venditum Thome Botoner[g] auie mee & T.Botoner filio suo primogenito,

Anno secundo regni Regis Henrici quarti. W.Wyrcestr pater meus[h] primo cepit in firmam tenementum Johannis Sutton super le bake in parochia sancti Jacobi[i] in quo tenemento W.Wyrcestre natus fuit

Anno[j] Christi .1412. Johannes Randolf obijt, & fecit executores Agnetam consortem suam & Willelmum Knokyn

Memorandum quod Adam Botoner de Coventre[k] fuit frater Thome Botoner aui mei. per relacionem Agnete Randolf auicie[l] me.[m] & ... [n] Bracy filie eius. Et dictus Adam habuit exitum Agnetam Botoner de laffordesyate. Bristollie. & obijt apud Coventre tempore magne pestilenciali. anno christi circa .1386.,[o] & misit filiam suam prefatam Bristollie ad Thomam

---

a *proxima* repeated
b Note breaks off
c *com* (for *commater?*) deleted
d *sic*
e Or possibly *Bemsham*
f *Bermondseystrete* (another confusion with London) deleted, and *Brodemede* written above
g *pat* (for *patri*) deleted
h *W.Wyrcestr pater meus* underlined by Talbot, who has put two marks, § and ⊕ in the margin opposite
i *v* (for *vbi?*) deleted
j *duodecimo* deleted
k *habuit* deleted
l *sic*, or possibly *amcie*, intended for *amicie*

(439) [continued]

Memorandum, that on Trinity Sunday next before the loss of the said ships,[1] Elizabeth Nicholl daughter of Isabel Nicholl was married to a certain merchant.

Memorandum, that on St Margaret's Day[2] in the year of Christ 1402, Matilda Botoner my grandmother died, and her executors were Thomas Botoner her son and William Worcestre her son-in-law; and she had issue the said William Botoner,[3] Elizabeth married to William Worcestre, and Alice married to Thomas Benisham.[4]

Memorandum, that in the month of July, in the fifth year of the reign of King Henry V,[5] William Worcestre[6] first occupied Colyns tenement in Broadmead.

In the 48th year of the reign of King Edward III,[7] my father's tenement in Broadmead was sold to Thomas Botoner my grandfather and Thomas Botoner his eldest son.

In the second year of the reign of King Henry IV,[8] W.Worcestre my father first leased the tenement of John Sutton upon The Back in St James's parish, in which tenement W.Worcestre was born.[9]

In the year of Christ 1412, John Randolf died and made Agnes his wife and William Knokyn [his] executors.

Memorandum, that Adam Botoner of Coventry was the brother of Thomas Botoner my grandfather, according to the account of Agnes Randolf my aunt and ... Bracy her daughter. And the said Adam had issue Agnes Botoner of Lawford's Gate, Bristol; and he died at Coventry at the time of the great plague about the year of Christ 1386, and sent his aforesaid daughter

---

1 Sunday 28th May 1430
2 20th July
3 *sic*, error for Thomas Botoner
4 Or possibly 'Bemsham'
5 July 1417
6 Father of the writer, who was then two or three years old
7 1374-5
8 1400-1
9 William Worcestre was born in 1415: J.H.Harvey, *The Genealogists' Magazine* xvi no.6 (June 1970), pp. 274-5 citing Bodleian MS. Laud Misc., 674 fo. 76

---

m *sic*
n Blank in MS
o Worcestre originally wrote *.1348.*, the year of the first great plague

(439) [continued]
Botoner fratrem suum. custodiendam. & quidam Johannes
Randolf de laffordesyate loder duxit dictam Agnetam ad tunc
etatis .4. annorum de Coventre ad Bristolliam

LIBER GRAMATICUS[a]
Memorandum de libro meo gramatico existente cum Magistro
scole[b] norwici ad recuperandum secundum relacionem Johannis
Cropp;
recuperat[c]

Memorandum de[d] nominibus Tychemerssh. prope villa
Wyrcestre vel prope villam de Ekyngton prope pershore quod
ipsi sunt de consanguinitate Willemi Botoner & Agnete Randolf
secundum suam relacionem;

> *[Here ends the main part of William
> Worcestre's Bristol notes, as now bound in
> C.C.C.C. MS 210, pp. 87–203]*

---

a   This note has been crossed through, presumably when the book was
    retrieved
b   ϴ by Talbot in margin opposite
c   Written in the margin, in different ink, on a later occasion
d   *T* (for *Tychemerssh*) deleted

(439) [continued]
to Bristol, to the care of Thomas Botoner his brother to be looked after; and a certain John Randolf of Lawford's Gate, carrier, brought the said Agnes, then aged 4 years, from Coventry to Bristol.

GRAMMAR BOOK
Memorandum, about my grammar book, being with the school master[1] at Norwich according to the account of John Cropp – to get it back.
Retrieved.

Memorandum about [persons] named Titchmarsh, near the town of Worcester, or near the village of Eckington[2] near Pershore: that they are kinsmen of William Botoner and Agnes Randolf, according to her account.

[Here ends the main part of William Worcestre's Bristol notes, as now bound in C.C.C.C. MS 210, pp. 87–203]

---

1 Harvey, *Itineraries*, p. 312 n.1 read this as *Magistro soole*, whom he identified as John Sowle, Carmelite friar of Norwich
2 The village of Eckington lies on the east bank of the Avon, about 3 miles south of Pershore

ADDITIONAL BRISTOL REFERENCES

[Sheets which were probably part of William Worcestre's 1480 Bristol notes, but which are now bound elsewhere in C.C.C.C. MS 210, together with other Bristol notes made on earlier visits. These are printed in the page order in which they are now bound] [a]

p.8　　　　　　　　　　　　　　　　　**[1478]**

(440)[b]
Memorandum
LONGITUDO RADCLIFFE ECCLESIE BRISTOLLIE
ā
longitudo tocius Ecclesie beate marie de Radclyffe continet .63. virgas preter Capellam beate Marie,[c]
longitudo capelle beate marie .13. virge .j. pedes[d] & dimidium
latitudo capelle 7 virge,
latitudo Ecclesie tocius .18. virge
Summa tocius longitudinis continet .77. virgas. Ecclesie Radclyffe
longitudo secundarie porte. ex parte boriali .v. virge
latitudo dicte Porche: 4 virge et quarta pars

Dominus Willelmus Canyngys ditissimus[e] ac sapientissimus mercator ville Bristollie predicta[f] decanus Ecclesie Westbery obijt .17. die Nouembris anno christi .1474. ut exaltatus fuit jn ordine presbiteratus .7. annis; & quinquies maior dicte ville fuit,
electus fuit pro re publica dicte ville

longitudo de crosse jsles continet in longitudine .38. virgas
latitudo trium Elarum voltarum cum lapidibus .14. virgas continet
latitudo cuiuslibet arcus jnfra columpnas continet .10. pedes
longitudo de le crosse jsle continet .8. arcus a boria in meridiem

---

a　Because these Bristol notes fall outside the main Bristol collection, they were all included in Harvey, *Itineraries* as indicated for each item
b　Item **(440)** was included in Harvey, *Itineraries*, pp. 52-55, with some variations in transcription and translation
c　.77. *virgas* (the overall length, as noted further down) has been inserted above *Capellam beate Marie*, deleted, and then marked *stet*
d　*sic*

ADDITIONAL BRISTOL REFERENCES

[Sheets which were probably part of William Worcestre's 1480 Bristol notes, but which are now bound elsewhere in C.C.C.C. MS 210, together with other Bristol notes made on earlier visits. These are printed in the page order in which they are now bound]

p.8 [1478][1]

(440)

Memorandum

THE LENGTH OF REDCLIFFE CHURCH, BRISTOL

The length of the whole church of the Blessed Mary of Redcliffe, except the Lady chapel, measures 63 yards.

The length of the Lady chapel: 13 yards 1½ feet.

The width of the chapel: 7 yards.

The width of the whole church: 18 yards.

The total of the whole length of Redcliffe church measures 77 yards.

The length of the secondary porch[2] on the north side: 5 yards.

The width of the said porch: 4¼ yards.

Sir William Canynges, a very rich and very wise merchant of the aforesaid town of Bristol, Dean of the church of Westbury, died the 17th day of November in the year of Christ 1474, when he had been raised to holy orders 7 years, and had been five times mayor of the said town.

He was chosen for the public service of the said town.

The length of the transepts measures 38 yards in length.

The width of the three aisles, vaulted with stone, measures 14 yards.

The width of each arch, between the pillars, measures 10 feet.

The length of the transept, from north to south, contains 8 arches.

---

1   The dates suggested by Harvey for these scattered notes are indicated at the start of each manuscript page

2   i.e. the outer north porch

---

e   Worcestre actually wrote *ditississimus*; § by Talbot in margin opposite

f   *sic*

(440) [continued]
ECCLESIA DE RADCLYFF
Et quilibet fenestra in le ovyrstorye continet .5. panellas glasetas;
Item quilibet fenestra in latitudine continet .10. pedes;
Item quilibet fenestra finis cuiuslibet ele continet .3. panellas glasetas vitreatas;

---

p.19   [1478]

(441)ᵃ
ᵇMemorandum de nauibus ad exspensas Domini Willelmi Canynghys de nouo fabricatis in villa Bristollie

Dominus Willelmus Canynges qui fuit maior Londoniensisᶜ .5. vicibus per octo annos exhibuit .800. homines jn nauibus occupatos et habuit operariosᵈ & carpentarios masons &c omni die .C. homines,

De nauibus habuit le mary canyngys de 400 doliate
    le mary Radclyff ponderis .500. doliatarum
    le Mary & John ponderis .900. doliatarum constabat
      sibi in toto .4000. marcas;
    le Galyot nauis ponderis .50. doliatarum
    le Cateryn ponderis .140 doliate
    le marybat ponderis 220 doliate
    le Margaryt de Tynly ponderis .200. doliate
    le Lytle Nicholas ponderis .140. doliate
    le Kateryn de Boston ponderis .220 doliate
    le ... ᵉ navis in Iselond perdita circa pondus .160.
    doliate,

Item vltra ista Edwardus Rex .4.ᵗᵘˢ habuit de dicto Willelmo .iij. milia marcarum pro pace sua habenda;

---

a Item **(441)** was included in Harvey, *Itineraries*, pp. 130-3, with some variations in transcription and translation
b Talbot has written *diues mercator post sacerdos and § master off Westbery college* (a rich merchant, afterwards a priest, and Master of Westbury College) above this item. O, also by Talbot, in the margin opposite
c *sic*, error for Bristol
d *navi* (for *navium*?) deleted
e *m* deleted, but otherwise blank in MS

(440) [continued]
THE CHURCH OF REDCLIFFE
And each window in the clerestory contains 5 glazed lights.
Also, each window measures 10 feet in width.
Also, each window at the end of each aisle contains 3 stained glass lights.

---

p.19   **[1478]**

(441)
Memorandum of the ships newly built in the town of Bristol at the cost of Sir William Canynges.

Sir William Canynges, who was mayor of London[1] for 5 terms, over eight years employed 800 men at work on ships, and had 100 men (workmen and carpenters, masons etc.) every day.

Of ships, he had the *Mary Canynges*, of 400 tons
     The *Mary Redcliffe* of 500 tons weight
     The *Mary and John* of 900 tons weight, cost him 4,000 marks in all[2]
     The *Galliot*,[3] a ship of 50 tons weight
     The *Catherine*, of 140 tons weight
     The *Marybat*,[4] of 220 tons weight
     The *Margaret* of Tynly,[5] of 200 tons weight
     The *Little Nicholas*, of 140 tons weight
     The *Katherine* of Boston, of 220 tons weight
     The ... , a ship lost off Iceland, weight of about 160 tons

Also, over above this, King Edward IV had 3,000 marks[6] from the said William, to have his peace.

---

1   *sic*, error for Bristol
2   £2,666 13s 4d (£2,666.66)
3   A *galliot* was a small galley, but Worcestre treats it as a ship's name
4   Possibly the Mary boat (*batus*)? There was a Batte family in Bristol at this time, but no link with Canynges or shipping has been noticed
5   *sic*: J.Sherborne, *William Canynges 1402-1474* (Historical Association Bristol Branch: Local History Pamphlets no.59, 1985) p. 12 n.22 suggests that *Tynly* is an error for Tenby
6   £2,000

p.31 [1478]

(442)[a]
longitudo capelle super pontem Bristollie .40.[b] steppys
latitudo vero, ... [c]
longitudo pontis Bristollie est .120. steppys,

(443)
ā
Longitudo navis Ecclesie fratrum minorum bristollie continet
54[d] steppys   latitudo continet .52. steppys

(444)
longitudo borialis partis cimiterij sancti Jacobi continet .220.
steppys   latitudo partis orientalis .124. steppys,

p.33 [1478]

(445)[e]
BRISTOLL
longitudo capelle pontis Bristollie .36.[f] steppys
longitudo pontis[g] Bristollie .140. steppys

(446)
longitudo porte Ecclesie Radclyffe ... [h] steppys

> *[An entry about Glastonbury abbey separates
> the two items about Redcliffe church]* [i]

(447)
RADCLYFF ECCLESIA
[j]Altitudo turris de Radclyfe continet 300. pedes de quo .100
pedes sunt per fulmen deiecti

(448)
BRISTOLL
Altitudo turris Ecclesie sancti Stephani Bristollie continet .125.
pedes et vltra .31. pedes infra terram,

---

a   Items **(442)**-**(444)** were included in Harvey, *Itineraries*, pp. 130-1, with
     some variations in transcription and translation
b   Worcestre originally wrote *.30.*, then wrote *4* over the *3*
c   Blank in MS
d   Worcestre originally wrote *53*, tried to convert it to *54* then deleted it
     and rewrote *54* in front of it

p.31   [1478]

(442)
The length of the chapel upon Bristol Bridge: 40 steps.
But the width ...
The length of Bristol Bridge is 120 steps.

(443)
The length of the nave of the church of the Friars Minor at
Bristol measures 54 steps. The width measures 52 steps.

(444)
The length of the north side of St James's churchyard
measures 220 steps. The width of the east side: 124 steps.

p.33   [1478]

(445)
BRISTOL
The length of the chapel of Bristol Bridge: 36 steps.
The length of Bristol Bridge: 140 steps.

(446)
The length of the porch of Redcliffe church: ... steps.

*[An entry about Glastonbury abbey separates
the two items about Redcliffe church]*

(447)
REDCLIFFE CHURCH
The height of the tower of Redcliffe measures 300 feet, of
which 100 feet have been thrown down by lightning.

(448)
BRISTOL
The height of the tower of St Stephen's church at Bristol
measures 125 feet, besides 31 feet below ground.

---

e   Items **(445)**-**(448)** were included in Harvey, *Itineraries*, pp. 128-131,
     with some variations in transcription and translation
f   *40* written above
g   *pontis* repeated
h   Blank in MS
i   See Harvey, *Itineraries*, pp. 128-9
j   *longitudo* deleted

Counter slip

Temple Cross

The Passage

Dr Whits Almshouse

Bear lane

Back

Water lane

Avon

Temple Street

Temple Chur

The Rackclose

The Ropeing House

Tower Harriot

Avon flu

Walke

Back

Avon

The Lime kilne

p.34　　　　　　　　　　　　　　　　　　　　　**[1478]**

(449)[a]
BRISTOLL
longitudo capelle pontis Bristollie continet .36. steppys
latitudo Capelle predicte .12. steppys[b]

　　　[Memorandum on the Lydbury family of
　　　Glastonbury] [c]

(450)
BRISTOLLIA
longitudo parochialis Ecclesie sancti Jacobi .54. steppys.
latitudo .40 steppys
longitudo prioratus Ecclesie predicte .40. steppys;
longitudo Capelle beate marie ibidem .40. steppys
latitudo eiusdem .12. steppys
latitudo Cimiterij[d] .130. steppys,

p.35　　　　　　　　　　　　　　　　　　　　　**[1478]**

(451)[e]
Expense Bristollie a die mercurij usque diem nativitatis beate
marie .8. die Septembris　Et vsque Tyntern per ... [f] dies 3.s
ijd

Item pro candelis cereis .2.d pro j bille de le forest 8d pro
papiro ob　pro vino & repastis .3.d　pro equis prebendis　.j.d.
pro ferrura .j.d.　Item reparacione celle &c[g] .6.d.　pro
medicina equi .2.d,
　　　　　　　Summa 21.d ob[h]

　　　[There follow expenses at Wells and
　　　Glastonbury, 9th–10th September 1478] [i]

---

a　Items **(449)–(450)** were included in Harvey, *Itineraries*, pp. 130-1 with
　　some variations in transcription and translation
b　*.12. steppys* repeated
c　This note was included in Harvey, *Itineraries*, pp. 128-9
d　*1210* deleted (probably a muddled correction of 120/130)
e　Item **(451)** was included in Harvey, *Itineraries*, pp. 40-1, with some
　　variations in transcription and translation
f　Blank in MS; see note 3 opposite

p.34 **[1478]**

(449)
BRISTOL
The length of the chapel of Bristol Bridge measures 36 steps.
The width of the aforesaid chapel: 12 steps.

> *[Memorandum on the Lydbury family of Glastonbury]*

(450)
BRISTOL
The length of the parish church of St James: 54 steps.
Width: 40 steps.
The length of the priory of the aforesaid church: 40 steps.
The length of the Lady chapel there: 40 steps.
Its width: 12 steps.
The width of the churchyard: 130 steps.

p.35 **[1478]**

(451)[1]
Expenses at Bristol from Wednesday[2] to the Nativity of the Blessed Mary on 8th day of September, and to Tintern for [three] days,[3] 3s. 2d.

Also for wax candles, 2d; for 1 bill of the forest, 8d.; for paper ½d.; for wine and refreshments, 3d; for horse fodder, 1d.; for shoeing, 1d. Also for repairs to the saddle etc., 6d.; for horse medicine, 2d.

Total 1s 9½d.[4]

> *[There follow expenses at Wells and Glastonbury, 9th–10th September 1478]*

---

1 These accounts partner **(454)**, Worcestre's diary of his 1478 Bristol visit,
2 2nd September 1478
3 3 days, 4th–6th September 1478: see **(454)**
4 In fact the total is 1s. 11½d.

---

g *2.d* deleted
h *sic*
i See Harvey, *Itineraries*, pp. 42–3

p.38   **[1478]**

(452)[a]
.18446744073709551615. numerus
tocius duplicacionis scaccarij qui est numerus tocius scaccarij
duplici.[b]

p.54   **[1478]**

(453)[c]
Memorandum, to[d] John Mey wexmaker yn Wynchestrete[e] that
hys chyld speke with the potmaker of Hanham to make .ij.
pottys as he made last safe only the mouth to besse[f] by j
quarter of an onch & aftir thys mesur of tree the mouth to
bere the brede
latitudo |———————————————————————|

mensura latitudinis oris olle pro distillatorio fiendo pro
dompno dan Water Brokware[g] yn Tynterne

p.60   **[1478]**

[Diary of Worcestre's travels in 1478]

(454)[h]
BRISTOLLIE[i]
Martis die primo .7.[bris] sancti Egidij equitaui per Mershfelde
vsque Bristolliam applicando ibi hora circa .6. post meridem,

Mercurij primo[j] .7.[bris] Bristollie

---

a Item **(452)** was included in Harvey, *Itineraries*, pp. 130-1, with some
   variations in transcription and translation. See note 1 opposite
b Followed by two or three illegible words in a later hand, not Talbot
c Item **(453)** was included in Harvey, *Itineraries*, pp. 76-9, with some
   variations in transcription and translation
d *the* deleted
e *to speke* deleted
f *sic*, error for *by lesse*, as suggested by Harvey?
g Smudged word, possibly *Gleth* or *Gheth*? Harvey read it as *Tlzoth*
h Item **(454)** was included in Harvey, *Itineraries*, pp. 36-7, 40-1, with
   some variations in transcription and translation. It partners his
   accounts for the same period, **(451)**
i *q'* (for *questio* or *query*?) in margin opposite beginning of this item
j *sic*: Worcestre's dates are, for several entries, one day out. The correct
   dates are shown opposite

p.38 [1478]

(452)
18,446,744,073,709,551,615
of the whole duplication of the exchequer, which is the number
of the whole duplication.[1]

p.54 [1478]

(453)
Memorandum, to John May, waxmaker in Wynch Street, that
his child[2] speak with the pot-maker[3] of Hanham,[4] to make 2
pots as he made previously, save only the mouth to be less by
¼ of an inch, according to this treen[5] measure, the mouth to
have the [same] width.
Width: |_____|

measure of the width of the mouth of the pot for the still
being made for Dom Dan Walter of Brockweir in Tintern.[6]

p.60 [1478]

[Diary of Worcestre's travels in 1478]

(454)[7]
BRISTOL
Tuesday the first day of September, St Giles's Day, I rode
through Marshfield to Bristol, arriving there about the hour of
6 in the afternoon.

Wednesday the first [2nd] of September: at Bristol.

---

1   While dated by Harvey to 1478, this note matches that made from a
    'little book' in St Stephen's Church, Bristol in 1480: see **(224)**; on this
    occasion there is no indication of the source
2   Perhaps *child* in the sense of errand-boy rather than offspring
3   Not a clay 'potter' as Harvey suggests, but a metal worker, making a
    copper pot for a still. This is an early reference to the metalworking
    industry east of Bristol which subsequently developed into the important
    brass-works of the Hanham, Conham and Keynsham area
4   Hanham was then a village 3½ miles east of Bristol, although the later
    brassworks were on R.Avon at Hanham Weir, 2 miles to the south
5   i.e. wooden: presumably carved to the correct size to fit the pipework
6   The hamlet of Brockweir lies 1½ miles upstream from Tintern. Harvey
    suggested that Dom Dan Walter may have been a Cistercian monk who
    had been at Oxford in 1442, and then at Buckfast. He was presumably
    a practising chemist, herbalist or distiller
7   This diary partners **(451)**, Worcestre's accounts for his 1478 Bristol
    visit

(454) [continued]
Jovis .2.ᵃ 7.ᵇʳⁱˢ jncepi equitare de Bristollia primo per aquam vsque ... ᵇ et postea equestrem vsque Austclyf ibidem pernoctando,

p.61 **[1478]**

Veneris .3. die .7.ᵇʳⁱˢ de Austclyff eundo per aquam vsque Chepstow nauigando ad prandium. applicando vsque abbathiam de Tyntern;

Sabbato .4. die .7.ᵇʳⁱˢ fui ibidem.

Dominica .5. die .7.ᵇʳⁱˢ fuiᶜ Tyntern abbey tota die Dominica. dicto die apud Tyntern.ᵈ

Lune .7. die Septembris. equitaui de Tyntern in mane
Lune predicto fui apud Chepstow

Lune predicto applicui vltra aquam per Austclyff usque Westbery

ᵉMartis die .7.ᵒ Septembrisᶠ nativitatis beate marie apud Westbery audiui diuina seruicia;
martis predicto post meridem applicui Bristollie,

Mercurij .9. Septembris de Bristollia hora meridiana applicui usque Wellys pernoctando

> *[The diary continues with Worcestre's journey to Cornwall and back, 9th–28th September 1478]* ᵍ

p.63 **[1478]**

Martis .29. die .7.ᵇʳⁱˢ die sancti michaelis de Wellys equitaui ad Bristolliam

mercurij primo die Octobris Bristollie

---

a   *sic:* Worcestre's dates are, for several entries, one day out.   The correct dates are shown opposite
b   Blank in MS
c   *Tynte* deleted
d   This would seem to be where Worcestre noticed his date error
e   *Dmc* (for *Dominica*?) deleted
f   *sic:* Worcestre gets his day and date out of step once again

(454) [continued]
Thursday 2nd [3rd] of September I began to ride from Bristol, first by water to ... ,[1] and afterwards on horseback to Aust Cliff, staying the night there.

p.61 [1478]

Friday 3rd [4th] day of September: going from Aust Cliff by water, sailing to Chepstow by lunchtime, [and] on to Tintern abbey.

Saturday 4th [5th] day of September I was there.

Sunday 5th [6th] day of September I was at Tintern abbey all day.
Sunday: the said day at Tintern.

Monday 7th day of September I rode from Tintern in the morning.
Monday aforesaid I was at Chepstow.

Monday aforesaid I arrived across the water, past Aust Cliff, to Westbury.

Tuesday 7th [8th] day of September, the Nativity of the Blessed Mary, I heard divine service at Westbury.
Tuesday aforesaid in the afternoon I arrived at Bristol.

Wednesday 9th September: from Bristol at noon; I arrived at Wells for the night.

> *[The diary continues with Worcestre's journey*
> *to Cornwall and back, 9th–28th September*
> *1478]*

p.63 [1478]

Tuesday 29th day of September, Michaelmas, I rode from Wells to Bristol.

Wednesday the first day of October: at Bristol.

---

1   Probably Shirehampton or Sea Mills, rather than the modern
    Avonmouth as suggested by Harvey

---

g   See Harvey, *Itineraries*, pp. 36-41

(454) [continued]
Jovis Bristollie .2. die Octobris

Veneris Bristollie .3. die vsque horam .4.[ta] horam[a] & applicui
ad Keynesham & applicui apud Bath

> *[Worcestre stayed overnight in Bath, and the
> diary continues with his journey to Winchester
> and back to London]*

p.66   **[1478]**

(455)[b]

Informacio Willelmi Powelle de Tyntern.

> *[Details of rocks and islands in the Severn
> estuary, on the Welsh side]*

5.d
Sancti Tiriaci anachorite, distat a kyngrode per .6. Miliaria in
parte Wallie; coram Mathern villa. Manerij Episcopi
Landauensis per vnum Miliare de Chepstow;

4.E
Kyngrode. distat a Seynt Tyryacle versus Bristolliam .x. Milia
& ad Bristolliam .6. Miliaria

Le Rokk vocata le Bynch vna rotunda Rupis in aqua savernie &
quando coperta est cum fluxu maris, tunc navis paratum est
velare ad Walliam;

Gystonclyffe durat in longitudine per tria Miliaria,

Memorandum isti articuli precedentes sunt in orientali parte
aque de Severn versus Bristolliam[c]

p.209   **[1480]**

> *[Notes on the church of Sheen Syon near
> Brentford, and the battle of Verneuil, 1424,
> from information of Nicholas Burton of
> Bristol]* [d]

---

a   *sic*
b   Item **(455)** was included in Harvey, *Itineraries*, pp. 74-7, with some
    variations in transcription and translation

(454) [continued]
Thursday 2nd day of October: at Bristol.

Friday 3rd day: at Bristol until 4 o'clock, and then I reached Keynsham and Bath.

> *[Worcestre stayed overnight in Bath, and the diary continues with his journey to Winchester and back to London]*

p.66 **[1478]**

(455)

Information of William Powell of Tintern:[1]

> *[Details of rocks and islands in the Severn estuary, on the Welsh side]*

St Tecla the anchorite: 6 miles from Kingroad on the Welsh side opposite Mathern, a village in the manor of the Bishop of Llandaff, one mile from Chepstow.

Kingroad: is 10 miles distant from St Tecla's towards Bristol, and 6 miles from Bristol.

The rock called The Bench[2] [is] a round rock in the river Severn; and when it is covered by the tide, then a ship is ready to sail for Wales.

Ghyston Cliff extends in length for 3 miles.

Memorandum, these preceding items are on the east side of the river Severn, towards Bristol.

p.209 **[1480]**

> *[Notes on the church of Sheen Syon near Brentford, and the battle of Verneuil, 1424, from information of Nicholas Burton of Bristol]*

---

1 Perhaps acquired during the journey from Aust Cliff to Tintern?
2 Probably Upper Bench, in mid-river between Aust Cliff and Beachley

---

c The rest of the page has been torn off
d See Harvey, *Itineraries*, pp. 334-5

(456)ᵃ
TURRIS QUADRATA SANCTI STEPHANI BRISTOLLIE
altitudo Turris sancti Stephani Bristollie continet in altitudine
from the grasse erthᵇ table to the Gargoyle est .21. brachia
idestᶜ .42. virgas idestᵈ
Et altitudo a le gargoyle vsqueᵉ le croppᶠ qui finit le stone
worke 31. pedes
Et latitudo eius ex parte orientali & occidentali .12 pedes &ᵍ
Et abʰ boriali in meridionali continet .14. pedes
Et a terra vsque fundamentumⁱ profundissimo continet .31.
pedes.
Et habet .4. storyes et ibi in quarta storia sunt campane
In superiori historia. tres orbe in qualibet panella
Inʲ
In secunda & tercia historia sunt due Orbe in qualibet panella
.4. panellarum
In jnferiori panellaᵏ sunt in duobus panellis in qualibet panella
south & west fenestre in alijs duobus panellis ex parte boriali &
orientali sunt due arche.

(457)ˡ
ECCLESIA DE RADCLIFF
longitudo Ecclesie beate Marie de Radclyff ville Bristollie
continet ... ᵐ
latitudo eius ... ᵐ
latitudo Brachiorum dicte Ecclesie viz a boria in meridiem
continet per altam crucem & per finem occidentalem chori cum
latitudine nauis continet sic .36. virgas
latitudo dictorum duorum brachiorum videlicet in duobus alis
ex parte boriali continet .11. virgas preter latitudinem duarum
capellarum. cum duobus arcubus in medio dictarum duarum
alarum;

---

a Items **(456)–(469)** were included in Harvey, *Itineraries*, pp. 401–3, in
　Latin only, with some variations in transcription
b　*erth* written above *grasse* but with no deletion or caret mark
c　*C* deleted: possibly Worcestre considered reckoning in feet (126)
d　Perhaps Worcestre intended to add *126 pedes*
e　*ad braz* (perhaps for *ad brattishing*) deleted
f　*ascendit* deleted
g　Note breaks off
h　*orientali* deleted
i　*continet* deleted

p. 209 **[1480]**

(456)
THE SQUARE TOWER OF ST STEPHEN'S, BRISTOL

The height of the tower of St Stephen's, Bristol, measures in height from ground level to the gargoyle 21 fathoms, that is 42 yards

And the height from the gargoyle to the 'crop'[1] which finishes the stonework: 31 feet.

And its width on the east and west sides: 12 feet, and

And from north to south it measures 14 feet.

And from ground level to the deepest foundation measures 31 feet.

And it has four storeys, and in the fourth storey there are the bells.

On the topmost storey [are] three blank panels on each side.[2]

On the second and third storeys are two blank panels on each side of the four sides.

On the lowest [storey] there are windows on two sides, [one] in each of the south and west sides; on the other two sides, on the north and east sides, there are 2 arches.

p. 210 **[1480]**

(457)
REDCLIFFE CHURCH

The length of the church of the Blessed Mary of Redcliffe, of the town of Bristol, measures ...

Its width ...

The width of the transepts of the said church, to wit: from north to south it measures past the high cross and past the west end of the quire, including the width of the nave: measures thus 36 yards.

The width of the said two transepts, to wit: the two aisles on the north side, measure 11 yards, without the width of the two chapels, but including the two arches in the middle of the said two aisles.

---

1 Probably parapet capping stones. The deletion (note e opposite) was possibly 'to the brattishing' (ornamental cresting)

2 *Orbe* are decorative blank panels within each larger *panella* or side panel of the structure

---

j The rest of the line, *superiori historia sunt orbe*, deleted as repetition

k Error for *historia*

l Items **(457)**–**(469)** were included in Harvey, *Itineraries*, p. 401-3, in Latin only, with some variations in transcription

m Blank in MS

(457) [continued]
latitudo alterius brachij ex parte meridionali cum duabus alis
cum .2. arcubus in dicta parte meridionali, in medio duarum
alarum preter latitudinem duarum alarum,[a] ... [b]

(458)
RADCLYFF
longitudo principalis porticus vbi sancta & beata Virgo
veneratur continet .12. virgas.   latitudo eius continet .6.
virgas

(459)
ECCLESIA CRIPPE SANCTI NICHOLAI BRISTOLLIE
longitudo volte sancti Nicholai continet preter capellam cum .7.
virgis pro latitudine[c] capelle sancte crucis[d] .31. virgas
latitudo eius continet .12. virgas vnum pedem & dimidium

(460)
longitudo Ecclesie fratrum sancti Francisci Bristollie cum .54.
gressibus[e] longitudinis[f] Chori. & .64. gressibus longitudinis
Navis dicte Ecclesie continet in toto .118. gressus[g]
latitudo navis dicte Ecclesie continet .55. gressus

p.214   [1480]

(461)
longitudo pontis B[ristollie][h] continet .140. gressus
latitudo eius continet ... [i]

(462)
longitudo de le Bake B[ristollie][h] continet .240. gressus
latitudo eius ... [i]

(463)
longitudo Marisci ex parte orientali videlicet a porta finis de le
bake vsque oppositum Ecclesie de Radclyff ad metam vnius
plancher de arbore ante locum vbi plures lapides congregantur
in aqua sunt sepcies .60.[ta] gressus idest .420. gressus,

---

a   This is contradictory, and is probably an error for *capellarum*
b   Blank in MS
c   *latitudine* is probably an error for *longitudine*; *cap* (for *capelle*) deleted
d   *.39.* deleted
e   Originally read *cum longitudinis Chori*, with *.54. gressibus* inserted after
f   *C* smudged and deleted
g   *.118.* repeated
h   Worcestre left space to fill in the rest of the name, but never did so
i   Blank in MS

(457) [continued]
The width of the other transept on the south side, with the
two aisles, including the 2 arches on the said south side in the
middle of the two aisles, without the width of the two aisles[1]
...

(458)
REDCLIFFE
The length of the main porch, where the Holy and Blessed
Virgin is worshipped,[2] measures 12 yards. Its width measures
6 yards.

(459)
THE CRYPT CHURCH OF ST NICHOLAS, BRISTOL
The length of the crypt of St Nicholas measures, excepting the
chapel, 31 yards, with 7 yards for the [length] of the chapel of
the Holy Cross.
Its width measures 12 yards 1½ feet.

(460)
The length of the church of the Franciscan Friars at Bristol:
including the quire 54 steps in length, and the nave 64 steps in
length, [the length] of the said church measures in all 118
steps.
The width of the nave of the said church measures 55 steps.

p.214 **[1480]**

(461)
The length of B[ristol] Bridge measures 140 steps.
Its width measures ...

(462)
The length of the Back of B[ristol] measures 240 steps.
Its width ...

(463)
The length of the Marsh on the east side, to wit from the gate
at the end of The Back as far as opposite Redcliffe church, to
the landmark of a timber post[3] in front of the spot where
many stones are heaped together in the water, is seven times
60 steps, that is 420 steps.

---

1 Error for chapels?
2 i.e. the north porch chapel
3 Gib Tailor, the marker post at the junction of R.Avon and R.Frome

(464)

ECCLESIA SANCTI AUGUSTINI

Chorus Ecclesie sancti Augustini Bristollie continet in longitudine .64. gressus vltra capellam beate marie

latitudo[a] navis chori cum duabus alis continet .50. gressus,

latitudo & longitudo quadrate ex omni parte continet .22. gressus

longitudo de le Frayterhous .26. gressus vel ... [b]

latitudo eius continet .16. gressus,

longitudo antique Ecclesia .80. gressus

latitudo eius continet 64. gressus

latitudo de le belfray .2[c]

longitudo de le Chapiterhous continet .56. gressus[d]

latitudo eius continet .18.[e] gressus

---

(465)

Capella sancti Georgij continet in longitudine .20. gressus vltra spacium cancelle

latitudo Capelle continet .12. gressus

---

(466)

longitudo navis Ecclesie fratrum carmelitarum continet in longitudine[f] .54. gressus

latitudo eius continet .27. gressus

---
[g]

(467)

ECCLESIA SANCTI JACOBI

Capella beate Marie sancti Jacobi continet in longitudine .21.[h] virgas[i]

latitudo eius continet .7. virgas

latitudo capelle sancte Anne continet .4. virgas,

longitudo dicte capelle continet .8. virgas

---

a   *Ecc* (for *Ecclesie*) deleted
b   Blank in MS
c   Probably intended for *.22.* steps, or a figure similar to that for the crossing
d   There is a large + at the end of this line
e   *.17.* deleted and *.18.* written above
f   *continet* repeated
g   There is a small + between the dividing line and the heading of **(467)**
h   *.31.* deleted and *.21.* written above
i   *.21.* repeated

(464)
ST AUGUSTINE'S CHURCH
The quire of St Augustine's church,[1] Bristol, measures 64
steps in length, besides the Lady chapel.
The width of the quire nave, with the two aisles, measures 50
steps.
The width and length of the square[2] measures 22 steps on each
side.
The length of the Frater-house: 26 steps or ...
Its width measures 16 steps.
The length of the old church:[3] 80 steps.
Its width measures 64 steps.
The width of the bell-tower: 2[-?].[4]
The length of the Chapter house measures 56 steps.
Its width measures 18 steps.

---

(465)
The chapel of St George measures 20 steps in length, besides
the area of the chancel.
The width of the chapel measures 12 steps.

---

(466)
The length of the nave of the Carmelite Friars' church: it
measures in length 54 steps.
Its breadth measures 27 steps.

---

(467)
ST JAMES'S CHURCH
The Lady chapel of St James's measures 21 yards in length.
Its width measures 7 yards.

The width of the chapel of St Anne measures 4 yards.
The length of the said chapel measures 8 yards.

---

1 The references to the Frater and the Chapter house, as well as its sheer
   size, make it clear that Worcestre is describing St Augustine's abbey
   church, and not St Augustine the Less parish church
2 i.e. the crossing under the central tower
3 i.e. the surviving remains of the small Norman nave, dwarfed by the
   spacious 14th century quire and east end
4 Probably intended for '22 steps': see note c opposite

(467) [continued]
longitudo navis Ecclesie[a] prioratus sancti Jacobi continet .15.
virgas & dimidium. vel .26. gressus
latitudo dicte navis continet .10. virgas. vel .16. gressus.

longitudo navis Ecclesie perochialis[b] sancti Jacobi annexa Navi
dicti prioratus continet .27. virgas vel .49. gressus
latitudo navis Ecclesie perochialis[b] annexe[c] Ecclesie navis dicti
prioratus continet .22. virgas vel .40. gressus

p.215   **[1480]**

(468)
ā
longitudo Ecclesie sancti Nicholai ... [d]
latitudo eius ... [d]
longitudo ... [d]

(469)
E[CCLESIA] OMNIUM SANCTORUM
ā
longitudo Ecclesie parochialis omnium sanctorum Bristollie
continet .74. gressus.
latitudo eius continet .33. gressus

p.218   **[1480]**

(470)[e]
ECCLESIA SANCTE KATERINE BRISTOLLIE
longitudo navis Ecclesie sancte katerine prope Bristollie
continet .16. virgas.
latitudo eius continet[f] .7. virgas cum dimidio
longitudo cancelle .9. virgas latitudo eius .5. virge cum
dimidio

1290 .a.
Dominus Robertus Barkle fundator & patronus hospitalis sancte
katerine qui obijt .3⁰. jdus Maij

:Λ

---

a   *presbitera* deleted
b   *sic*
c   *ad* deleted
d   Blank in MS

(467) [continued]
The length of the nave of the priory church of St James measures 15½ yards or 26 steps.
The width of the said nave measures 10 yards or 16 steps.

The length of the nave of the parish church of St James, annexed to the said of the said priory, measures 27 yards or 49 steps.
The width of the nave of the parish church annexed to the nave of the said priory church measures 22 yards or 40 steps.

p.215   [1480]

(468)
The length of St Nicholas's church ...
Its width ...
The length ...

(469)
ALL SAINTS CHURCH
The length of the parish church of All Saints, Bristol, measures 74 steps.
Its width measures 33 steps.

p.218   [1480]

(470)
ST KATHERINE'S CHURCH, BRISTOL.
The length of the nave of St Katherine's church near Bristol measures 16 yards.
Its width measures 7½ yards.
The length of the chancel: 9 yards; its width, 5½ yards.

1290 (a)
Sir Robert Berkeley, founder and patron of St Katherine's hospital, who died 3 Ides May.[1]

:∧

---

1   13th May

---

e   Item **(470)** was included in Harvey, *Itineraries*, pp. 334-5, with some variations in transcription and translation
f   *.16.* deleted

(470) [continued]
ASSHTON
Dominus Ada de heyron Militis ville de Asshton
Thomas hayron antecessor suus qui dedit ... ᵃ
Alexander de Alneto antecessor & successorum suorum
Willelmi lyons antecessorum & successorum suorum

.b. :∧ᵇ Dominus Thomas de Barkle Miles frater dicti Roberti
qui dedit terras & tenementa in Bysshopworth & dictam
fundacionem per eundem Robertum confectam. confirmauit

DE BRISTOLLIE
Willelmi Comyn de Bristollie
Ricardi Dyer.   Julliane Suse   Johannis filius Aurifabri
Christiane Roo.   Johannis Stryglynge
Dominis Johannas Thorp presbiter

p.223   [1480]

*[Astrological charts for two horoscopes cast
for William Worcestre on 3rd September 1480,
presumably while he was at Bristol or Tintern]* ᶜ

p.319   [1479]

(471)ᵈ
ā
Matheus de Gornay miles comitatus Somersetie obijt die .28.
Augusti,ᵉ

(472)
ā
.1215.
Pons Bristollie primo fundatur per Johannem Regem Anglie qui
continet in longitudine 140 gressus Worcestre,ᶠ

---

a   Blank in MS
b   This note .*b.* is intended to follow on from note .*a.* above, with linking
   caret marks :∧
c   These are reproduced in Harvey, *Itineraries*, pp. 300-1. They have no
   other Bristol relevance
d   Items **(471)** and **(472)** were included in Harvey, *Itineraries*, pp. 248-9,
   with some variations in transcription and translation
e   ⊖ by Talbot in the margin opposite
f   O and § by Talbot in the margin opposite

(470) [continued]
ASHTON
Sir Adam de Heyron, knight, of the village of Ashton.
Thomas Hayron his ancestor who gave ...
Alexander de Alnetus his ancestor[s] and successors.
William Lyons his ancestors and successors.[1]

(b) :ʌ Sir Thomas de Berkeley, knight, brother of the said Robert, who gave lands and tenements in Bishopsworth, and confirmed the said foundation made by that same Robert.[1]

OF BRISTOL
William Comyn of Bristol
Richard Dyer, Juliana Suse, John son of the goldsmith
Christine Roo, John Strigling
Sir John Thorp, priest[1]

p.223 [1480]

[Astrological charts for two horoscopes cast for William Worcestre on 3rd September 1480, presumably while he was at Bristol or Tintern] [2]

p.319 [1479]

(471)
Matthew de Gurney, knight, of the county of Somerset, died 28th day of August.

(472)
1215
Bristol Bridge, which measures 140 of Worcestre's steps in length, was first founded by King John of England.

---

1   All benefactors of St Katherine's hospital
2   See note c opposite. For Worcestre's diary, 3rd–4th September 1480, see **(454)**

APPENDIX:
SYMBOLS & ABBREVIATIONS

MARKS & SYMBOLS USED BY WILLIAM WORCESTRE

William Worcestre used a number of marginal marks and symbols in his Bristol notes:

ā probably standing for *animadvertit*, against items of special interest to him, or needing further investigation; usually a clear ā, it sometimes degenerates to a simple pointer a–

\+ probably serving a similar purpose

q' (for *questio* or *query*?) seems to be put in the margin where a space has been left for figures which may or may not have been filled in afterwards; or where facts and figures needed further checking

∴ and other linking symbols, as shown, indicate the correct sequence of notes that have been scattered around a page for lack of space

.a., .b., .1., .2. are used similarly to indicate the correct order of notes.

Worcestre occasionally underlines words of importance, usually with a line that has a characteristic 'swan neck' at the left end: 2⎯⎯⎯⎯ . This makes it possible to distinguish Worcestre's underlinings from the more ragged lines of later commentators. All these marks are indicated in the text. Together with his copious use of brackets and 'boxes' (not shown) to organise overcrowded pages of notes, they indicate Worcestre's concern to order what at first sight appears to be a random collection of material.

LATER NOTES BY OTHER PEOPLE

Some time after Worcestre's death, the manuscript came into the possession of Robert Talbot (c.1505–58), Treasurer of Norwich Cathedral 1547–58, poet and antiquary, and a close friend of the topographer John Leland.[1] Talbot made copious underlinings and annotations, particularly of items that were comparable with Norwich. He also showed an interest in the derivation of words, in place–names and family names (pursuing, for example, a spurious connection between The Weir in Bristol and the de la Warre family) and in William Worcestre's background. Talbot used his own selection of

---

1 Kendrick, *British Antiquity*, pp. 135–6; Harvey, *Itineraries*, p. xix

marginal symbols, chiefly a mark resembling the musical 'natural' sign, rendered §, and a selection of circles O, ⊕, ⊗. With the exception of **(33)** and **(50)** (see below), these annotations are indicated in footnotes to the text.

The manuscript subsequently passed to Henry Aldrich, Fellow of Corpus Christi College, Cambridge, 1569–79 and grammar teacher in Norwich 1583, who died 1593.[1] He used blank areas for pen trials and unrelated jottings.

Two items relating to Worcestre's childhood and family, **(33)** and **(50)**, have been so heavily annotated by other people that only Worcestre's own markings are included in the main text. Annotations by others are shown separately, below.

(33)
VENELLA PARVA DE HYGHSTRETE PER CIMITERIUM OMNIUM SANCTORUM

Venella parvissima et stricta eundo de hyghstrete prope altam Crucem inter Ecclesiam omnium sanctorum & officium artis Cocorum ville extendo per cimiterium eiusdem Ecclesie et meridionalem partem dicte Ecclesie. iuxta murum noue ale edificatum diebus juuentutis mee per hostium meridionalem Ecclesie predicte. et iuxta quem[a] murum <u>Dominus Thomas Botoner presbiter</u>[b] fuit sepultus in parte orientali hostij meridionalis sed credo ossa dicti domini Thome sunt remota tempore edificationis nove <u>ale.</u>[c] et Tumba de Frestone eius similiter est remota, Et dicta stricta venella in longitudine extendit ad parvam et Curtam viam in occidentali parte dicte Ecclesie ad finem hospicij alti <u>prioris Collegij vocati</u>[d] lez kalenders vbi <u>dictus dominus Thomas Botoner</u>[e] fuit vt supponitur consocius. et in domo prioratus hospicij obijt ex <u>certa scientia Elizabet fratris sue matris mee</u>[f] michi relate.

---

1   Harvey, *Itineraries*, p. xx

Taking Worcestre's own writing as hand 1:
a   X in a different, darker ink (hand 2) in the margin opposite
b   Underlined as shown by hand 2
c   Underlined, with *Noua aula* written in the margin alongside, in a different ink and a considerably later hand (hand 3)
d   Underlined, probably by hand 3. The underlining includes the *fratrum* deleted by Worcestre
e   Underlined by hand 2
f   Underlined, probably by Talbot (hand 4) with a marginal note alongside:
        this sir thom. botiner erat eius auunculus id est frater matris
    (this Sir Thomas Botoner was his uncle, that is the mother's brother)

(33) [continued]

circa etatem juuentatis mee quinque vel sex annorum vt suppono; quia quamvis fui presens secum die mortis sue cum matre mea. vale faciendo die vltimo vite sue non habui discrecionem ad noticiam persone sue. Et vt credo Carte & evidencie tam hereditatis sue in tenemento suo prope yeldehall in Bradstrete ex parte meridionali dicte Gyldhall necnon de hereditate eius per Thomam Botoner patrem eius et matris mee in villa de Bokyngham in Westrete jacentem versus aquam in parte ... ^a scitam ac in villis adiacentibus iacent de racione deberent remanere quando queratur de priore kalendarij si remanent inter eorum evidencias de evidencijs <u>Domini Thome Botoner consocij</u>^b eorum;

(50)

At Newyate vbi quondam scola gramatica per magistrum Robertum Land^c principalem didascolum cum ... ^d <u>leyland magistri gramaticorum</u>^e in Oxonia dicebatur fuisse flos gramaticorum^f & poetarum temporibus annis plurimis revolutis. & tempore quo primo veni ad Oxoniam universitatem scolatizandi obijt in termino pasche anno christi .1432. circa mensem Junij quando generalis Eclipsis die sancti Botulphi accidebat

---

a Blank in MS
b Underlined by Talbot (hand 4) with § in margin alongside
c O in margin by Talbot (hand 4)
d Blank in MS
e Underlined, with § in margin by Talbot (hand 4)
f *flos gramaticorum* refers to the popular saying about John Leyland the elder, grammarian (d.1428), noted in full by Talbot (hand 4) at the foot of the page:

> *vt Rosa flos florum sic Leland gramaticorum*
> (as the Rose is the flower of flowers,
> so is Leland the flower of grammarians)

Talbot has drawn a wavy vertical line down the left hand side of the note, from opposite *flos...* to the end

INDEX
of
Persons, Places and selected Subjects

Bold numbers in brackets refer to **item** numbers in the manuscript, and plain numbers to pages of this book.

The index is based on the modernised English translation. Worcestre's original spellings are included only where modern spelling or identification are uncertain, thus: *Rydelyngfelde.*

Bristol: specific references to the town are indexed under 'Bristol', but as most of the text is concerned with Bristol, streets, buildings and topographical features are indexed under their own names, and are in Bristol unless indicated otherwise. Architectural details of a building are not indexed separately unless of particular importance.

Names of streets in 1673 (J.Millerd plan) or 1828 (G.C.Ashmead map) or at the present day are included where Worcestre gives no name, and where it clarifies a reference. These later names are in square brackets, thus: [Ivie Lane].

[Jacob Street or Jacob's Lane] **(179)**, **(184)**
Jaffa [Joppa, Tel-Aviv] **(248)**
Jay, Joan, sister of William Worcestre **(394)**, **(417)**; house of **(294)**, **(364)**; land of **(395)**
Jay, John, brother-in-law of William Worcestre **(417)**
Jay, John the younger, voyage to Brazil of **(418)**
Jerusalem, Order of St John of *see* St John of Jerusalem
Jerusalem, voyage to **(143)**, **(248)**
Jewish synagogue **(46)**, **(200)**, **(270)**, **(320)**, **(353)**, **(369)**
[Jewrie Lane] **(46)**, **(107)**
Jews **(56)**; *see also* synagogue
John son of the goldsmith **(470)**
Joppa *see* Jaffa
jousting-place, the **(192)**

Kalendars, College and Fraternity **(33)**, **(81–2)**, **(387)**; library **(266)**; prior **(33)**; prior's lodgings **(33)**, **(34)**; water-conduit house beneath the hall **(82)**
Key, The **(5)**, **(16)**, **(32)**, **(36–9)**, **(46)**, **(48–9)**, **(103–4)**, **(107)**, **(128)**, **(200)**, **(223)**, **(268–9)**, **(320)**, **(351–3)**, **(358)**, **(369)**, **(391)**; Broad Key **(369)**, **(391)**; corner house of Henry Vyell (Vyell's Place)/stone house/great corner place at start of **(37)**, **(200)**, **(269)**, **(369)**; covered walkway along **(38)**, **(320)**; height of inner town above **(102)**; houses on **(369)**; jettied houses upon **(38)**; lanes leading off *see* St Stephen's church, lanes around; ship-building on **(39)**, **(369)**, **(391)**; towers on **(369)**, **(391)** *and see also* walls, town: Key; triangle or triangular roadway or space on **(5)**, **(32)**, **(37–8)**, **(48)**, **(102–5)**, **(108)**, **(223)**, **(242)**; warehouses on **(39)**; water-conduit tower on **(5)**, **(32)**, **(38)**, **(48)**, **(104)**, **(108)**, **(223)**
Keynsham **(454)**
Kidwelly **(251)**
King Street (east Bristol) **(61)**, **(70)**, **(91)**, **(280)**, **(290)**, **(300)**
Kingroad **(52)**, **(248)**, **(406)**, **(418)**, **(439)**, **(455)**
Kings, dates of obits of **(286)**
Kingswood, Forest of **(186)**

Knapp's chapel *alias* Chapel on The Back, Chapel of St John the Evangelist **(124–5)**, **(181)**, **(219–20)**, **(249–50)**, **(252)**, **(260)**, **(342)**
Knapp, T[homas], merchant **(220)**, **(252)**, **(260)**
Knifesmith Street *see* Christmas Street
Knights of St John of Jerusalem *see* St John of Jerusalem
Knights Templar *see* Templars
Knokyn, William **(439)**
Knole **(395)**
Knoll Field, land in **(395)**

Ladies' Mirror, The, book belonging to William Worcestre **(437)**
Lands End **(52)**
latrines: Bristol Bridge **(118)**; the Marsh **(4)**; Pithay **(98)**
Laugharne **(251)**
Lawford's Gate **(184–6)**, **(191)**, **(214)**, **(397)**, **(402)**; roads at **(187–8)**; *see also* Holy Trinity hospital
Leads rocks, The [in Avon Gorge] **(69)**, **(240)**
Leigh, Ashton- *alias* [Abbots], Somerset **(64)**, **(69)**, **(406)**
Leland (Leyland), John, grammarian **(50)**, 286
Lewinsmead **(92)**, **(156)**, **(192)**, **(273–4)**, **(301–2)**, **(394)**, **(401)**; hospital in **(401)**; stile at **(77)**
Leycestre, John, burgess and merchant, mayor **(49)**, **(439)**
Lisbon, Portugal **(122)**
Little Back *see* St James's Back
Llandaff, Bishop of **(455)**
Llanstephen **(251)**
Lloyd, master mariner, voyage to Brazil of **(418)**
Lokbridge (*Lokbrygge*) at Earlsmead **(71)**, **(423)**
Lollards of Prague (Hussites of Bohemia) **(119)**
Lombard, Moses, house of **(426)**
Londe, Robert, grammar school master **(50)**, **(237)**, 286
London **(259)**, **(308)**, **(395)**, **(439)**, **(441)**; Bermondsey Street **(439)**; Charing Cross **(22)**; Lime Street **(321)**; Milk Street **(394)**; road to **(186)**, **(402)**; Tower of **(19)**; Westminster **(166)**
Long Ashton *see* Ashton, [Long]
[Long Row] **(310)**, **(361–2)**
Lundy, island of **(52)**
Lyons, William **(470)**

A BRIEF GLOSSARY
of Worcestre's
architectural and measuring terms

ashlar	dressed blocks of building stone **(421)**
bowtel	a boltel, plain round moulding, shaft of a clustered pillar **(86)**, **(225)**, **(421)**
braz...	brattishing, ornamental cresting? **(456)**
casement	a large, shallow hollow moulding; a 'lowryng' casement is a lowering casement, according to Harvey, *Itineraries*, pp. 332-3 **(225)**, **(421)**
champ	chamfer, bevelled edge **(421)**
course	continuous layer or row **(421)**
cropp	parapet capping stones? **(456)**
entayle	carving **(421)**
fillet	a narrow flat band separating two mouldings **(225)**, **(421)**
garlond	decorative band of stonework round a spire **(226)**
genlese	cusps **(421)**
gradus	a stair, or the step of a stair **(68)** *passim*
gressus	Worcestre's pace, heel to toe, of c.22 inches (56 cms.) **(3)** *passim*
historia	storey **(456)**
ogee	an S-shaped, double curved moulding **(225)** **(421)**
orbe	decorative blank stone panels **(456)**
pana	panel **(112)**, **(226)**
panella	sides of a structure **(456)**
ressant, ressaunt	an ogee or S-shaped moulding **(225)**; ressaunt lorymer, an ogee drip according to Harvey, *Itineraries*, p. 332-3 **(421)**
sconcus	sconchon, a splayed angled stone **(112)**

A SELECT BIBLIOGRAPHY
of books and articles relating to William Worcestre.

Bettey, J.H., 'Late-medieval Bristol: from town to city', *Local Historian* vol.28 no.1 (February 1998), pp. 3-15

Bettey, J.H., *St Augustine's Abbey, Bristol* (Bristol Branch of the Historical Association, 1962)

Burgess, C., *The Pre-Reformation Records of All Saints', Bristol: Part I* (Bristol Record Society vol. XLVI, 1995)

Dallaway, J., *Antiquities of Bristow* (1834)

Gray, I., *Antiquaries of Gloucestershire and Bristol* (1981)

Harvey, J.H., 'William Worcestre', *The Genealogists' Magazine* XVI no. 6 (June 1970) pp. 274-5

Harvey, J.H., *English Mediæval Architects* (1954)

Harvey, J.H., *William Worcestre: Itineraries* (1969)

James, M.R., *Descriptive Catalogue of the Manuscripts in the Library of Corpus Christi College, Cambridge* (1912)

Jones, R.H., *Excavations in Redcliffe 1983-5* (1986)

Kendrick, T.D., *British Antiquity* (2nd edn., 1970)

Leech, R.H., 'Aspects of the Medieval Defences of Bristol' in *From Cornwall to Caithness: papers presented to Norman V.Quinnell*, ed. M.Bowden, D.Mackay and P.Topping (1989)

Leech, R.H., 'The Medieval Defences of Bristol Revisited', in *'Almost the Richest City': Bristol in the Middle Ages*, ed. L.Keen (British Archæological Association Conference Transactions XIX, 1997)

Leech, R.H., *The Topography of Medieval and Early Modern Bristol: Part I* (Bristol Record Society vol. XLVIII, 1997)

McFarlane, K.B., 'William Worcestre, a Preliminary Survey' in *Studies presented to Sir Hilary Jenkinson*, ed. J.C.Davies (1957), pp. 196-221

Nasmith, J., *Itineraria Symonis Simeonis et Willelmi de Worcestre* (1778)

Neale, F., 'Worship Street Bristol: A puzzle street-name', *Bristol Archaeological Research Group Bulletin* vol.5 no.1 (1974), p.6

Orme, N., 'The Guild of Kalendars, Bristol', *Transactions of the Bristol & Gloucestershire Archæological Society* XCVI (1978), pp.32-52

Ponsford, M.W., *Bristol Castle* (M.Litt. thesis, Bristol 1979)

Ralph, E., 'Bristol c.1480 by Robert Ricart', in *Maps and Plans of Medieval England*, ed. P.Harvey and R.Skelton (1971), pp. 309-16

Sherborne, J.W., *The Port of Bristol in the Middle Ages* (Bristol Branch of the Historical Association 2nd edn., 1971)

Sherborne, J.W., *William Canynges 1402-1474* (Bristol Branch of the Historical Association, 1985)

Smith, M.Q., *St Mary Redcliffe* (1995)

Toulmin Smith, L., *The Maire of Bristowe is Kalendar by Robert Ricart* (Camden Society n.s.V, 1872)

Wadley, T.P., *Notes of Bristol Wills* (1886)